Collins

AF655593

Enhanced Collins English Grammar and Composition 7

With SAFAL assessments

Grammar is the foundation of good English; good composition follows. *Enhanced Collins English Grammar and Composition* provides a thorough grounding in the English language. The exercises help students acquire proficiency in language skills.

Ruskin Bond

Author | K. Padmini Shankar
Series Editor | Samson Thomas

HarperCollins*Publishers*
Publishing operations in 17 countries and 120+ imprints globally

William Collins' dream of knowledge for all began with the publication of his first book in 1819. A self-educated mill worker, he not only enriched millions of lives, but also founded a flourishing publishing house. Today, staying true to this spirit, Collins books are packed with inspiration, innovation and practical expertise. They place you at the centre of a world of possibility and give you exactly what you need to explore it.

Published by Collins Learning
An imprint of HarperCollins*Publishers* India
Building No. 10, Tower A, 4th Floor, DLF Cyber City, Gurugram, Haryana 122002, India

First edition: 2018
Enhanced edition: 2024
Reprint edition: 2024
ISBN: 978-93-6213-418-9

Artwork, typesetting and layout by **Seedbox 6 and Q2A Media Services Pvt. Ltd.**
Cover layout by **Misha Gurnanee Gudibanda**
Printed and bound by Thomson Press India Ltd

Browse the complete Collins catalogue at www.collins.in.
For any queries/feedback, please write to us at SCHOOLSUPPORT@harpercollins.co.in.

Preface

Enhanced Collins English Grammar and Composition is a carefully graded series spanning eight levels which aims to enable learners to master the rules of the English language. Current developments in cognitive psychology suggest that effective learning depends on a relaxed learning atmosphere, a combination of discovery learning and direct instruction, and a variety of tasks to suit the major learning styles. This series takes these insights into account to facilitate effective intervention in the teaching-learning of English grammar at the word, sentence and discourse levels. It also recognizes the importance of communication as a life skill and the key role of language in teaching and learning, as outlined in the National Curriculum Framework, 2023.

Key Features

Each unit starts with the **Let's Get Started** section, featuring a rhyme, a short narrative, a dialogue or a few questions that acts as an introduction to the topic, drawing upon the learner's existing understanding of the language. The learner's response is then used to explicitly teach the topic.

Definitions of key grammar terms are given in simple, clear language, and are highlighted and placed in a box for easy recognition. The definitions are accompanied by examples to explain the concept through usage. Each unit is accompanied by **extensive exercises** and practice drills to reinforce concept acquisition. The tasks aid a variety of learning methods: teacher-driven instruction, discovery learning, incidental teaching, and activities promoting unconscious acquisition of grammatical structures. Recycling of items ensures high retention.

The **Grammar Bytes** feature highlights additional facts related to the topic covered. The **Watch Out!** section cautions learners against erroneous application of the rule, points out exceptions to rules and usage errors. The **Don't Forget!** section at the end of the unit does a quick recap of the important points.

The **Let Us Write** section at the end of the unit includes a guided writing task. It requires learners to apply the grammar concept just learnt, besides alerting them to the usefulness of the concept in day-to-day communication.

From level 2 onwards, each book starts with a **Self-Assessment Test** to help the learner determine his/her current competency level and spot specific gaps in understanding. Remedial measures and level adjustment are suggested based on the learner's score in the test.

The **Grammar on the Go** units revisit important grammar items by focusing on usage. The **Vocabulary** units cover common usage structures encountered in speech and writing.

Each book includes three **Tests**, which help learners evaluate the acquisition of concepts covered.

Graded **composition** units hone learners' skills in creative writing. Each composition unit has guidelines for the topic, sample pieces for reference as well as guided and independent writing tasks.

The books also include extensive **comprehension** practice, with the passages ranging from fiction to non-fiction and poetry.

The books are supported by Teacher's Manuals with detailed lesson plans, and digital resources for additional reinforcement.

Grammar is the framework within which language thrives. The aim of this series, ultimately, is to equip learners to read and write English correctly. We hope that it will be a useful resource for the autonomous learner as well as teachers and parents.

**

Authors

K. Padmini Shankar is a Professor at the English and Foreign Languages University, Hyderabad. She has taught at the undergraduate and post-graduate levels for over two decades. Her research interests include classroom-based research, and teacher training and development.

The Series Editor, **Samson Thomas**, is a Professor of English at the English and Foreign Languages University, Hyderabad. He has authored several English language books.

KEY FEATURES

Enhanced Collins English Grammar and Composition aims to make the English language accessible for all learners by equipping them to use language as a tool of communication and of exploration of literature and knowledge. In doing so, the series is aligned with the National Education Policy, 2020 through the following elements.

Let's Get Started is an introductory activity featuring rhymes, short narratives, dialogues and questions.

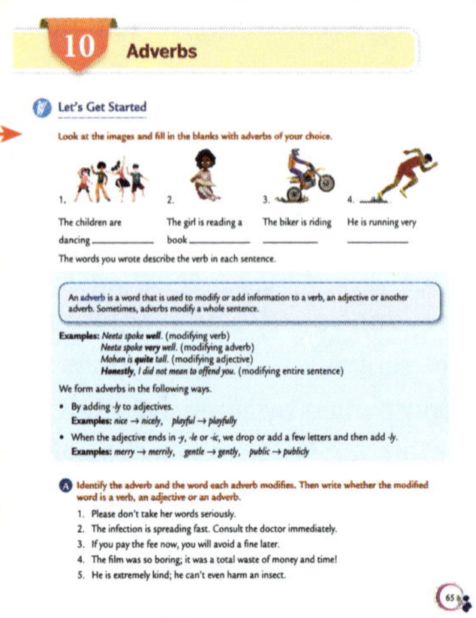

10 Adverbs

Let's Get Started

Look at the images and fill in the blanks with adverbs of your choice.

1. The children are dancing ________
2. The girl is reading a book ________
3. The biker is riding ________
4. He is running very ________

The words you wrote describe the verb in each sentence.

An **adverb** is a word that is used to modify or add information to a verb, an adjective or another adverb. Sometimes, adverbs modify a whole sentence.

Examples: *Neeta spoke* ***well***. (modifying verb)
Neeta spoke ***very*** *well*. (modifying adverb)
Mohan is ***quite*** *tall*. (modifying adjective)
Honestly, *I did not mean to offend you*. (modifying entire sentence)

We form adverbs in the following ways.

- By adding *-ly* to adjectives.
  Examples: *nice → nicely*, *playful → playfully*
- When the adjective ends in *-y*, *-le* or *-ic*, we drop or add a few letters and then add *-ly*.
  Examples: *merry → merrily*, *gentle → gently*, *public → publicly*

A **Identify the adverb and the word each adverb modifies. Then write whether the modified word is a verb, an adjective or an adverb.**

1. Please don't take her words seriously.
2. The infection is spreading fast. Consult the doctor immediately.
3. If you pay the fee now, you will avoid a fine later.
4. The film was so boring; it was a total waste of money and time!
5. He is extremely kind; he can't even harm an insect.

65

Definitions of key grammar terms are given in simple and clear language. These are accompanied by examples.

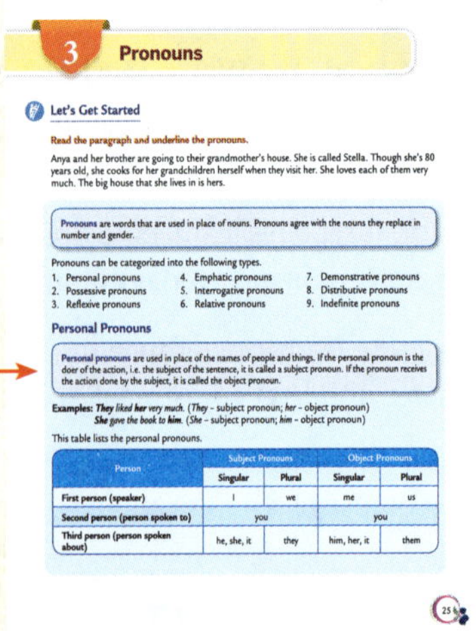

3 Pronouns

Let's Get Started

Read the paragraph and underline the pronouns.

Anya and her brother are going to their grandmother's house. She is called Stella. Though she's 80 years old, she cooks for her grandchildren herself when they visit her. She loves each of them very much. The big house that she lives in is hers.

Pronouns are words that are used in place of nouns. Pronouns agree with the nouns they replace in number and gender.

Pronouns can be categorized into the following types.

1. Personal pronouns
2. Possessive pronouns
3. Reflexive pronouns
4. Emphatic pronouns
5. Interrogative pronouns
6. Relative pronouns
7. Demonstrative pronouns
8. Distributive pronouns
9. Indefinite pronouns

Personal Pronouns

Personal pronouns are used in place of the names of people and things. If the personal pronoun is the doer of the action, i.e. the subject of the sentence, it is called a subject pronoun. If the pronoun receives the action done by the subject, it is called the object pronoun.

Examples: ***They*** *liked* ***her*** *very much*. (*They* - subject pronoun; *her* - object pronoun)
She *gave the book to* ***him***. (*She* - subject pronoun; *him* - object pronoun)

This table lists the personal pronouns.

Person	Subject Pronouns		Object Pronouns	
	Singular	**Plural**	**Singular**	**Plural**
First person (speaker)	I	we	me	us
Second person (person spoken to)	you		you	
Third person (person spoken about)	he, she, it	they	him, her, it	them

25

Grammar Bytes highlights additional facts related to the topic.

Grammar Bytes

Describing words tell us these things about a naming word:

- the number
- the colour
- the shape
- the size

Watch Out! lists common usage errors and points out exceptions to rules.

Watch Out!

We do not use *a* or *an* when we talk of more than one thing.

a telephones (✗)
a telephone (✓)
the telephones (✓)
telephones (✓)

Don't Forget! includes a quick recap of the important points at the end of the unit.

Don't Forget!

1. Naming words can show number. Singular naming words show one. Plural naming words show more than one.
2. Singular naming words can be changed into plural naming words by adding *-s*, *-es*, *-ies* and *-ves* at the end.

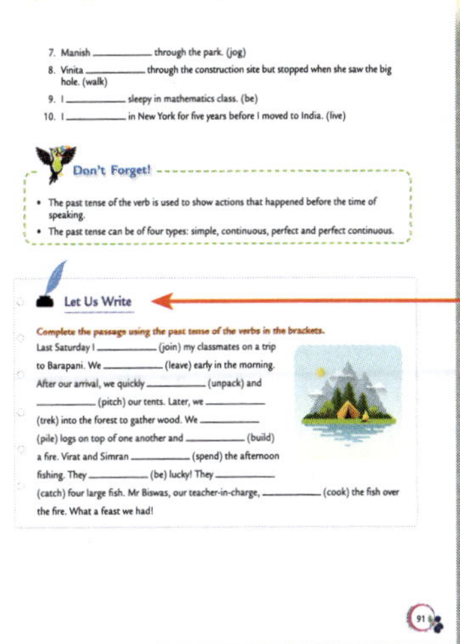

The **Test** pages assess learners on what they have just studied. They foster conceptual understanding.

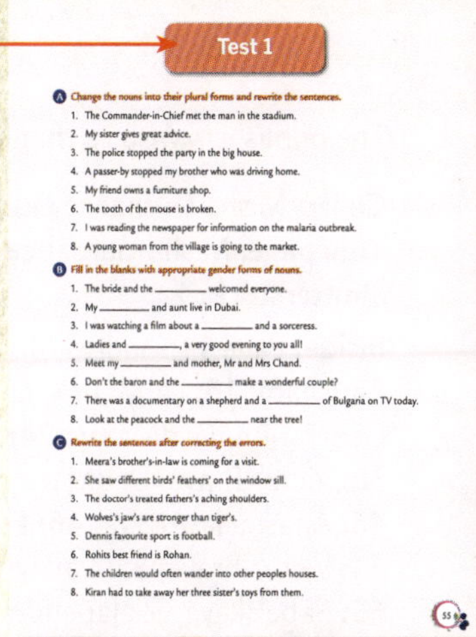

Let Us Write includes guided or independent writing tasks related to the unit.

The **Vocabulary** units include words and common usage structures in speech and writing.

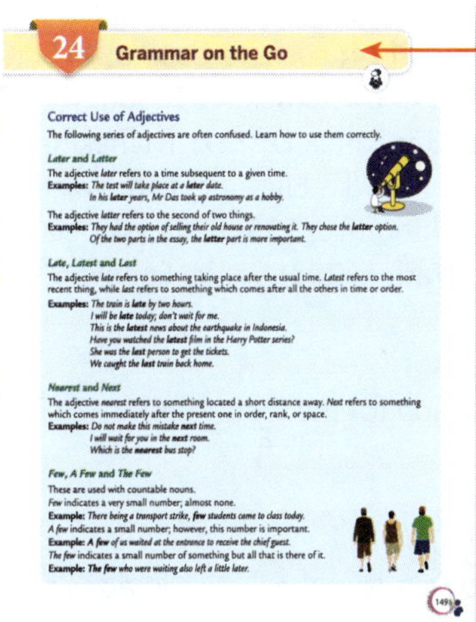

Grammar on the Go revisits important grammar items with focus on usage.

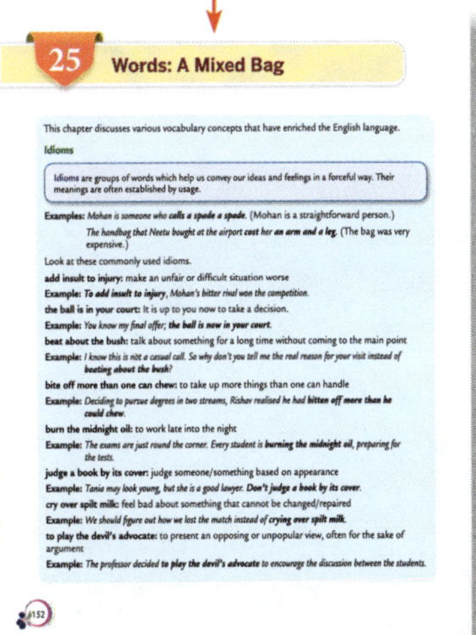

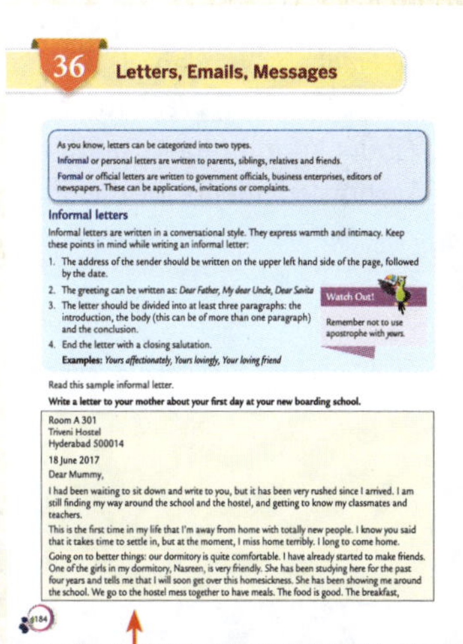

Comprehension units include passages ranging from fiction to non-fiction and poetry. They help learners practise reading comprehension skills.

The **Composition** units hone learners' skills in creative writing, thus encouraging creativity and critical thinking.

Acknowledgements

The publishers wish to thank and acknowledge the following for granting us permission to use copyright material:

Cover: Misha Gurnanee Gudibanda
Title page: Misha Gurnanee Gudibanda
Shutterstock:

Inside: Page **11:** Andres Moncayo; **12:** Davdeka; **13:** Olga_Serova, Pretty Vectors; **14:** Dvo; **15:** Allies Interactive, Aarisham; **16:** Lady Luck, Luisa Venturoli; **19:** Lorelyn Medina, MatiasDelCarmine; **21:** Sparkstudio; **23:** Visual Generation, DedMazay; **24:** Moriz; **27:** Moriz; **29:** Ivan Aleshin; **30:** Iconic Bestiary, **31:** Crisan Rosu; **32:** Pushkin; **38:** Victor Brave, DedMazay; **39:** Allies Interactive; **41:** Muhammad Desta Laksana; **44:** MatiasDelCarmine; **45:** Anastacia-Azzzya; **46:** Esenin Studio; **48:** Dojdis; **49:** Olga1818; **51:** Teguh Mujiono; **52:** Pewara Nicropithak; **54:** Victor Brave; **55:** Pallavi_Patil; **58:** Byskop/Shuttterstock; **60:** M.Svetlana, Arbit; **61:** Igor Kaplunovich; **65:** Sabelskaya, Skalapendra, Sabelskaya, Sportpoint; **66:** Artisticco; **67:** Laurent Renault; **68:** Teguh Mujiono; **69:** Portare Fortuna; **73:** RomMashkaVector; **78:** Sabelskaya; **79:** JonahWong, Noraneko Design; **80:** Zhelunovych, Victor Brave; **84:** BaboonChe, Anna.zabella; **85:** Artisticco; **86:** Macrovector, Cosmaa; **87:** Aleutie; **89:** Holly Braun; **91:** Vecton; **92:** Manas_ko; **93:** Jana Guothova; **95:** Lorelyn Medina; **96:** Lorelyn Medina; **99:** Dirk Ercken; **106:** Ori Artiste; **107:** Lorelyn Medina; **109:** Kittikiti, Lineartestpilot; **110:** Aarisham; **111:** Stocklifemax; **112:** Pushkin, Artisticco; **113:** Nadya Art; **114:** Luciano Cosmo; **115:** Kimazo, Pittore; **116:** HappyPictures; **117:** BlueRingMedia; **120:** Saiko3p; **121:** Flowerstock; **122:** SofiaV; **127:** Hans Wagemaker; **128:** Creative Mood; **130:** Ayelet Keshet; **131:** Stellarstock; **133:** Sahua D; **137:** Thanakim Thanomton; **139:** AboliC; **141:** Evgeny Bornyakov; **145:** Emjay Smith; **147:** Selena1981, Ellegant; **148:** VolsKinvols; **149:** Lorelyn Medina, File404; **153:** Stockakia; **154:** Lorelyn Medina, NotionPic; **155:** Bedlovska Liana; **156:** Lady-luck; **163:** Rad Radu; **176:** Nachiketa Bajaj; **197:** Visual Generation; **203:** Vadim Sadovski.

iStock: Page **169:** ruvanboshoff

The publishers have applied for permission for the following:
Mr Franks by Vandana J. Bist
The Cobbler by R. Venkatnarayan
'Count Your Jumbos', published by *The Telegraph*
Acknowledgments for the above will be made in the future editions of the book.

Contents

Self-Assessment

Complete the test to find out how much you already know.

A Underline the transitive verbs and circle the intransitive verbs. **(10×1)**

1. Mona will move to Delhi this summer.
2. He moved the furniture to his new house.
3. I like chicken manchurian.
4. She likes to spend time with her puppy.
5. She baked some bread.
6. He kicked the ball hard.
7. They laughed loudly.
8. We have received the invitation.
9. The dog barked at the stranger.
10. They were received warmly.

B Identify the non-finite verbs in the sentences and say whether they are infinitives, participles or gerunds. **(10×1)**

1. Mona wanted to go to the beach but her brother insisted they go to the zoo.
2. Sonali saw the kneeling devotees through the window of the temple.
3. Rock climbing is what Krishna does every summer.
4. Tired and annoyed, I started redoing the assignment.
5. Shall I help you carry the luggage?
6. Finding honest people is difficult these days.
7. Hibernating animals are cold-blooded.
8. I suggest you book the tickets early if you want front-row seats.
9. Deven went to Mumbai to attend an interview.
10. Kirti loves making sandcastles.

C Underline the verbs in the following sentences and state their tenses. **(10×1)**

1. She has been working in this school for the past twenty years. She is the senior-most teacher.
2. Steffi had an appointment with the dentist. She left the office early.
3. Ipshita looks after her aged parents very well.
4. She is writing her third novel at the moment. Her two earlier novels were bestsellers.
5. Revanth had messaged his friend many times before he left for Chennai.
6. They were watching TV when their uncle arrived.
7. I had been waiting for a long time before I received her call.
8. The students are writing the test.
9. I have finished my geography project.
10. By this time next year, I will have finished writing my novel.

D Convert the sentences from the direct to indirect speech. **(10×1)**

1. Divya said to Dinesh, 'How kind of you to drop me home!'
2. Mother said to Veena, 'Polish your shoes.'
3. Roopa said to Mini, 'I love your new frock.'
4. Tarun said, 'We shall give Mummy a surprise gift.'
5. Gopal said to Simi, 'When will you come back from Goa?'
6. They said, 'Alas! We lost the match.'
7. Tabitha said to Robin, 'Will you take Dan to the doctor tomorrow?'
8. Vandana said to Bhavan, 'Come home early.'
9. Sita said to Laxman, 'Go and look for your brother.'
10. The teacher said, 'Staple the answer scripts carefully.'

E Write whether the sentences are in active voice (A) or passive voice (P). **(10×1)**

1. She boiled some eggs for dinner. ☐
2. We are being taught about the Mauryan Empire in class. ☐
3. The invitations have been sent. ☐
4. The washing machine is leaking. ☐
5. He has won the first prize. ☐
6. The bird has built the nest skilfully. ☐
7. The order for the meal has been placed. ☐
8. The dog was licking the bone. ☐
9. Rats have made holes here. ☐
10. The dam has been repaired. ☐

The answers are given on page 201.

Assessment

1. If you score 7 or more in each section, you are ready to start the new chapters.
2. If you score less than 6 in section A, revise 'Transitive and Intransitive Verbs'.
3. If you score less than 6 in section B, revise 'Infinitives, Gerunds and Participles'.
4. If you score less than 6 in section C, revise 'Tenses'.
5. If you score less than 6 in section D, revise 'Direct and Indirect Speech'.
6. If you score less than 6 in section E, revise 'Active and Passive Voice'.

1 Nouns

Let's Get Started

Look at this picture of a café. Write down all the nouns that you see and state whether they are countable or uncountable.

____

____

____

____

How many nouns did you find? Compare your list with that of your partner's and check if you both noted down the same nouns.

A **noun** is a word that indicates the name of a person, a place, an animal, a thing or an idea.

The two main types of nouns are proper nouns and common nouns.

Proper and Common Nouns

Proper nouns are words which refer to the particular names of people, animals, places and things. Proper nouns always begin with a capital letter.

Examples: *The Mesopotamian civilization developed on the banks of the* ***Tigris*** *and the* ***Euphrates****.*

Jupiter *is the largest planet in the solar system.*

Common nouns are words that refer to persons, animals or things of the same kind or general category.

Examples: *The* ***students*** *listened attentively while the* ***teacher*** *explained the* ***problem****.*

He owns a ***shop*** *on the main* ***street*** *of the* ***town****.*

Grammar Bytes

These are proper nouns.

- names of people
- days of the week
- months of the year
- names of towns, cities, streets, states, countries

Watch Out!

We generally do not use an article (*a, an, the*) before a proper noun.

The India [✗]
The January [✗]

Look at these common nouns and their corresponding proper nouns.

Common nouns	Proper nouns
river	Godavari
mountain	Mount Everest
girl	Nandini
boy	Vivek
state	Himachal Pradesh

A **Underline the nouns in the following passage. Write (P) for proper nouns and (C) for common nouns.**

Many kings ruled ancient India over the ages. Among the greatest of them was Emperor Ashoka. He was known as a fierce and brave warrior. But the war of Kalinga brought a complete change in him. He was deeply disturbed by the many lives lost in the war. From that time, he gave up violence and became a follower of the Buddha. He sent his children – his daughter Sanghamitra and son Mahindra – to spread Buddhism to Sri Lanka, a far-off foreign land. The spread of Buddhism in Asian countries such as China, Japan, Cambodia and Laos is because of the efforts of Ashoka.

Countable and Uncountable Nouns

Common nouns can be classified into countable and uncountable nouns.

Countable nouns are names of things that can be counted. They can be singular or plural.

Examples: *In our class, there are twenty* ***boys*** *and twelve* ***girls****.*
In our ***classroom****, there are thirty-two* ***chairs*** *and two* ***cupboards****.*

A **singular** noun is the name of a single person or thing.
Examples: *satellite, volcano*

A **plural** noun is the name of more than one person or thing.
Examples: *emperors, fountains*

Uncountable nouns are names of things that cannot be counted. They do not have singular or plural forms.

Examples: *I have* ***curd*** *every day in summer.*
Please add more ***sugar*** *in my* ***coffee****.*
Buy some ***bread*** *when you go out.*

We can indicate the quantity of uncountable nouns in two ways.

1. With units of measurements such as *litre* and *kilo*.
   Examples: *two* ***kilos*** *of sugar, five* ***litres*** *of water, two* ***loaves*** *of bread*
2. With words such as *little, a little, some* and *much*.
   Examples: ***a little*** *rice,* ***much*** *happiness,* ***some*** *juice*

Grammar Bytes

Singular countable nouns always need an article or words like *my, your, this* and *which* before them.
I have apple every morning. [✗]
I have an apple every morning. [✓]

Uncountable nouns are usually liquids (*milk*), grains (*rice*), feelings (*happiness*), abstract ideas (*justice*), natural phenomena (*rain*) and states of being (*youth*).

Watch Out!

Some nouns are always singular.
Examples: *scenery, furniture, progress, information, money, outlook, rainfall, haircut*
Some nouns always take the plural form.
Examples: *scissors, trousers, pants, goods, savings, glasses, spectacles*
Certain nouns are always used in a singular sense, although they have a plural form.
Examples: *news, physics, athletics, billiards, crossroads*
Certain nouns are always used as plural nouns although they have a singular form.
Examples: *cattle, police, poultry, data*
Some nouns have the same singular and plural forms.
Examples: *fish, deer, offspring, spacecraft*

B **Read the sentences and write whether the nouns given in italics are countable (C) or uncountable (U).**

1. How much *cheese* do you need?
2. Meenu has *friends* all over the neighbourhood.
3. I like strawberry *milkshake*.
4. They needed gallons of *water* to put out the *fire*.
5. Abbas always has orange *juice* in the morning.
6. Dogs are faithful *animals*.
7. Neelam eats brown *rice* three times a *week*.
8. Delete all the old *messages* on your mobile phone.

Concrete and Abstract Nouns

Concrete nouns refer to things that we can touch or see. They can be both countable and uncountable.

Examples: *box, bag, bottle, car, keys, table, milk, oil, butter*

Abstract nouns refer to things which we cannot see or touch but only feel. They include feelings, experiences, states, qualities and ideas.

Examples: *love, hate, pride* (feelings and emotions)
comfort, chaos, courage (states)
freedom, truth, belief (qualities, ideas)
adventure, drought (events, experiences)

Collective Nouns

Collective nouns are nouns that refer to a group of people or things.

Examples: *The **committee** arrived at the decision together.*
*The **audience** cheered for the performers loudly.*
*The **class** maintained complete silence while the principal was in the room.*

Other collective nouns include *army, jury, troop* and *family*.

C **Fill in the blanks with the correct options.**

gaggle horde bundle crowd bunch swarm bouquet gang

1. a ________________ of thieves
2. a ________________ of geese
3. a ________________ of clothes
4. a ________________ of flowers
5. a ________________ of grapes
6. a ________________ of locusts
7. a ________________ of people
8. a ________________ of barbarians

D **Identify the nouns in the following sentences. Then, write if they are proper (P), common (C), collective (CO) or abstract (A).**

1. Hard work never goes to waste.
2. There is no shortcut to success.
3. The police have caught the criminal.
4. The committee has prepared the petition.
5. Emperor Vikramaditya was a great patron of the arts.
6. The cattle are grazing in the field.
7. She sent me a bouquet of flowers.
8. Hyderabad is the capital of the newly-formed state of Telangana.
9. Faith can create miracles.

Material Nouns

Material nouns refer to materials or substances used to make things.

Examples: *paper, glass, gold, wood, iron, wool*

E **Underline the material nouns in these sentences.**

1. Gold is a good conductor of heat.
2. Jute is one of the cheapest natural fibres.
3. The child is sailing a boat made of paper.
4. Plastic is not good for the environment.
5. Rubber is a bad conductor of electricity.
6. Some people think that food tastes better when cooked in utensils made of clay.

Compound Nouns

Compound nouns are nouns that are formed by combining two or more words.

Compound nouns are formed by combining words belonging to different parts of speech.

1. noun + noun (tooth + brush = toothbrush)
2. adjective + noun (green + house = greenhouse)
3. noun + verb (hair + cut = haircut)
4. verb + adverb (take + off = take-off)

Compound nouns can be written as a:

a. single word (*firewood, bedroom, pancake*)

b. hyphenated word (*check-in, dry-cleaning, jack-in-the-box*)

c. spaced word (*bus stop, water bottle, post office*)

Plurals of compound nouns can be formed in different ways.

Rule	Examples
By adding -*s* to the main noun	*mothers-in-law, editors-in-chief*
By adding -*s* to the end word	*assistant directors, water bottles*
By making both nouns plural	*menservants*
By adding -*s* or -*es* to the end of the word when there is no obvious principal noun	*forget-me-nots, toothbrushes*

F **Write the plural forms of the following compound nouns.**

1. passer-by
2. ladybird
3. water tank
4. printer cartridge
5. washing machine
6. daughter-in-law

G Choose the correct nouns to complete the sentences.

1. They are buying ______________ (furniture/furnitures) for their new house.
2. This railway track is used for ______________ (goods/good) trains.
3. I have no further ______________ (information/informations) regarding her arrival.
4. He is older than his brother by two and a half ______________ (year/years).
5. She lost her bunch of ______________ (key/keys) in the train yesterday.
6. The accident was seen by many ______________ (passer-bys/passers-by).
7. He has seven ______________ (son-in-laws/sons-in-law).
8. The two former ______________ (chiefs of staff/chief of staffs) are attending the meeting.

Don't Forget!

1. Nouns can be classified into common and proper, countable and uncountable, abstract and concrete, collective, material and compound nouns.
2. Abstract nouns refer to names of feelings, experiences, states, qualities and ideas. Concrete nouns refer to things which we can touch and see.
3. Material nouns are names of substances used to make things.
4. Compound nouns are nouns formed by combining two or more words. They can be a combination of either two nouns, or an adjective and a noun, or a noun and a verb, or a verb and an adverb.

Let Us Write

Use these nouns to write a paragraph with the given beginning. You can also add nouns of your own.

cart	goods	heap	brass	aluminium	seller
eatables	crowd	unwillingness	help	gratitude	peanuts

Harish and Himadri were best friends. One day, as the two boys were walking past the post office, they heard a loud noise.

Then, write the type of each noun you have used.

2 Adjectives

Let's Get Started

Underline the adjectives in the passage.

The grey elephant was walking behind a white taxi. Suddenly, it raised its large trunk and let out a loud trumpet. A little girl peeked out from the old taxi. As soon as the elephant saw her, he brought his trunk down and waited. The girl stepped out of the taxi. She had two bananas in her small hands. The elephant took the yellow bananas, ate them and walked away on the dusty road.

An **adjective** describes, identifies or quantifies a noun or a pronoun. Adjectives describe nouns or pronouns by giving some information about a person's or an object's size, shape, age, colour, origin or material.

Examples: *Irfan is a **hardworking** student.*
*It's a **windy** day.*
*That is an **old** table.*
*He wanted to sit on the **wooden** chair.*

Grammar Bytes

Adjectives can come after the noun they describe.

*Our neighbours are **kind**.*

Kinds of Adjectives

Adjectives can be of different types depending on the type of information they give about a noun or a pronoun.

Adjectives of Quality

Adjectives of quality describe the quality of a noun, its shape, size, colour, state or condition. They answer the question *what kind of*.

Examples: *Neeta does not like the smell of **ripe** jackfruit.*
*The boy wearing a **blue** jacket is my brother.*
*Draw a **big** circle.*
*The cookies are in the **round** box, not the **square** one.*

Adjectives of Quantity

Adjectives of quantity specify the quantity of the noun being talked about. They answer the question *how many* in the case of countable nouns and *how much* in the case of uncountable nouns.

Examples: *I have **many** friends.*
*There is **enough** food for everyone.*

*There are **several** students waiting to meet the principal.*
*She has **little** money to support herself.*

Demonstrative Adjectives

Demonstrative adjectives are used to point out a specific noun or pronoun. The four demonstrative adjectives are *this*, *that*, *these* and *those*.

Examples: ***Those*** *bananas are ripe, while **these** ones are raw.*
That *question has a simple answer.*
This *argument is convincing.*

Grammar Byte

This and *that* are used with singular nouns. *These* and *those* are used with plural nouns.

Interrogative Adjectives

Interrogative adjectives are used to ask questions and are always followed by a noun.

Examples: ***Which*** *topic are you going to talk about?*
Whose *papers are you checking?*
What *problems are you facing?*

Possessive Adjectives

Possessive adjectives indicate ownership or possession and always come before the noun. They answer the question *whose*.

Examples: ***Their*** *children live in the USA.*
Her *son is studying in Chennai.*
My *parents are arriving today.*

Adjectives of Number

Adjectives of number indicate the number of the noun. They are of four types: indefinite, distributive, cardinals and ordinals.

Indefinite adjectives don't specify a particular number.

Examples: ***Some*** *people like red more than black.*
*Give me **any** pen.*

Distributive adjectives are used to refer to a person or thing separately.

Examples: ***Each*** *student was given a kit.*
Neither *boy was invited to the party.*
Every *boy in the room wanted to have ice cream.*

Cardinal numbers mention the exact number of the noun.

Examples: *I called you **three** times.*
*Do you have **twenty** rupees?*

Ordinal numbers mention rank, position or order of a noun in a series.

Examples: *Rahul is the **first** boy to reach school.*
*This is the **third** time I am calling you.*

Proper Adjectives

Proper adjectives are formed from proper nouns.

Examples: *I love **Shakespearean** dramas.*
*There are many **Indian** restaurants in Manchester.*
*My uncle married an **Irish** woman.*

Watch Out!

Always use a capital letter for a proper adjective.
Examples: *Indian students, African forests, British merchants, American youth*

Emphasizing Adjectives

Emphasizing adjectives are used to lay stress on a noun.

Examples: *You are the **very** person I am looking for.*
*Mind your **own** business!*
*Is that your **actual** name?*

A Underline the adjectives in the following sentences and mention their types.

1. My niece is a jovial person; everyone likes her.
2. We have five pens; we need to buy three more.
3. Indian films are loved all over the world.
4. Many people know that she is the daughter of a famous film star.
5. Which shirt do you like more, this one or that one?
6. The audience was spellbound by the tricks of the skilful magician.
7. I have photocopied those documents.
8. If you go to the market, buy some sugar and a dozen eggs.
9. Our luggage is packed; we are ready.
10. I had a busy day in office today; there were several meetings.

B Fill in the blanks with the appropriate adjectives.

1. Sit in your ______________ chair. (actual/own/very)
2. The ______________ tea ceremony is a beautiful cultural activity. (Japan/Japanese)
3. There are ______________ options available. (none/own/six)
4. What a ______________ flower! (some/all/pretty)
5. ______________ of the women were upset. (Any/Some/One)
6. She looks ______________. (Europe/European/Europe-like)
7. I bought ______________ mangoes from the seller. (actual/nine/sixth)
8. The ______________ house from the left is Mr Mukherjee's. (fourth/own/four)

Formation of Adjectives

Some adjectives are formed from nouns and others are formed from verbs. Look at these examples.

From nouns

anger (noun) → *angry* (adjective)

danger (noun) → *dangerous* (adjective)

From verbs

accept (verb) → *acceptable* (adjective)

create (verb) → *creative* (adjective)

C Fill in the blanks with adjectives formed from the given words.

1. The teacher often scolds Reba because she is ______________. (talk)
2. My uncle was a ______________ (book) child. He would always be found in the school library.
3. Pam always looked ______________ (cheer). No one knew that she had a ______________ (tragedy) history.
4. Though his relatives denied it, Shamik was the ______________ (law) owner of the property.
5. His ______________ (haste) decision cost him the respect of his ______________ (love) ones.

Compound Adjectives

A **compound adjective** is formed when two or more words are joined together to modify the same noun. The words are usually separated with a hyphen.

Examples: *He submitted a* ***ten-page*** *assignment.*
Don't give me ***half-baked*** *ideas!*
They have a ***two-year-old*** *daughter.*

Watch Out!

If the first part of the compound adjective ends in *-ly*, then there is no hyphen in between the words.

I had to eat from a *badly cleaned* plate.

D Fill in the blanks with the given compound adjectives.

state-of-the-art   mouth-watering   weak-kneed   man-eating   long-lasting   strong-willed

1. We have ______________ laboratories in our school.
2. Martin Luther King Jr's speech had a ______________ impact on humanity.
3. My aunt is a ______________ woman; she is not easily influenced by external pressure.
4. Among the many attractions of old Delhi is its ______________ street food.
5. The ______________ tiger entered the village silently.
6. The ______________ lord does not have the courage to speak up for the interests of his men in front of the king.

Order of Adjectives

When more than one adjective is used to describe a noun, it usually follows a particular order.

Look at the table below to understand the usual order of adjectives.

1	2	3	4	5	6	7	8	9	10
quantity	general opinion	specific opinion	size	temperature	shape	age	colour	nationality	material

Examples: *They have a* ***ferocious, big, two-year-old, black*** *dog.*
She bought a ***lovely, spacious, four-bedroom*** *flat.*
She stores her jewellery in a ***tiny, square, red, Spanish*** *box.*
She bought ***four expensive, square, wooden*** *tables for her office room.*
They are selling their ***magnificent ten-year-old, Italian rosewood*** *rocking chair.*

E Choose the option that has the correct order of adjectives.

1. I am going to wear my __________ shirt for my cousin's wedding.
   a. new, silk, purple   b. new, purple, silk
   c. silk, purple, new   d. purple, new, silk

2. We need to recycle the __________ cans.
   a. six, plastic, round   b. round, plastic, six
   c. six, round, plastic   d. plastic, six, round

3. Raman is a __________ man.
   a. tall, generous, thin   b. thin, tall, generous
   c. generous, tall, thin   d. generous, thin, tall

4. I am going to drink tea from a __________ cup.
   a. small, English, china   b. English, small, china
   c. small, china, English   d. china, small, English

5. The __________ teacher spoke for hours.
   a. interesting, German, old
   b. interesting, old, German
   c. old, interesting, German
   d. German, interesting, old

Degrees of Comparison

Adjectives have three degrees of comparison: positive, comparative and superlative.

Examples: *hot* *hotter* *hottest*
quiet *quieter* *quietest*

The **positive degree** is the base form of the adjective. In other words, a positive degree offers no comparison.

Examples: *Our house is **large**.*
*Delhi is an **expensive** city.*

For negative comparisons with *not*, we use the positive degree of comparison.

Example: *These flowers are **not as fresh as** those flowers.*

When we want to compare two things or groups of things, we use the **comparative degree**. The comparative degree is formed by adding *-er* to the base adjective or adding *more* before an adjective.

Grammar Byte

Some adjectives form the degrees of comparison differently.

Positive	Comparative	Superlative
good	*better*	*best*
bad	*worse*	*worst*
little	*less*	*least*
many	*more*	*most*

Examples: *This room is **brighter** than that room.*
*I am **more surprised** than you are.*

We use the **superlative degree** to compare three or more nouns. The superlative degree is formed by adding *-est* to the base adjective or adding *most* before an adjective. We use *the* before the superlative degree of an adjective.

Examples: *The Nile is the **longest** river in Africa.*
*Sumit is the **shortest** boy in our class.*
*Grace is the **most trustworthy** friend that I have.*

Watch Out!

Avoid double comparatives.

He is more better than you are. [✗] *She is more cleverer than I am.* [✗]

Use *many* for countable nouns and *much* for uncountable nouns

I have much problems. [✗] *I have many problems.* [✓]

There is not many sugar in the jar. [✗] *There is not much sugar in the jar.* [✓]

Watch Out!

Last means 'the previous one'; *latest* means 'the most recent one'.

Give me the last novel. [✗] *Give me the latest novel.* [✓]

Quantifiers like *half, both* and *all* are used before the possessive.

Both their sons are doctors. *You used up half your time.*

Words like *senior, junior, inferior, superior, anterior, posterior* and *prior* are already in the comparative form. Use *to* and not *than* with them.

No one is superior to others here. *Afra is senior to me by four years.*

There is no comparative or superlative form for some adjectives because you cannot grade them as more or less.

Examples: *unique, perfect, infinite, impossible, absolute, inevitable, sufficient, main, complete, unanimous, universal, ideal, fatal, dead*

This is a more universal problem. [✗] *This is a universal problem.* [✓]

He is the most perfect leader. [✗] *He is a perfect leader.* [✓]

F Fill in the blanks with the comparative form of the given adjectives.

1. There is ________________ (little) water in this bottle than in that one.
2. Baishali is a ________________ (wise) woman today than she was five years ago.
3. Villages are usually ________________ (polluted) than cities.
4. He is in a ________________ (good) state today than yesterday.
5. ________________ (many) often than not, people make this mistake.
6. Children are usually ________________ (intelligent) than we think they are.
7. The resort is at the ________________ (far) end of the street.
8. You have never met a ________________ (generous) person than Stephen.
9. Rekha is the ________________ (pretty) of the two sisters.
10. Of these two pairs of shoes, which one looks likely to be ________________ (long-lasting)?

G Complete the following sentences using the appropriate degree of comparison of the given adjectives.

1. She is ________________ than her brother. (smart)
2. Ritu is the ________________ student in class. (soft-spoken)
3. Arun's handwriting is quite ________________. (neat)
4. This dress is not really as ________________ as that one. (pretty)
5. China is a ________________ country. (large)
6. *The Sign of Four*, a Sherlock Holmes mystery, is the ________________ book I have read. (thrilling)
7. Take the ________________ of the two ropes. (short)
8. Mani Bakery sells the ________________ muffins in town. (good)

Don't Forget!

1. Adjectives are of the following types: adjectives of quality, quantity, interrogative adjectives, distributive adjectives, demonstrative adjectives, possessive adjectives, adjectives of number, proper adjectives and emphasizing adjectives.
2. Adjectives can be formed from nouns, verbs and other adjectives.
3. Adjectives in a sentence follow the order: quantity, general opinion, specific opinion, size, temperature, shape, age, colour, nationality, material.
4. Adjectives usually form the comparative and superlative degrees by adding *-er* and *-est* at the end, or by adding *more* and *most* before the adjective.

Let Us Write

Describe the following in a sentence using adjectives of your choice.

1. A bus with a lot of people in it.
   The bus was packed, noisy and hot.
2. A fruit and vegetable market ______________________________
3. A school concert ______________________________
4. The last day of the year ______________________________
5. Christmas ______________________________
6. Diwali ______________________________
7. Your school in the morning ______________________________

3 Pronouns

Let's Get Started

Read the paragraph and underline the pronouns.

Anya and her brother are going to their grandmother's house. She is called Stella. Though she's 80 years old, she cooks for her grandchildren herself when they visit her. She loves each of them very much. The big house that she lives in is hers.

Pronouns are words that are used in place of nouns. Pronouns agree with the nouns they replace in number and gender.

Pronouns can be categorized into the following types.

1. Personal pronouns
2. Possessive pronouns
3. Reflexive pronouns
4. Emphatic pronouns
5. Interrogative pronouns
6. Relative pronouns
7. Demonstrative pronouns
8. Distributive pronouns
9. Indefinite pronouns

Personal Pronouns

Personal pronouns are used in place of the names of people and things. If the personal pronoun is the doer of the action, i.e. the subject of the sentence, it is called a subject pronoun. If the pronoun receives the action done by the subject, it is called the object pronoun.

Examples: ***They*** *liked* ***her*** *very much.* (*They* – subject pronoun; *her* – object pronoun)
She *gave the book to* ***him***. (*She* – subject pronoun; *him* – object pronoun)

This table lists the personal pronouns.

Person	Subject Pronouns		Object Pronouns	
	Singular	**Plural**	**Singular**	**Plural**
First person (speaker)	I	we	me	us
Second person (person spoken to)	you		you	
Third person (person spoken about)	he, she, it	they	him, her, it	them

A Fill in the blanks with the correct personal pronouns.

1. __________ are good friends from now on. (You and I/Me and you/I and you/You and me)
2. My mother has made chicken stew and *appams* for __________. (my friends and me/I and my friends/me and my friends/my friends and I)
3. The teacher is very angry with __________. (us/we/they/he)
4. __________ are going to start a business soon. (Lina and I/I and Lina/Me and Lina/Lina and me)
5. The workers have put in long hours. The employers have promised __________ a holiday next week. (them/we/you/I)
6. Her dog loves __________. (me and her/I and her/us/we)
7. __________ are the winners of the musical contest. (Mohan and I/Mohan and me/Me and Mohan/I and Mohan)
8. __________ are going on a trip to Sri Lanka. (She and I/She and me/I and she/Me and she)

Watch Out!

I always comes last when a set of pronouns and nouns are used together.
She and I [✓]
Tina, Ramesh and I [✓]
I, Tina and Ramesh [✗]

Do not use *me* in place of *I*, when *I* is part of the subject of the sentence.
Anish and I are siblings. [✓]
Anish and me are siblings. [✗]

Possessive Pronouns

Possessive pronouns show ownership. They tell us who or what something belongs to.

Examples: *We bought two hats. The blue one is Meena's and the pink one is* ***mine****.*
Suresh and Rina have two cars. The jeep is ***his*** *and the sedan is* ***hers****.*

Look at this list of possessive pronouns.

Person	Possessive pronouns	
	Singular	**Plural**
First person	mine	ours
Second person	yours	
Third person	his, hers	theirs

Watch Out!

Its is not a possessive pronoun.

Do not add apostrophe before *s* in *ours, yours, theirs* and *hers*.

Reflexive Pronouns

Reflexive pronouns are used when we want to refer back to the subject of the sentence. In some cases, they can act as the object of the sentence if the subject and the object are the same.

The reflexive pronouns are *myself, yourself, himself, herself, itself, ourselves, yourselves* and *themselves*.

Examples: *I looked at* ***myself*** *in the mirror.*
Please help ***yourself****; there's plenty of ice cream.* (direct object)
The students solved the problems ***themselves****.*

Emphatic Pronouns

Emphatic pronouns are used to emphasize the action of the subject. They have the same forms as reflexive pronouns.

Examples: *I **myself** agreed to organize the picnic.*
*The children **themselves** joined their parents in helping out their aged neighbours.*
*She **herself** admitted her mistake.*

Grammar Bytes

- If the gender of an animal is known, usually *she* or *he* is used instead of *it*.
- We often use possessive pronouns after the preposition *of*.

Example: *Rehan is one of my favourite cousins. = Rehan is a favourite cousin of **mine**.*

B **Fill in the blanks with suitable pronouns.**

1. I can only help you so much. You have to do the rest __________
2. Tony was ashamed of __________ because he had lied to his parents.
3. People who take care of __________ have a better chance of staying healthy.
4. All of you have done a very good job. You should be proud of __________
5. Aryan did his homework by __________
6. Anish exclaimed, 'The tyres of our car are punctured! Where shall we go to get __________ repaired?'
7. 'Don't __________ worry, sir! I can do __________. It's a really easy job for __________,' replied the watchman.
8. She said, 'If __________ are ready, __________ can all start.'
9. '__________ have lost a lot of weight. Look at __________,' my mother said to me.
10. We, along with our neighbours, had bought two LCD TVs last month from the same shop. My neighbours say that __________ is working fine, but __________ often has problems.

Interrogative Pronouns

Interrogative pronouns are used to ask questions. The five interrogative pronouns are *who, what, which, whom* and *whose*.

Examples: ***Who** went to pick up grandpa?*
***What** are you searching for?*
***Which** of these books are you going to buy?*
***Whom** do you want to meet?*
***Whose** is this car?*

C **Fill in the blanks with suitable interrogative pronouns.**

1. __________ will come with me to the market?
2. __________ are these books?
3. __________ of these shirts do you like?
4. __________ will pay the bill?

5. __________ do you want?

6. __________ is this purse?

7. __________ is the matter with you?

8. __________ is the road to the metro station?

Relative Pronouns

Relative pronouns are used to refer to nouns mentioned earlier in the sentence. They also help us join two sentences. The relative pronouns are *who, whom, whose, that* and *which*.

Look at the way the different relative pronouns are used.

Relative pronoun	Used for	Examples
who whose whom	people	*The passenger* ***who*** *sat next to the old lady helped her unbuckle the seat belt.* *The man* ***whose*** *house you are buying is my neighbour.* *The guests* ***whom*** *you met at the party are from Malaysia.*
which	animals and things	*The snake* ***which*** *bit the boy has been caught.* *The car* ***which*** *they bought is expensive.*
that	both people and things	*The people* ***that*** *I met on the way were very friendly.* *The problem* ***that*** *you are talking about can be easily solved.*

We also use *what* as a relative pronoun in the sense of 'that which' or 'the thing which'.

Examples: ***What*** *you want cannot be given to you.* (that which)
You got ***what*** *you deserved.* (the thing which)

Whose is used as a relative pronoun for inanimate objects too.

Examples: *The bottle* ***whose*** *cap is broken is leaking.*
The house ***whose*** *roof is broken was abandoned several years ago.*
The blanket, ***whose*** *edges are embroidered with lace, belongs to me.*

Watch Out!

We often incorrectly use *who* in place of *whom*. Remember that *who* functions as a subject and *whom* functions as an object in a sentence.

Doctors ***who*** *care for their patients are respected.* (The relative pronoun is a subject, so we use *who*.)

Patients want doctors ***whom*** *they can trust.* (The relative pronoun is an object, so we use *whom*.)

D Fill in the blanks with suitable relative pronouns.

1. The director __________ made this film passed away two years ago.
2. She won the finals of the tough competition, __________ no one had expected her to.
3. Tell me __________ your friends are and I will tell you what kind of a person you are.
4. The swimmer __________ won the gold medal trained for many years.
5. The sweater __________ I bought yesterday shrank after a wash.

6. The names of the eleven players __________ made it to the national team will be announced tomorrow.
7. Roti, __________ we eat for dinner, is part of our staple diet.
8. Where did you buy the earrings __________ you gave Minu?
9. Salman Rushdie's latest book, __________ was published last year, was an instant bestseller.
10. The tea shop __________ we used to visit often has closed down suddenly.

Omission of Relative Pronouns

The relative pronoun is omitted if it acts as the object. In such cases, we change the position of the preposition in the sentence.

Examples: *The boy to **whom** you gifted the books did very well in the exams.*
The boy you gifted the books to did very well in the exams. (The position of the preposition *to* changes.)
*These are the colours with **which** he painted the walls.*
These are the colours he painted the walls with. (The position of the preposition *with* changes.)

E Rewrite the following sentences omitting the relative pronouns. Change the position of the prepositions.

1. This is a house in which you can maintain a big lawn.
2. The person about whom you are asking is known to our family.
3. This is the road beside which the Ganga flows.
4. *Zootopia* is the animated film about which I was telling my brother.
5. Cynthia is the girl with whom I shared a room during our school trip.
6. This is the organization in which my brother works.
7. The professor with whom we requested a meeting has not arrived yet.
8. This is the museum beside which the restaurant is located.
9. Who is the person with whom you discuss your troubles?
10. The hill on top of which the monastery is situated is very high.

Demonstrative Pronouns

Demonstrative pronouns point to specific people and things. These are *this, that, these* and *those.*

Examples: ***This** is the boy who is a member of the music group.*
***That** is the lake where we can go rowing.*
*These cookies are tastier than **those** in the jar.*

Distributive Pronouns

Distributive pronouns are used to talk about people or things as individual members of a pair or of a group. A distributive pronoun is always singular and is therefore followed by a singular verb.

Some of the common distributive pronouns are *each*, *either* and *neither*.
Each is used to denote every one of a number of persons or things taken singly.
We use *either* and *neither* to refer to individuals in a pair.
When used as a distributive pronoun, *each*, *either* and *neither* are followed by plural nouns and singular verbs. Note that when they are used as distributive pronouns, they are used by themselves, without a noun after them.

Examples: *Of the ten students shortlisted,* ***each*** *received an award.*
Two buses stop near my house. ***Either*** *can take you to the railway station, but neither goes to the airport.*
Each *of the pastries has a unique flavour.*
Either *of the books is a good choice for a gift.*
Neither *of the two speakers was knowledgeable about the subject.*

Indefinite Pronouns

Indefinite pronouns are used to talk about people or things in general. They do not refer to specific things.

They include:
anyone, anybody, anything — *someone, somebody, something* — *no one, nobody, nothing*
everyone, everybody, everything — *one, all, some, few, many, none*

Examples: ***Anyone*** *can apply for the course.*
Anything *can happen.*
Something *is wrong.*
No one *knows what happened.*
Nothing *is more important than peace of mind.*

F Fill in the blanks with the correct pronouns.

1. We were all so tired that __________ wanted to have dinner. (anybody/nobody)
2. __________ is at the door. Go and open it. (Everybody/Somebody)
3. I cannot buy __________ of these shirts. Both are costly. (either/any)
4. __________ are the changes you have to make. (These/Each)
5. __________ of you who have finished the work may leave. (Those/Any)
6. Do you see the boy sitting in the last row? __________ is the student we met at the science fair. (This/That)
7. The plot of the book __________ I took from you is fast-paced. (what/which)
8. The dentist __________ pulled out my tooth was an expert. (whom/who)

9. The boy __________ pen you borrowed has left the exam hall. (whose/whom)
10. __________ are you angry with? (Whom/That)
11. __________ are you thinking about? (What/Where)
12. Of these two sizes, __________ fits you better? (which/what)
13. Don't blame me; you did it __________. (yourself/myself)
14. __________ of them is interested in going for the picnic. (Anybody/Neither)
15. Are you still writing the essay? I finished __________ long ago. (yours/mine)
16. The book __________ (that/whom) you had ordered has arrived.
17. The man __________ (that/who) met with the accident has been taken to hospital.
18. The woman __________ (who/whose) purse was stolen is arguing with the police officer.

Let Us Write

Complete the dialogue between Nitin and his mother using suitable pronouns.

Mother: Nitin! Where are ________?
Nitin: ________ am here, Mother. Do ________ need something?
Mother: ________ am looking for your sister's shirt. ________ asked ________ to iron ________.
Nitin: ________ don't know where ________ is. Why don't ________ ask ________?
Mother: ________ has gone for her dance class. Afterwards, ________ is going out with some friends of ________. ________ will all be coming back to the house for dinner at 8 p.m.
Nitin: Did ________ try messaging ________?
Mother: No, ________ did not. ________ will do it now.

4 Transitive and Intransitive Verbs

Let's Get Started

Underline the verbs which have a noun or pronoun that receives the action of the verb.

1. Ranjini sold her old typewriter to the antique collector.
2. Smita danced beautifully.
3. Prem saw a rare species of vulture on his travels.
4. We walked on the beach and ate ice creams.

Verbs can be transitive or intransitive depending on whether they need an object to make complete sense. Let us learn more about the object of the verb.

Direct and Indirect Objects

Verbs can have two objects: direct and indirect.

A **direct object** is a noun or pronoun that receives the action of the verb. It is identified by asking the question *who* or *what* in relation to the verb.

Example: *The teacher opened* ***the book****.* (answers the question *opened what?*)

The **indirect object** is a noun or pronoun that tells us *to whom* or *for whom* the action of the verb is performed.

Example: *The tailor showed* ***her*** *a beautiful dress.* (answers the question *showed whom?*)

Remember that for a verb to have an indirect object, there must also be a direct object.
The indirect object usually appears before the direct object.

Look at these sentences.

Subject	Verb	Indirect object	Direct object
She	gave	me	a book.
He	brought	her	some flowers.

A Underline the direct object and circle the indirect object in the following sentences.

1. He bought her an expensive pen.
2. The judge awarded the criminal a life sentence.
3. They sent you a mail.

Grammar Byte

Though the indirect object usually comes before the direct object, we can reverse this order by using a preposition (*to*, *for*) with the indirect object.

She gave ***me*** *a book.*
She gave a book ***to me****.*

4. My mother taught me English.
5. She showed us all the gifts.
6. My father gifted me a nice watch.
7. Shaila stitched a dress for her baby sister.
8. Deepak lent his friend his binoculars.
9. Renu fed her dog biscuits.
10. Prema told me about her holiday plans.

Transitive and Intransitive Verbs

A **transitive verb** is a verb which needs an object to complete its meaning.

Example: *They* ***bought*** *some vegetables.*
Here, *vegetables* is the direct object of the verb *bought*. It answers the question, *what did they buy?* *Bought* is a transitive verb because it has the object, *vegetables*.

An **intransitive** verb makes complete sense by itself. It does not need an object to complete its meaning.

Example: *The race* ***began****.*

Here, the subject is *race* and the verb is *began*. The sentence does not have an object, but makes complete sense. The verb *began* does not need an object to complete its meaning and hence, is an intransitive verb.

Look at some more examples of transitive and intransitive verbs.

The cat ***chased*** *the mice.* (transitive)
The cat ***is sleeping*** *on the couch.* (intransitive)
Rabbits ***love*** *carrots.* (transitive)
The rabbit ***is going*** *into its burrow.* (intransitive)
My mother ***stitched*** *a skirt for me.* (transitive)

Watch Out!

The same verbs can be transitive or intransitive, depending on how the verb is used.

Water **boils** at 100 degrees Celcius. (intransitive)

Mother **boils** eggs for breakfast. (transitive)

B Identify the verbs in the following sentences and write 'T' for transitive verbs and 'IT' for intransitive verbs.

1. He kicked the ball.
2. Prema shouted loudly.
3. You park the car.
4. You parked in the wrong place.
5. She met him in the evening.
6. They called his name many times.
7. The envelope contained important papers.
8. ISRO sent 104 satellites to space at one go.
9. I forgot all about it.
10. We won the match out of sheer good luck.
11. The lawyer argued the case cleverly.
12. The winners received many prizes.

Verbs of Incomplete Predication

In the last exercise, you may have noticed that some verbs, though intransitive (without an object) need other words to complete their full meaning in the sentence.

Look at these sentences.

Sanjay **seems** *angry*.

Here, the word *angry* completes the meaning of the sentence. It tells us *how* Sanjay seems.

King Krishnadeva Raya **was** *wise*.

Here, the word *wise* tells us the kind of king Krishnadeva Raya was.

The adjectives *angry* and *wise* help complete the meaning of the sentences. They are complements of the verbs.

The verbs *seems* and *was* require the help of the given complements to complete their meaning. They are intransitive verbs of incomplete predication.

> Words which help to complete the meaning of the verb form the **complement of the verb**. As they tell us something important about the subject, they are called **subjective complements**.
>
> Intransitive verbs which need words other than objects to complete their meaning are called **intransitive verbs of incomplete predication**.

Transitive verbs too take complements.

The prince ***appointed*** him *minister*.

Here, the pronoun *him* is the object.

The noun *minister* tells us *what* the man was appointed as.

Pritha ***found*** the extra classes *useful*.

Here, the noun *classes* is the object.

The adjective *useful* tells us how Pritha found the classes.

The words *minister* and *useful* are complements of the verbs in the sentences. They are objective complements.

Grammar Byte

Subjective complements are used with intransitive verbs. Objective complements are used with transitive verbs.

> Complements that give information about the object of the verb are called **objective complements**.
>
> Transitive verbs which need the help of other words to complete their meaning are called **transitive verbs of incomplete predication**.

As the examples show, the complement can be a noun, an adjective or an adverb.

C **Write whether the verbs in these sentences are transitive or intransitive. Underline the object of the transitive verbs and circle the complements, if any. Mention whether they are subjective or objective complements.**

1. The excitement soon died down.
   died: intransitive verb, down: subjective complement
2. They all shouted happily.
3. The surgeon is very skilful.
4. I found the conversation disturbing.
5. She will leave soon.

6. They are theatre artists.
7. He cannot reach the jar on the top shelf.
8. When the game ended, the teams broke up.
9. I will meet you at the guest house.
10. The door of the log cabin was damaged during the storm.
11. The detective found the ruined building empty.
12. I invited my cousins to my house.

Don't Forget!

1. Verbs can be transitive or intransitive.
2. Transitive verbs need objects to complete their meaning. Intransitive verbs make complete sense without an object.
3. Some intransitive verbs need other words to complete their meanings. These are verbs of incomplete predication.
4. The words used to complete the meaning of verbs are called complements.
5. Subjective complements give information about the subject of a sentence. Objective complements give information about the object of a verb.

Let Us Write

A Identify the transitive (T) and intransitive (I) verbs in the story.

The little boy stood still. He saw three woodcutters; they had been felling trees. It was illegal in this forest. He felt pity for the trees. He saw axes lying around. The men were sitting at a distance. They had their backs to him. They were eating their lunch. He crept closer and picked up the axes one by one. He placed the axes in his sack and ran away, unseen. He then reported the matter to the forest department. Officers immediately went looking for the woodcutters and caught them. The little boy became a hero. Indeed, he had acted bravely.

B Write down the direct and the indirect objects in the story.

Direct objects: ____________________

Indirect objects: ____________________

5 Agreement of Subject and Verb

Let's Get Started

Read the dialogue and fill in the blanks with the correct form of the verbs. Then, for each verb, underline the noun which decides the number and tense of the verb.

Mukul: Both Shyam and I __________ (like) collecting coins.

David: Do you both collect Indian coins?

Mukul: Shyam __________ (collect) some Indian coins, but I __________ (collect) other kinds of coins. Most of our coins __________ (be) either commemorative or period collections.

For a sentence to be grammatically correct, the main verb should agree with the subject in person and number. When the subject is singular, the verb should be singular. When the subject is plural, the verb is also plural. The verb also takes different forms depending on whether the noun is in first, second or third person. This is called the **agreement of the subject and verb**.

Examples: *Valli **likes** to build robots as a hobby.* (singular subject: *Valli*, singular verb: *likes*)
*Swati and Swaroop **are** writers.* (plural subject: *Swati and Swaroop*, plural verb: *are*)
*I **speak** Telugu, but Ajith **speaks** Kannada.* (*I:* first person; *Ajith:* third person)

Rules of Subject-Verb Agreement

1. Two or more subjects joined by *and* take a plural verb.
   Examples: *Sunil, Renu, Medha and I **are** good friends.*
   *Bread, butter and jam **are** common breakfast items.*
2. In some sentences, the subject and the verb may be separated by several other words. In such cases, identify the subject and verb correctly.
   Example: *The <u>noise</u> of the chirping crickets **was** a constant feature in the forest.*
3. Collective nouns when thought of as a single unit, take a singular verb. Collective nouns may be followed by 'of + noun' or be a single word.
   Examples: *A team of expert lawyers **is investigating** the case.*
   *A pile of clothes **is waiting** to be washed.*
   *The committee **has agreed** to meet next Wednesday.*
4. When the members of a collective noun are thought of as individual units, it takes a plural verb.
   Example: *The jury **were** divided in their opinion about the guilty verdict. (members of the jury as individual persons)*
5. Subjects that have the phrase *pair of* take a singular verb as pair refers to one thing, even though the noun is plural. **Examples:** *A pair of jeans **is** all that he bought from the shop.*
   *A pair of scissors **is** needed to cut the ribbon.*

6. Two singular nouns joined by *or*, *either ... or* and *neither ... nor* take a singular verb.
   Examples: *Mary or John* ***is*** *going to escort the chief guest.*
   Neither Janani nor Jatin ***is*** *ready with the presentation.*

7. When the subject is made up of two or more nouns joined by correlative conjunctions, the verb agrees with the noun or pronoun that is placed closest to it.
   Examples: *Either my friends or my brother* ***is*** *going to book the tickets.*
   Either my brother or my friends ***are*** *coming to pick me up from the station.*

8. Indefinite pronouns such as *much, many, anything, nothing, everything, something, either* and *neither* usually take a singular verb.
   Examples: *Neither of the two houses* ***has*** *a balcony.*
   Everything ***is*** *very expensive these days.*
   Much money ***has*** *been spent on renovating the house.*

9. Singular subjects followed by words such as *as well as, along with* and *besides* take a singular verb. When the subject is plural, the verb will also be plural. Look at these sentences.

   The teacher, along with her students, **sits** down to watch a film.
   A good book as well as the company of friends **makes** her happy.
   The dolphins, along with the orca, **are swimming** together in the ocean.

   In these sentences, the verbs, *sits* and *makes*, agree with the singular subjects (*teacher*, *book*), whereas the verb *are swimming* agrees with the plural noun *dolphins*. The underlined words are considered extra information, which do not alter the meaning of the sentence when removed. The nouns in it don't affect the subject-verb agreement in the sentence.

Grammar Byte

Note the number of the verb when used with *many* and *many a*.

Many days ***have*** *passed since I met Hari.*

Many a day ***has*** *passed when I have thought of Hari.*

Watch Out!

For nouns preceded by 'one of', we use a singular verb even though the noun is always plural.

One of my friends ***works*** *for Google.*

One of the good things about summer ***is*** *that you get plenty of mangoes.*

10. Distances, periods of time and sums of money, when considered as a single unit, take a singular verb.
    Examples: *Ten miles* ***is*** *a long distance to walk.*
    Five years ***is*** *a long time to not meet your friends.*
    Ten thousand dollars ***is*** *the prize money offered in the game show.*

11. Words that indicate quantity such as *all, none, some, most, more, enough, plenty,* and *a lot of* take a singular verb when the subject is singular and a plural verb when the subject is plural.
    Examples: *A lot of the two chocolate fudge cakes* ***have*** *already* ***been served****.*
    All the boys ***have taken*** *the vaccine.*
    Some of the cake ***is*** *in the fridge.*
    Plenty of new dishes of food ***are*** *left for any guests who arrive later.*

12. Titles of books always take a singular verb even if the name has plural nouns.
    Examples: A Tale of Two Cities ***is*** *a popular novel by Charles Dickens.*
    The Arabian Nights ***is*** *a book that we all love to read.*

A Rewrite the sentences after correcting the errors.

1. Professor Jaya Shekar and Professor Maya Patkar is doing a combined project.
2. Neither the teacher nor the students is present in the class.
3. My friend, philosopher and guide are my father.
4. The list of invitees are ready.
5. Anusha and her sisters is at university.
6. Neither my father nor my mother are coming for the meeting.
7. Gregory and Tamannah doesn't want to be late for their meeting.
8. The cute puppy live on my street.
9. Everybody know that stray animals needs homes.
10. The host and hostess greets the guests warmly.
11. Your pants is in the washing machine.
12. All his mother's hopes rests on his shoulders.
13. Each of these books are for sale.

B Identify the errors in the sentences and rewrite them correctly.

1. Many a student have had a hard time with mathematics.
2. Satyajit Ray, the filmmaker, music director, writer and illustrator, were a talented man.
3. Either of the two trains go to Indore.
4. The jury declare the accused to be guilty.
5. Every one of the students have the potential to do well in life.
6. The soldiers as well as the king is fighting bravely in the battle.
7. Three hundred and sixty five make up the number of days we have in a year.
8. The principal, along with the teacher, greet the chief guest warmly.
9. Solomon and Sally doesn't like to play in the park.
10. Neither the director nor the actor were patient or reasonable.
11. The philosopher and the poet is dead.
12. The monsoon have arrived in Kerala.
13. *Ghost Tales From the Raj* are written by Ruskin Bond.

C Fill in the blanks with the correct options.

1. Each of the boys ____________ (is/are) smart.
2. None of the books ____________ (is/are) available.
3. Moni and her brother ____________ (has/have) watched the film.
4. Either Dhoni or Kohli ____________ (is/are) going to captain the team tomorrow.
5. The standard meal of roti, rice, vegetables and dal ____________ (is/are) available at the mess for lunch.
6. Rs 20,000 ____________ (is/are) the price of this computer.

7. Neither my brother nor my parents __________ (know/knows) about my grade card.
8. Mrs Samuels, along with the rest of the neighbours, __________ (was/were) waiting to hear about the commotion last night.
9. Most of the pie __________ (has/have) already been eaten.
10. Some of the jury members __________ (is/are) in a meeting right now.
11. Nothing __________ (is/are) worth losing sleep over.
12. A team of scientists __________ (is/are) visiting the laboratory.
13. The right pair of shoes __________ (is/are) all you need to complete your outfit.
14. *American Gods* __________ (is/are) a book by Neil Gaiman that has been adapted for television.
15. Where __________ (is/are) my new pair of spectacles?

Don't Forget!

1. In a sentence, the subject must always agree with the verb.
2. A singular subject takes a singular verb and a plural subject takes a plural verb.
3. Collective nouns can take both singular and plural verbs depending on the context.
4. *Either, neither, either ... or, neither ... nor* take singular verbs.
5. A collective noun takes a singular verb when it is considered a single unit and a plural verb when its members are thought of as individual entities.

Let Us Write

Do you have a sibling? Write a paragraph discussing the similarities and the differences between you and them.

You can use the following points:

- age and appearance
- relationship with parents
- hobbies and extracurricular activities
- studies
- behaviour during a notable incident

You can use these words.

pronouns like *both, some, any, many, none*
conjunctions like *or, either ... or, neither ... nor*
phrases like *as well as, along with*

6 Primary and Modal Auxiliaries

Let's Get Started

Read the conversation. Then, underline the verbs which are joined with another verb to complete the meaning of the sentence.

Shalini: I might go for a jog today.
Mother: Can you buy a carton of milk on your way back?
Shalini: Sure, I will. I should help you more at home.
Mother: Thank you, Shalini. If there's anything you would like for breakfast tomorrow, buy it as well.

Main Verbs and Auxiliary Verbs

Read these sentences.

Black clouds **covered** the sun before the storm broke.
I **shall** finish my work by evening.

In the first sentence, the verb *covered* can stand on its own. In the second sentence, the verb *shall* requires another verb – *finish* – to complete its meaning. *Covered* is a main verb, while *shall* is an auxiliary verb.

Verbs can be categorized into main and auxiliary (helping) verbs.

Main verbs are those which can stand on their own in a sentence.

Examples: *I* ***flew*** *a kite. Nila* ***threw*** *the papers away.*

Auxiliary or **helping verbs** are those which are used with other verbs to complete the meaning of a sentence.

The most commonly used auxiliary verbs are:

be and its forms: (*is, am, are, was* and *were*)
do and its forms: (*does, did*)
have and its forms: (*has, had*)

shall, should; will, would
can, could; may, might
must; ought; dare; need

Examples: *I* ***should play*** *the drums.* (*should*: helping verb; *play*: main verb)
I ***will see*** *a doctor.* (*will*: helping verb; *see*: main verb)

A **Underline the main verbs and circle the helping verbs in these sentences.**

1. He is preparing for his exam.
2. She is getting ready for the interview.
3. They have invited many friends to the party.
4. We can travel in two days.
5. You filled in the form correctly.
6. I have been working for the past four hours.
7. The volcano has erupted.
8. My sister has completed her assignment.
9. Mayank should help Mandira.
10. What do we get Tasneem on her birthday?

Primary Auxiliaries

The verbs *be*, *have* and *do* are the **primary auxiliaries**. They can act as main verbs or as helping verbs. As helping verbs, they show the number and person of the subject. They are also used to form questions and negative sentences.

Examples: *The teachers* ***are*** *busy finalizing the syllabus for next year.* (helping verb)
The countries ***have*** *signed a pact to reduce carbon dioxide emission.* (helping verb)
I ***do*** *yoga to keep myself fit.* (main verb)

The verb *be* (*is, am, are, was, were*) is used to show a state of being. It forms the present and the past continuous tenses.

The verb *do* (*do, does, did*) is used to emphasize, ask a question, or form negatives in the simple present and the simple past tenses.

The verb *have* (*have, has, had*) is used to show that an action has already been completed. It forms the present perfect and the past perfect tenses. It also indicates ownership.

Examples: *Anita* ***is*** *a teacher.* (*is* acts as the main verb; it indicates the state of Anita as a teacher.)
She ***is*** *correcting the answer scripts of her students.* (*is* acts as the helping verb; it indicates the tense and shows the number and person of the pronoun, *she*.)
She ***has*** *Rs 5,000 in the bank.* (indicates ownership)
Do *you know the way to the bank?* (forms a question in the present tense)

B **Underline the primary auxiliaries in these sentences. Mention whether they act as the main verb or as the helping verb.**

1. Tina has a pet dog called Fanny.
2. They are making a film about Malavath Purna, the youngest person to climb Mt Everest.
3. The prices of vegetables have shot up in summer.
4. We are ready to leave now.

5. Do you like horror stories?
6. She did her work before anyone else.

Modal Auxiliaries

Modal auxiliaries or **modals** are auxiliary verbs that give additional information about the function of the main verbs that follow them. They indicate likelihood, ability, capability, willingness, possibility, permission and obligation.

Grammar Byte

Modals do not change form according to the number or person of the subject or the tense of the main verb. The exceptions are *can, shall* and *may*. Modals are always followed by the main verb.

Let's look at the uses of these modal auxiliaries.

Modal	What it indicates	Examples
Can	ability	*I **can** paint.*
	possibility	*The river **can** overflow its banks any day.*
	suggestion	*You **can** try on the red pair of jeans if you like it.*
	permission	*Yes, you **can** use my phone.*
Could	ability	*I **could** jog for an hour when I was young.*
	possibility	***Could** I get knee pain if I did this exercise?*
	suggestion	*You **could** fix an appointment with the doctor for next Monday.*
	permission	***Could** I come and meet you tomorrow in your office?*
Will	future action	*I **will** visit them next month.*
	general truth	*This bottle **will** hold up to one litre of water.*
	resolve	*I **will** never speak to her again.*
Would	future action	*Sunny said that he **would** meet me next week.*
	future possibility	*If it rains, you **would** need an umbrella.*
	past habit	*When I was little, I **would** sing to myself.*
	preference	*I **would** rather go to the library today.*
	to express a wish	*I **would** like to have some more rice, please.*
Shall	future action	*We **shall** meet again next month.*
	resolve	*I **shall** finish my assignment before I go to bed.*
	suggestion	***Shall** we get him a gift before he leaves?*

Modal	What it indicates	Examples
Should	advice	*You* ***should*** *practise hard in order to excel in tennis.*
	probability	*Are you ready? The taxi* ***should*** *be here in a minute.*
	preference	*I* ***should*** *like to take a break.*
	seek opinion	*What* ***should*** *I do about this project?*
	obligation	*You* ***should*** *be wearing a seat belt.*
May	possibility	*It* ***may*** *rain any time today.*
	permission (formal)	***May*** *I leave now?*
Might	possibility	*I* ***might*** *not be able to come to your party.*
	suggestion	*You* ***might*** *visit the palace during your visit.*
	conditional	*I* ***might*** *come with you, if I don't have a prior appointment.*
Must	obligation	*You* ***must*** *sign a contract with us for two years.*
	prohibition	*You* ***must*** *not enter the premises without permission.*
	strong possibility	*She came home and fell asleep immediately. She* ***must*** *be very tired.*
	strong recommendation	*You* ***must*** *exercise for an hour every day.*
	deduction (based on evidence)	*The ground is wet. It* ***must*** *have rained at night.*

Ought, *need* and *dare* are known as 'semi' or 'quasi' modal auxiliaries. *Ought* and *need* are always followed by *to*.

Examples: *You* ***ought*** *to pay more attention to your health.*
We ***ought*** *to spend less time watching television.*
You ***need*** *to spend more time on this chapter.*
They ***need*** *not go to school tomorrow.*
He ***dare*** *not wake up the ogre.*
How ***dare*** *he disobey the king!*

Grammar Byte

The modals *can, will, shall, may* in direct speech become *could, would, should, might* in indirect speech.

He said, 'You ***can*** *use the upper floor.'*
He told her that she ***could*** *use the upper floor.*
Raina said, 'I ***may*** *join another summer camp.'*
Raina said that she ***might*** *join another summer camp.*

C Fill in the blanks with suitable modals based on the given hints.

1. You __________ use this place till 6 p.m. (permission)
2. You __________ come again tomorrow. (suggestion)
3. We __________ be late if we do not start now. (possibility)
4. The thief __________ have been someone known to the family. (deduction based on evidence)
5. __________ I enter my name for the competition? (seek opinion)
6. I __________ climb the stairs two at a time last year. (past habit)

D Fill in the blanks with the most suitable modals.

1. Due to some urgent work, they __________ not meet me as we had planned.
   a. would   b. should   c. could   d. might
2. You __________ leave the room at once.
   a. may   b. could   c. must   d. can
3. She __________ contact me only if it is absolutely necessary.
   a. should   b. can not
4. __________ you please teach me how to use the first aid kit?
   a. could   b. should   c. must   d. might
5. You __________ do well in your exams!
   a. must   b. dare
6. I'm not sure if I can reach in time for dinner; it __________ be very late by the time I finish my dance class.
   a. should   b. might
7. We __________ all be fine; don't worry about us.
   a. must   b. will   c. may   d. can
8. I __________ certainly meet you before you leave for Toronto.
   a. might   b. must   c. will   d. may

E Rewrite the sentences using the given modals.

1. It is possible that this painting was created by Leonardo da Vinci. (may)
   This painting may have been created by Leonardo da Vinci.
2. I am sure you are joking. (must)
3. No one has the courage to disobey the headmaster. (dare)
4. It is very important that we reach home by 9 p.m. (ought)
5. Tani knows how to speak Marathi, Punjabi and Telugu. (can)
6. I would advise you to walk for half an hour in the morning and evening. (should)

Don't Forget!

1. Auxiliaries are helping verbs.
2. The primary auxiliaries are *be, have* and *do*. They can act as main verbs or as helping verbs and change forms depending on person and number.
3. Modal auxiliaries include *can, could, may, might, must, shall, should* and *will*. Except for *can, may* and *shall,* they never change their forms and can suggest various meanings depending on the context.

7 Expressing the Present

Let's Get Started

Write one sentence for each of the given situations.

1. a universal truth ____________________
2. an ongoing action ____________________
3. an action completed in the recent past ____________________
4. an action that started in the past but continued into the present ____________________

The sentences you wrote use the various tenses that a verb can have.

Tense

Look at this paragraph.

Mohan **loves** his grandparents. They **live** in the other end of the city. Mohan **visits** his grandparents every Sunday. But this Sunday, he **had** a special class in school. So he **missed** the trip. He **will** definitely **go** next week.

Watch Out!

Except a verb, no other part of speech has tense.

The highlighted verbs indicate the time of the action. They express a **tense**.

The **tense** of a verb indicates present, past and future time. The tense also indicates whether the action is complete, is going on, has been completed in the recent past or whether it started earlier and has continued into the present.

Look at this table which shows the various forms of the three tenses using the verb *make*.

Form	Present	Past	Future
Simple	*Remya **makes** cookies.*	*Remya **made** cookies yesterday.*	*Remya **will make** cookies tomorrow.*
Continuous	*Remya **is making** cookies now.*	*Remya **was making** cookies yesterday.*	*Remya **will be making** cookies tomorrow.*
Perfect	*Remya **has made** cookies.*	*Remya **had made** cookies yesterday.*	*Remya **will have made** ten batches of cookies by 5:00 p.m.*
Perfect continuous	*Remya **has been making** cookies since yesterday.*	*Remya **had been making** cookies yesterday.*	*By 5:00 p.m tomorrow, Remya **will have been making** cookies for two days.*

We use the simple present and the present continuous tenses to describe an action in the present time.

Simple Present Tense

The **simple present tense** is used to talk about things that happen regularly or are universal truths.

Examples: *We always **have** dessert after dinner.*
*The sun **gives** us heat and light.*

The simple present tense is used for the following.

1. To express habitual or repeated actions.
   Examples: *She **speaks** politely.*
   *He **goes** to the market on Sundays.*
2. To express general truths and scientific facts.
   Examples: *Dogs **make** excellent guide animals for the visually-impaired.*
   *Water **boils** at 100 degree centigrade.*
3. In proverbs.
   Examples: *All that **glitters** is not gold.*
   *Birds of a feather **flock** together.*
4. To express planned future.
   Examples: *The train **arrives** at 6 a.m.*
   *My uncle **retires** in two years.*
5. To give instructions or directions.
   Examples: ***Drive** for a kilometre and then **take** a right turn.*
   *First **take** the yellow sheet and then **fold** it in half.*

Look at the forms of the simple present tense.

	Form	Examples
Affirmative	*I/We/You/They* + base form of verb *He/She/It* + base form of verb + *-s/-es*	*I **play** the guitar.* *She **plays** the guitar.*
Negative	*I/We/You/They* + *do not* + base form of verb *He/She/It* + *does not* + base form of verb	*I **do not play** the guitar.* *She **does not play** the guitar.*
Interrogative	*Do* + *I/we/you/they* + base form of verb *Does* + *he/she/it* + base form of verb	*Do you **play** the guitar?* *Does she **play** the guitar?*

A Fill in the blanks with the simple present tense of the given verbs.

1. The train __________ (arrive) in another ten minutes.
2. The Aurora Borealis __________ (light) up the night sky in the Arctic regions.
3. Pranesh __________ (draw) water from the well and __________ (water) his plants every day.

4. The next season of this drama __________ (begin) in September.
5. Copper __________ (conduct) heat better than iron.
6. __________ (can) we wait until he __________ (finish) his work?
7. The Orion constellation __________ (resemble) a warrior with a sword.
8. The meeting __________ (start) at 10 a.m. Please __________ (do) not be late.

Present Continuous Tense

The **present continuous tense** is used to describe a continued or an ongoing action in the present time. It is also known as the progressive tense as it refers to an action that is in progress at the time of speaking.

Examples: *I **am drinking** hot chocolate.*
*The child **is playing** with the puppy.*

The present continuous tense is used for the following.

1. To describe actions happening at the time of speaking.
   Examples: *We **are learning** grammar now.*
   *The children **are playing** in the garden.*
2. To describe actions which have been going on for a period of time, but which may not necessarily be happening at the time of speaking.
   Examples: *They **are changing** the telephone cables in our locality.*
   *She **is preparing** for the examinations.*
3. For actions that may take place in the near future.
   Examples: *The guests **are arriving** in the evening.*
   *We **are buying** a new TV next month.*

Grammar Bytes

- With the simple present tense, we use expressions of time such as *always, never, often, usually, sometimes, every day.*
- With the present continuous tense, we use expressions of time such as *now, today, at the moment.*

Look at the different forms of the present continuous tense.

Type of sentence	Form	Examples
Affirmative	*I* + *am* + verb + *-ing* *You/We/They* + *are* + verb + *-ing* *He/She/It* + *is* + verb + *-ing*	*I **am sleeping**.* *You **are sleeping**.* *She **is sleeping**.*
Negative	*I* + *am* + *not* + verb + *-ing* *You/We/They* + *are not* + verb + *-ing* *He/She/It* + *is not* + verb + *-ing*	*I **am not sleeping**.* *You **are not sleeping**.* *She **is not sleeping**.*
Interrogative	*Am* + *I* + verb + *-ing* *Are* + *you/we/they* + verb + *-ing* *Is* + *he/she/it* + verb + *-ing*	***Am** I **sleeping**?* ***Are** you **sleeping**?* ***Is** she **sleeping**?*

B **Fill in the blanks with the present continuous tense of the given verbs.**

1. Hurry up! Amit __________ for us. (wait)
2. I __________ Janaki today. (meet)
3. I hate to be disturbed when I __________. (work)
4. Do you know the boy who __________ on the platform by himself? (stand)
5. Let me warn you that you __________ a mistake. (make)
6. We __________ (study) for tomorrow's exam.
7. Zubin __________ the plants. (prune)
8. We __________ the dough for the cake. (prepare)

Simple Present or Present Continuous Tense

We use the present tense and not the present continuous with the following types of verbs.

1. Verbs of senses, such as *see, hear, smell* and *taste*

Examples: *The pudding **tastes** delicious. (The pudding is tasting delicious. [✗])*
*I **see** the point. (I am seeing the point. [✗])*

2. Verbs of feeling, such as *like, care, fear, love, hate*

Examples: *Raju **cares** deeply about his pets. (Raju is caring deeply about his pets. [✗])*
*She **wants** more pocket money. (She is wanting more pocket money. [✗])*

3. Verbs such as *believe, agree, disagree, differ, doubt, think, trust, suppose, understand, recollect, remember, mean, know* and *imagine*

Examples: *He **knows** many people in the apartment complex. (He is knowing many people in the apartment complex. [✗])*
*I **think** she is unwell. (I am thinking she is unwell. [✗])*

4. Verbs showing possession, such as *own, belong, possess, has* and *have*

Examples: *She **has** two brothers. (She is having two brothers. [✗])*
*This house **belongs** to my uncle. (This house is belonging to my uncle. [✗])*

5. Verbs such as *cost, contain, seem, appear* and *resemble*

Examples: *The tins **contain** processed fish. (The tins are containing processed fish. [✗])*
*You **seem** quite tired. (You are seeming quite tired. [✗])*

Watch Out!

We use the present continuous with *have* when we use it in the sense of eating or drinking, having an experience, performing a particular action and others.

*I **am having** a sandwich.* [✓]
*We **are having** a screening of the film tomorrow.* [✓]
*Shireen **is having** a swim in the pool downstairs.* [✓]

We do not use it in the sense of ownership or when referring to a physical condition.

I am having a house in Coimbatore. [✗]
I am having a cold. [✗]

C **Fill in the blanks with the simple present or the present continuous forms of the given verbs.**

1. I __________ (work) now. In the evening, I __________ (play) the guitar in a show with my band. I can talk to you after the show.
2. Mary __________ (love) orange juice. She always __________ (have) some with breakfast.

3. They __________ (vacate) the house tomorrow. They __________ (pack) at the moment.
4. Archana always __________ (ride) her bicycle to school as she __________ (live) nearby.
5. The moon __________ (revolve) around the earth. The moon __________ (shine) brightly tonight.
6. Our neighbour, Mr Sinha, __________ (go) for a jog in the park every day.
7. I __________ (think) I __________ (have) a fever.
8. Can't you see Ritika? She __________ (read) under the banyan tree.
9. Our school's annual play __________ (start) at 6 p.m.
10. My mother always __________ (go) to the market herself, but today my father __________ (accompany) her.

D **Rewrite the sentences after correcting the errors.**

1. I am not understanding this sum. Can you please help me?
2. Devika sleeps now. She will not come out to play.
3. I know I run late. I am apologizing for keeping you waiting.
4. The baby is liking to eat bananas.
5. Jeevan will help you if you are asking him.
6. We are reading the newspaper online these days.
7. Keeping fit is depending on regular exercise.
8. The lasagne is tasting delicious. How did you make it?
9. How terrible the weather is! I am hearing that it's going to get even hotter.
10. My father usually is giving me a present for Diwali.

Present Perfect Tense

The **present perfect tense** is used to talk about an action completed in the recent past but whose effects still remain.

The present perfect tense is used for the following.

1. To talk about an action that has been completed in the recent past.
   Examples: *They **have** just **arrived**.*
   *She **has** just **finished** lunch.*
2. To talk about an action that was completed at some time in the past, but whose exact time of completion may not be known.
   Examples: *I **have visited** the Taj Mahal.*
   *She **has posted** the letter.*
3. To talk about a past action that has some impact in the present.
   Examples: *She **has made** the tea.* (so we can have it now)
   *The tailor **has stitched** the jacket.* (so you can collect it now)

4. To describe something that started in the past and has continued into the present.

Examples: *Medha **has been** a teacher in this school for the past five years.*

*My grandmother **has stitched** dresses for us every year since we were children.*

Look at the different forms of the present perfect tense.

Type of sentence	Form	Examples
Affirmative	*has/have* + past participle form of the verb	*The bird **has built** the nest.* *The players **have returned** to the field.*
Negative	*has/have* + *not* + past participle form of the verb	*The boy **has not done** the work.* *We **have not seen** the film yet.*
Interrogative	*has/have* + subject + past participle form of the verb	***Has** she **returned** my book?* ***Have** they not **come**?*

E Complete the passage with the present perfect tense of the given verbs.

Shyamal __________ (always love) coming to the forest near his ancestral village. He __________ (see) many animals here at close range and __________ (spend) many afternoons studying the flora and fauna. He __________ (also bring) some of his friends during summer holidays every year. Together, they __________ (explore) the area. It is safe because no one __________ (sight) any predators in the area, save the odd jackal. The forest __________ (be) part of the elephants' trail for decades, but the villagers __________ (always deal) with it. Sadly, now that the authorities __________ (plan) to build a road through the forest, Shyamal is worried that his beloved haunt will no longer be the same.

Present Perfect Continuous Tense

The **present perfect continuous tense** is used to talk about an action that started in the past but is still going on at the time of speaking.

Grammar Byte

We usually use words like *since* (to indicate a point of time) and *for* (to indicate a period of time) with the present perfect continuous tense.

*I have been waiting to hear from him **since** morning.*
*I have been waiting for his call **for** two hours.*

The present perfect continuous tense is used to describe an action that began in the past and is still going on.

Examples: *She **has been trying** to solve the puzzle for half an hour.*

*They **have been building** the road for six months now.*

Look at the different forms of the present perfect continuous tense.

Type of sentence	Form	Examples
Affirmative	*has/have been* + *-ing* form of the verb	*The bird* ***has been building*** *its nest.* *The girls* ***have been playing*** *basketball since morning.*
Negative	*has/have not* + *been*+ *-ing* form of the verb	*The baby* ***has not been sleeping*** *well.* *We* ***have not been rehearsing*** *for the last two days.*
Interrogative	*has/have* + subject + *been* + *-ing* form of the verb	***Has*** *she* ***been missing*** *class for the last one week?* ***Have*** *they* ***been digging*** *up the ditch?*

Present Continuous or Present Perfect Continuous

The present continuous is used for an action that is going on at the time of speaking.

The present perfect continuous is used when we want to indicate the duration for which the action has been going on. The duration is also often indicated by a time expression in the sentence.

Example: *The bird* ***is building*** *a nest.* (action going on at the present moment)
The bird ***has been building*** *the nest for the past one hour.* (The action began an hour ago and is still going on.)

F Fill in the blanks with the present continuous or the present perfect continuous tense of the given verbs.

1. Mary __________ (draw) water from the new well for washing clothes.
2. Sujan __________ (draft) the letter at the moment.
3. The kids __________ (play) computer games for two hours now.
4. It __________ (snow) all week in Srinagar.
5. We __________ (wait) for Trisha since 9 a.m.
6. What is that sound? I wonder if the neighbour's baby __________ (cry) again.
7. You look very sleepy. __________ (you, get) enough sleep lately?
8. Our maths teacher __________ (feel) unwell for the past week.
9. Tulika is fluent in Chinese now. She __________ (go) for weekly Chinese classes.
10. Sweta __________ (watch) films all day. No wonder she can barely keep her eyes open now!

Don't Forget!

1. The present tense takes four forms: simple present, present continuous, present perfect and present perfect continuous.
2. In the simple present tense, the base form of the verb is used.
3. The present continuous tense takes the form *is/are* + *-ing* form of the verb.
4. The present perfect tense takes the form *have/has* + *-past participle* form of the verb.
5. The present perfect continuous tense takes the form *have/has been* + *-ing* form of the verb.

8 Expressing the Past

Let's Get Started

Match the actions in column A with the descriptions of the actions in column B.

Column A

1. By the time Pratim turned fifty, he had been painting for forty years.
2. Pratim painted only landcsapes until last year.
3. Pratim had painted a cityscape of Mumbai last year which sold for a huge sum.
4. Pratim finished a painting yesterday.

Column B

a. an action which happened in the recent past
b. habitual past action
c. action going on over a period of time in the past
d. an action that took place before another action in the past

The options in Column B tell us about the situations in which the various forms of the past tense are used.

We use the various forms of the past tense to talk about past actions. These forms are the simple past, past continuous, past perfect and past perfect continuous.

Simple Past Tense

The simple past tense is used for the following.

1. To express an action that has already been completed and usually has a time reference.
   Examples: *The producers **released** the film last week.*
   *I **met** my friend six months ago.*
2. To talk about actions that took place over a period of time in the past.
   Examples: *We **stayed** in Sydney for a week.*
   *They **paid** back the bank for their loan over many months.*
3. To talk about past habits.
   Examples: *We **listened** to the children's programme on All India Radio on Sundays.*
   *My eldest sister **went** for summer camps every year when she was in school.*

4. To make requests and ask questions.
   Examples: *I **wanted** to ask you for help.*
   ***Did** you **want** to talk to me?*

Look at the forms of the verb in various types of sentences in the simple past tense.

Type of sentence	Form	Examples
Affirmative	past form of the verb	*The baby **slept**.* *I **woke up** at 5 a.m. today.*
Negative	*did not* + base form of the verb	*The boy **did not play**.* *The traffic **did not move** for another ten minutes.*
Interrogative	*did* + subject + base form of the verb *wh-* word + *was/were* + subject	***Did** they **come** home last night?* ***Who was** the stranger at the door?*

A Complete the passage with the simple past tense of the given verbs.

It ________________ (be) a wonder of nature. Three leopards in an African forest ________________ (play) with a young fawn, but they ________________ (do) not harm him. The fawn ________________ (walk) around the predators on unsteady legs, while they ________________ (lick) the little thing. After a while, they ________________ (let) it go. Was it one of those incredible stories of predators who ________________ (turn) nurturers? The wildlife photographer who ________________ (capture) the incredible incident ________________ (disagree). 'I think both parties were just curious.' The photos soon ________________ (make) their way into social media. 'Leopards show Bambi some love', ________________ (declare) the newspaper headlines.

Used to for Past Actions

We use *used to* for describing actions which happened often in the past but no longer occur in the present.

Examples: *Sheeba **used to** have long hair when she was young.*
*My mother **used** to play badminton in college.*

B Read the sentences and rewrite them with *used to*.

1. Grandma walked four kilometres every day in the morning to go to school.
2. She studied hard and did well in class.
3. She went to St Mary's School.
4. She played with her friends in the evening.
5. She listened to stories told by her mother at night.

The Simple Past Tense and the Present Perfect Tense

The simple past tense and the present perfect tense both describe an action that has already happened. The simple past describes a completed action while the present perfect describes an action completed in the past whose effects can still be felt in the present.

Example: *The teacher **scolded** the students.* (simple past; the action is complete.)
*The principal **has asked** the students to wear blazers in winter.* (present perfect; the action was done in the past, but its effects remain.)

To decide whether a verb should be in the simple past or the present perfect tense, check whether the sentence includes an expression of past time. If it includes such an expression, the verb will be in the simple past tense.

We use these common expressions of time with the two tenses.

Simple Past: *yesterday, the week before, last month, in 2006*
Present Perfect: *already, just, yet, before, after, still, for, since*

Watch Out!

We do not use expressions indicating past time with the present perfect tense.

I have gone to Taiwan in 2011. [✗]
I went to Taiwan in 2011. [✓]
I have gone to Taiwan. [✓]

C **Fill in the blanks with the simple past or the present perfect tense of the given verbs.**

1. Rupa ______________ (finish) her MA in 2015. She ______________ (join) the University of Reading for her PhD.
2. She ______________ (never go) to the United Kingdom but she ______________ (live) in the USA for a year as an exchange student.
3. While walking down a crowded street, she loudly exclaimed, 'Oh no! I ______________ (lose) my phone!'
4. Jonas ______________ (read) seven books last week.
5. Thomas ______________ (visit) Australia when he was young.
6. The ship's crew ______________ (launch) the lifeboats as soon as they noticed that the vessel had developed a fault.
7. Sana and Rosa ______________ (live) in eight countries, so they know a lot about the cultures of different nations.
8. Ouch! I just ______________ (cut) my hand using the can opener.

Past Continuous Tense

The **past continuous tense** is used to talk about actions that went on for some time in the past.

The past continuous tense is used for the following.

1. To talk about an action that started and continued for some time in the past.
   Examples: *It **was raining** heavily.*
   *They **were discussing** the plans all through the day.*

2. To talk about the earlier action when two past actions are described.
   Examples: *I **was ironing** my uniform when the doorbell rang.*
   *She **was getting** ready when the guests arrived.*

Look at the forms of the verb in the past continuous tense.

Type of sentence	Form	Examples
Affirmative	*was/were* + *-ing* form of the verb	*She **was dancing**.* *Mike **was riding** a horse.*
Negative	*was/were* + *not* + *-ing* form of the verb	*They **were not enjoying** the pizza at all.* *She **was not sleeping** very well.*
Interrogative	*was/were* + subject + *-ing* form of the verb	***Was** he **waiting** for me?* ***Were** George and Ringo **buying** guitars?*

D **Fill in the blanks with the simple past or the past continuous tense of the given verbs.**

1. When I __________ (reach) home, everyone __________ (sleep).
2. While travelling to Delhi by train, we __________ (make) lots of new friends.
3. Although it __________ (snow), the plane __________ (take off).
4. Katrina __________ (cycle) when she __________ (have) an accident.
5. The grandchildren __________ (wrap) birthday gifts when their grandfather __________ (walk) into the room.
6. I __________ (walk) home yesterday evening when the lights __________ (go) off.
7. Sindhu __________ (sit) in a café when you __________ (call).
8. Who __________ (wait) for Vinod when he __________ (arrive) at the dentist's clinic?

Past Perfect Tense

The **past perfect tense** is used to talk about a past action that was completed before another past action began.

The past perfect tense is used for the following.

1. To talk about an action which was completed in the past before another action began. For the other past action, we use the simple past tense.
   Examples: *She **had** just **got** the ingredients for dinner together when the oven broke down.*
   *I **had** just **entered** the auditorium when the dance programme began.*

2. To describe a past action in the reported speech.
   Example: *Megha said that they **had bought** a new car.*
3. With some verbs such as *hope, expect* and *think*, when we want to talk about a past hope, desire or intention that has not been realized in the present.
   Examples: *I **had expected** India to win the match, but we lost.*
   *We **had hoped** that she would stay with us for a few days.*

Look at the forms of the verb in the past perfect tense.

Type of sentence	Form	Examples
Affirmative	*had* + past participle form of the verb	*The dog **had dug** a hole.*
Negative	*had* + not + past participle form of the verb	*The mason **had not finished** the work on time.* *Shweta **had not remembered** to water the plants.*
Interrogative	*had* + subject + past participle form of the verb	***Had** they **slept** in the guest bedroom last night?*

E **Fill in the blanks with the simple past or the past perfect tense of the given verbs.**

1. I'm sure I __________ (turn) the gas off before I __________ (go) to the gym.
2. She __________ (think) of inviting many people to the party initially, but she __________ (change) her mind later.
3. Geeta __________ (live) in Delhi all her life until she __________ (move) to Kolkata.
4. Dhanush told us that he __________ (already sell) his house.
5. I __________ (already wait) for the taxi for an hour before I __________ (realise) that it wasn't coming.
6. The students __________ (complete) several chapters by the time the teachers __________ (inform) them that the exam had been cancelled.
7. James __________ (exclaim) that he __________ (forget) to bring the birthday gift.
8. Suneet __________ (finish) his assignments, so he __________ (come) to watch a film with us.

Past Perfect Continuous Tense

The **past perfect continuous tense** is used to talk about an action that took place in the past and continued for a period of time before it was completed.

Examples: *She was very angry when she met you because she* ***had been waiting*** *for two hours.*
Surya ***had been writing*** *the exam for three hours. When he came home, he felt exhausted.*

Look at the forms of the verb in the past perfect continuous tense.

Type of sentence	Form	Examples
Affirmative	*had been* + *-ing* form of the verb	*The bird* ***had been building*** *the nest for two days.*
Negative	*had not been* + *-ing* form of the verb	*The baby* ***had not been sleeping*** *all evening.*
Interrogative	*had* + subject + *been* + *-ing* form of the verb	***Had*** *the workers* ***been digging*** *the well?*

F **Fill in the blanks with the simple past or the past perfect continuous tense of the given verbs.**

1. My sister __________ (try) to repair the cooler all day.
2. Sidney __________ (sing) for two years before he __________ (meet) David and they __________ (form) a band together.
3. I __________ (study) for two hours by the time the clock __________ (strike) one.
4. When I __________ (become) friends with Dinesh and Shobhna in 2009, the brother-sister duo __________ (take) care of animals at their shelter for ten years.
5. Sarah __________ (practise) her badminton shots for an hour.

6. Eighty-year-old Savitri __________ (narrate) stories of her childhood in Lahore to her granddaughter when the little girl __________ (ask) her a question.

G **Complete the passage with the correct past tenses of the given verbs.**

The ferry ________ (wait) at its usual post by the ghat. It ________ (be) 1 o'clock. By that time, the flower seller ________ (peddle) her wares for two hours, the fruit seller ________ (do) brisk business through the day. His mangoes ________ (be) especially popular. No one knew when it ________ (happen), but all of a sudden, there ________ (be) a shrill cry, followed by shouts of 'Help! Get him out of the water!' The cry ________ (be) that of a mother. A minute ago, she ________ (mind) her younger son and ________ (not notice) that the elder one ________ (inch) towards the water as he ________ (play). The boy's saviour ________ (be) an unlikely one. One of the stray dogs who ________ (hang) around the ghat in the hopes of scraps thrown by passers-by ________ (jump) into the water as soon as he ________ (see) the boy fall in. The brave creature ________ (hold) on to the boy's shirt by his teeth and ________ (drag) him back to the ghat. Why ________ (do) he do it? Perhaps it ________ (be) the universal kindness that binds all of God's creatures together.

Don't Forget!

1. The past tense takes four forms: the simple past, past continuous, past perfect and past perfect continuous.
2. The past continuous tense takes the form *was/were* + *-ing* form of the verb.
3. The past perfect tense takes the form *had* + past participle form of the verb.
4. The past perfect continuous tense takes the form *had been* + *-ing* form of the verb.

Let Us Write

Complete the following sentences meaningfully.

1. Vimal had finished his breakfast before ____________________
2. Meenal went to the USA after she ____________________
3. Teena hadn't studied French before ____________________
4. My mother didn't say anything until ____________________
5. By the time he got a taxi ____________________
6. She lived here for four years before ____________________

9 Expressing the Future

Let's Get Started

Complete this passage on what you will be doing in the future.

Right now, I am __________ years old. Ten years from now, I __________ years old. I will be a __________. I __________ studying __________ . I will __________ . In fifteen years, I will be __________ years old. I __________ living __________. I __________ be working __________ . In twenty years, I __________ be __________ years old.

The **future tense** is used to talk about actions that will take place in the future.

Examples: *Rajan **will go** to London to attend his brother's wedding.*
*I **will be preparing** for the competition from tomorrow.*

Look at the various forms of the future tense.

Tense	Form	Examples
Simple future	*will/shall* + base form of the verb	*The school **will conduct** essay competitions next week.* *She **will return** after one hour.*
Future continuous	*will be* + base form of the verb + *-ing*	*She **will be meeting** the children on Friday.* *Our teacher **will be correcting** our answer scripts all of tomorrow.*
Future perfect	*will have* + past participle form of the verb	*My elder brother **will have completed** his tenth grade by 2020.* *My parents **will have completed** twenty five years of marriage by 2018.*

Uses of *Will* and *Shall*

Will and *shall* are used for the following.

1. to talk about something we have just decided to do.
   Example: *I didn't know I had to submit my assignment today.*
   *I **will** send it right away.*
2. to talk about something we hope or expect will happen.
   Example: *I hope we **will** go for a long holiday.*
3. to express willingness to do something.
   Example: *I **will** help you organize your birthday party.*
4. to express an intention.
   Example: *I **will** finish my homework today.*

Using *Going to* for Future Time

You have already learnt how the simple present tense can be used to talk about the future. Now, look at these sentences.

She **is going to leave** for Chennai tonight.
She **will be leaving** for Chennai tonight.

In both these sentences, the action will happen in the future. However, in the first sentence, the verb is in the present continuous tense.

Going to is often used to refer to actions that will happen in the future. It performs the same function as *shall* and *will*. However, in some cases, they mean different things in the way they refer to future time.

Example: *I **will/shall** call you.* (refers to an indefinite time in the future)
*I am **going to** call you.* (indicates definite intention in the near future)

So, we use *going to* for the following.

1. To talk about something we have already planned or decided to do.

   Examples: *We are **going to** spend the holidays at my grandmother's house.*
   *I am **going to** help my mother in the kitchen today.*

2. To talk about something we expect to happen in the immediate future.

   Examples: *The clouds are very dark. It is **going to** rain.*
   *Watch out! That tree is **going to** fall!*

A Underline the correct options to complete the sentences.

1. Are you *going to/Will you* answer the phone for me, please? I'm working.
2. I hope Sachin *will/is going to* visit us soon.
3. *I shall/I'm going* to help you with that in ten minutes.
4. As decided, we *will/are going to* watch a film tonight.
5. Watch out! That vase *will/is going to* fall on you!
6. Please take an umbrella. It looks like it *will/is going to* rain.
7. If you want, I *will/am going to* bring a cake for the get-together.
8. Shyam and Ritesh *will/are going to* collect all the newspapers and recycle them.

Simple Future Tense

The **simple future tense** is used for actions that will happen at some point of time in the future.

Examples: *Bipin **will play** as the main striker in the football match.*
*Pratyusha **will perform** in the concert.*

Using the Simple Present for Future Time

The simple present tense can be used to describe future actions or events, especially actions that take place in the future as part of a schedule.

Examples: *My birthday **is** next week.*
*The construction for the new school building **begins** in a few months.*
*My train **leaves** at eight o'clock.*
*The bookstore **opens** in half an hour.*

The simple future tense is used in the following situations.

1. To predict an event in the immediate or near future.
   Examples: *It **will rain** tomorrow.*
   *The tree **will bear** fruit soon.*

2. To express a decision or willingness to do something.
   Examples: *We **will buy** the house.*
   *She **will fetch** the bag for you.*
3. To make an offer or a suggestion.
   Examples: ***Shall** I **get** some coffee for you?*
   ***Shall** we **go** to the park?*
4. To ask for advice or instructions.
   Examples: *What **shall** I **make** for dinner?*
   *Where **shall** we **go** for our vacation?*

Using the Present Continuous for Future Time

The present continuous may also be used to refer to future events or actions, especially when they are part of a definite plan.

Examples: *We **are having** a birthday party on Saturday.*
*I **am meeting** my cousins today.*
*He **is leaving** for Chandigarh at 8 o'clock tonight.*
*Rahul **is getting** the graphic novel he wanted for his birthday.*

B Read these sentences and write if they refer to present or future actions.

1. The film starts at 8 p.m. tonight.
2. Tara is having lunch with me in the afternoon.
3. Our school re-opens after vacations next week.
4. We are visiting our cousins next week.
5. The mall closes at 6 p.m. today.
6. We are having dinner.
7. I begin my music classes soon.
8. I visit my friends on weekends.

Future Continuous Tense

The **future continuous tense** is used for actions that will start in the future and continue for some time.

Examples: *Prerita **will be starting** dance classes from next week.*
*By this time next year, Sumedha **will be studying** in the ninth standard.*

C **Fill in the blanks using the future continuous tense of the given verbs.**

1. I have severe toothache. I __________ the dentist. (visit)
2. Dina __________ for the birthday party. (come)
3. We __________ our holidays in Delhi this year. (spend)
4. We __________ lots of mangoes from Mumbai. (get)
5. By this time next week, I __________ in Singapore. (work)
6. __________ you __________ the concert this year? (attend)
7. The Ghosh family __________ to Kerala this summer. (fly)
8. __________ Tandra __________ with you in April? (stay)

Future Perfect Tense

The **future perfect tense** is used to talk about a future activity that will be finished by or before a specific time in the future.

Examples: *By 4 o'clock tomorrow, the train* ***will have left.***
By the time you get home, I ***will have made*** *dinner.*

D **Complete the sentences using the future perfect form of the given verbs.**

1. Tarun and Aditi __________ by this time tomorrow. (arrive)
2. I __________ my homework by tomorrow. (complete)
3. Daniel __________ a complaint against his landlord by this evening. (lodge)
4. Sunita's mother __________ her lunch before she leaves for work. (pack)
5. The old man __________ the puppy by noon. (feed)
6. The parrot __________ a new song by this time next week. (learn)

Future Perfect Continuous Tense

The **future perfect continuous tense** is used to talk about an ongoing activity which has not yet been completed but will be at a specified time in the future.

Examples: *Next month, Kiran* ***will have been taking*** *singing lessons for ten years.*
By this time next year, Mridul ***will have been playing*** *professional football for two years.*

E **Fill in the blanks using the future perfect continuous form of the given verbs.**

1. By next June, we __________ on the project for three months. (work)
2. I __________ the house for two hours when it strikes ten. (clean)
3. The class __________ on over one hour by the time the bell rings. (go)
4. Come August, we __________ in Mumbai for five years. (live)
5. By the time I attend the next school reunion, I __________ for nearly five years. (work)

6. By 2017, Sarojini ________ as a professional singer for a decade. (perform)
7. They ________ abroad for two years by this time next year. (stay)
8. By today, it ________ for three days continuously. (rain)

Don't Forget!

1. In future time, the verb takes four forms: the simple future, future continuous, future perfect and future perfect continuous.
2. The verb in the simple future tense takes the form *will + verb*.
3. The verb in the future continuous tense takes the form *will be + verb + -ing*.
4. The verb in the future perfect tense takes the form *will have + past participle of verb*.
5. The verb in the future perfect continuous tense takes the form *will have been + verb + -ing*.
6. *Going to*, the present continuous tense and the simple present tense are also used to show future time.

Let Us Write

Vinita is writing a letter to her brother, Sameer. Complete the letter with the stated form of the given verbs.

10, Shaheed Captain Bhan Marg
Delhi - 110092

18 July 2020

Dear Sameer,

How ____________ (you be, present perfect)? ____________ (you come, simple future) home next month? I ____________ (write, present continuous) to you for some advice. I ____________ (think, present continuous) of taking up a summer job as an intern with an NGO. I ____________ (apply, future continuous) to HelpAge India. ____________ (you know, simple present) of any others that I ____________ (can, simple present) apply to? I ____________ (also look, simple future) at other options for summer employment.

By this time next year, I ____________ (volunteer, future perfect continuous) at NGOs for two years. I ____________ (gain, future perfect) useful experience, but I ____________ (want, simple present) to do more.

Since you ____________ (do, present perfect) such work before, please ____________ (send, simple present) me some suggestions.

With love,

Vinita

Test 1

A **Underline the nouns in the following sentences. Then, identify whether they are common, proper, collective or abstract nouns.**

1. Zeenat went for a picnic last Sunday with her family.
2. Gloria won two gold and three silver medals in the inter-school competition.
3. Anna had some great memories of the time she had spent with her family.
4. We recorded the song in front of a live studio audience.
5. She sent me a bouquet of flowers.
6. Everyone could see Aditya's determination to finish the race.

B **Rewrite the sentences after correcting the errors in the use of adjectives.**

1. There aren't much students in the class.
2. It's growing cold and cold by the day.
3. Mohit is more greedier than Ronit.
4. That boy is strong than Hari.
5. Veena is junior than Vinod by five years.
6. We are discussing a more major issue.

C **Fill in the blanks with suitable pronouns.**

1. She looked at __________ in the mirror and said, 'How beautiful __________ look in this new dress!'
2. He went to the visa office to submit his application but could not submit __________ because __________ did not have all the documents.
3. Neeti told me that a friend of __________ was going to Sydney next week.
4. Let's change the tyres __________. It will be much cheaper.
5. __________ repaired the car for you? Did you do it __________ ?

D **Fill in the blanks with appropriate modal auxiliaries.**

1. If you don't like the blue shirt, you __________ (can/shall/will) try the grey one.
2. She __________ (could/should/might) easily lift weights of 60 kilos when she was young.
3. __________ (Will/May/Shall) I come in, please?
4. You __________ (would/must) not leave the campus without informing your teacher.
5. If I were you, I __________ (would/could/can) ask for a refund.
6. In future, people __________ (will/can/could) send and receive messages using more efficient ways of communicating.

E **Underline the direct objects and circle the indirect objects in these sentences.**

1. The patient sent the doctor a 'thank you' note.
2. The teacher gave all the students chocolates.
3. His grandmother sends him a gift for his birthday every year.
4. Did Jai give you the passes for the play?
5. The school awarded Ravi a full scholarship.
6. We wrote a poem for Aunt Shanti.

F **Correct the errors in subject-verb agreement in the following sentences.**

1. Many a soldier are hurt in the battlefield.
2. Ten thousand rupees are a lot of money to carry in cash.
3. Each of the gifts are wrapped beautifully.
4. People says the house is beautiful.
5. None of the children in this group are older than twelve.
6. Everyone in the class have a copy of the handout.

G **Fill in the blanks with the correct present tense form of the verbs.**

1. He __________ (wake) up at 5 a.m. every day to play cricket.
2. I __________ (meet) her before.
3. It __________ (rain) since morning.
4. I __________ (watch) the film, *The Sound of Music* now. It __________ (has) beautiful songs.
5. I __________ (play) tennis daily for two weeks since my doctor advised me to lose weight.
6. Shankar's health __________ (improve) greatly since yesterday.

H **Fill in the blanks with the correct past tense form of the verbs.**

1. She __________ (finish) cooking before the guests __________ (arrive).
2. I __________ (watch) TV when I heard a sudden noise outside.
3. Surya told me that he __________ (book) the tickets.
4. When she realized I __________ (look) at her, she turned away.
5. Rohit __________ (wait) for an hour by the time his mother __________. (call)
6. At the conference, the scientists announced that they __________ (find) a cure for cancer.

I **Fill in the blanks with the correct future tense form of the verbs.**

1. Tomorrow's English class __________ (continue) for about 30 minutes.
2. Meet me at the park tomorrow. I __________ (sit) close to the main gate.
3. The trophy __________ (go) to the best team.
4. By this time next year, my sister __________ (start) going to her new school.
5. Sia __________ (wait) for Reema at her house for over two hours now.
6. I __________ (visit) my grandmother next summer.

10 Adverbs

Let's Get Started

Look at the images and fill in the blanks with adverbs of your choice.

1. 

The children are dancing ____________

2. 

The girl is reading a book ____________

3. 

The biker is riding ____________

4. 

He is running very ____________

The words you wrote describe the verb in each sentence.

An **adverb** is a word that is used to modify or add information to a verb, an adjective or another adverb. Sometimes, adverbs modify a whole sentence.

Examples: *Neeta spoke **well**.* (modifying verb)
*Neeta spoke **very** well.* (modifying adverb)
*Mohan is **quite** tall.* (modifying adjective)
***Honestly**, I did not mean to offend you.* (modifying entire sentence)

We form adverbs in the following ways.

- By adding *-ly* to adjectives.
  Examples: *nice → nicely*, *playful → playfully*
- When the adjective ends in *-y*, *-le* or *-ic*, we drop or add a few letters and then add *-ly*.
  Examples: *merry → merrily*, *gentle → gently*, *public → publicly*

A Identify the adverb and the word each adverb modifies. Then write whether the modified word is a verb, an adjective or an adverb.

1. Please don't take her words seriously.
2. The infection is spreading fast. Consult the doctor immediately.
3. If you pay the fee now, you will avoid a fine later.
4. The film was so boring; it was a total waste of money and time!
5. He is extremely kind; he can't even harm an insect.

6. It was a terrible accident; many people were seriously injured.
7. They heard a loud noise and were very afraid.
8. She was an able administrator who knew the strengths of her staff well.

Types of Adverbs

Adverbs can tell us how, where, when and how many times an action occurs, as well as about the intensity of the action. Adverbs are classified into different types based on these functions.

Adverbs of manner tell us *how* the action takes place.

Examples: *Let's move **faster**.*
*He was driving **slowly**.*
*She spoke **loudly**.*

Adverbs of place tell us *where* the action takes place.

Examples: *They will come **here**.*
*Sit **near** me.*
*Leave your shoes **outside**.*

Grammar Byte

When an adverb qualifies an adjective, it is usually placed before it.

*She was **so** happy to meet her grandson after ten years.*

Adverbs of time tell us *when* the action takes place.

Examples: *The guests will arrive **now**.*
*We'll go shopping in the **evening**.*
*Let's start **tomorrow**.*

Adverbs of frequency tell us *how often* the action takes place.

Examples: *She **seldom** eats sweets.*
*They **regularly** watch films at the multiplex.*
*The train **always** leaves on time.*
*She pays her rent on a **monthly** basis.*

Grammar Byte

Some words are used both as adjectives and adverbs.

*There is **enough** food in the fridge.* (adjective; modifies the noun *food*)

*You have worked **enough** for the day.* (adverb; modifies the verb *have worked*)

Adverbs of degree tell us *how intensely* the action takes place.

Examples: *She was **quite** sick for a week.*
*She found the question paper **extremely** difficult.*
*Rashmi was **so** tired that she fell asleep at 6 p.m.*

B **Underline the adverbs and mention their types.**

1. She goes to the gym daily; she rarely skips the routine. ____________
2. She was so shy that she rarely spoke in class. ____________
3. Leave the umbrella outside; it will dry faster. ____________
4. We shall meet again tomorrow. ____________
5. Shyam once borrowed money from his friend and forgot to pay him back. ____________
6. Suhas spoke eloquently at the morning assembly. ____________
7. They are extremely decent people; they never speak ill about anyone. ____________
8. You have done very well in maths. ____________
9. I clearly remember keeping the keys on the table. ____________
10. I don't want the injection. It's extremely painful! ____________

Adverbs that ask questions about the time, place and manner of the action and the reason for the action are called **interrogative adverbs**. These are *when, where, how* and *why.*

Examples: ***When*** *will you get ready?* (time)
Where *are we going?* (place)
How *will we go?* (manner)
Why *are you up so late at night?* (reason)

Adverbs that confirm or deny the action of a verb are called **adverbs of affirmation or negation**, respectively.

Some commonly used adverbs of affirmation are *definitely, surely, absolutely* and *undoubtedly*.
Some commonly used adverbs of negation are *no, can't, don't, not* and *never*.

Examples: *Sita said she would* ***definitely*** *attend the ceremony.* (affirmation)
I am ***not*** *taking up your offer.* (negation)

C **Underline the adverbs and state what type they are.**

1. No, they are not going to come. ____________
2. Tia is undoubtedly the sweetest girl in the class. ____________
3. She asked Kainaz how she had been. ____________
4. When shall we eat? I'm quite hungry. ____________
5. You are not training enough for the upcoming swimming competition. ____________
6. I am extremely sorry for forgetting the task you asked me to do. ____________

D Fill in the blanks with suitable adverbs.

1. She thinks she is ____________ correct. (adverb of affirmation)
2. Neha ran ____________ fast but could not catch the bus. (adverb of degree)
3. He is lazy; he ____________ does any work. I have ____________ told him to change his ways but he ____________ listens. (adverbs of frequency)
4. We reached the venue for the competition ____________ time. (adverb of time)
5. I had ____________ fallen asleep when a loud noise woke me up. (adverb of degree)
6. Eat ____________, there's plenty of time. (adverb of manner)
7. The dog barked ____________ and ____________ at the sight of the strangers. (adverb of manner)
8. Speak ____________; I can't hear you. (adverb of manner)
9. Look! How ____________ the peacock is dancing! (adverb of manner)
10. ____________ are you planning to leave for the concert? (interrogative adverb)

Position of Adverbs

Adverbs of manner, place and time are usually placed after the verb. If the verb has a direct object, the adverb is placed after it.

Examples: *The lion roared* ***angrily***. (adverb of manner)

The mechanic repaired the car ***easily***. (adverb of manner; direct object: *car*)

I met my friend ***here***. (adverb of place; direct object: *friend*)

I will finish the work ***tonight***. (adverb of time; direct object: *work*)

Adverbs of frequency and degree are often placed between the subject of the sentence and the verb.

Examples: *I* ***always*** *have breakfast by 8 a.m.*

I ***just*** *remembered that I have to meet my friend today.*

If the verb consists of two words, then the adverb is placed between the two words.

Example: *I had* ***almost*** *forgotten that we have to attend a birthday party tomorrow.*

E Insert the adverbs in the correct place.

1. I remember to wear my watch. (seldom)
2. The foal trotted beside its mother. (calmly)
3. Fred walked the house to check that all the doors were locked. (around)
4. I am getting on the bus. (now)
5. Salma was satisfied with her work. (quite)
6. I have discussed this matter with him. (already)

7. There is no chance of our reaching the venue on time. (almost)
8. Farah spoke to the man who had misplaced her bags. (angrily)

Degrees of Comparison of Adverbs

Adverbs, like adjectives, also have three degrees of comparison – positive, comparative and superlative.

Adverbs form their comparatives and superlatives by adding *-er* and *-est* to the base form or by adding *more* and *most*.

Examples: *The lion ran* ***fast****.* (positive degree)

I reached early, but my sister had reached ***earlier****.* (comparative degree)

The children have performed ***most delightfully****.* (superlative degree)

Sometimes, the word *as* is used to show comparison.

Examples: *He can shout* ***as*** *much as you can.*

She cooks ***as*** *well as my mother.*

There are some adverbs that form the comparative and superlative irregularly.

Examples: *little → less → least*

well → better → best

badly → worse → worst

Grammar Bytes

Adverbs that end in *-ly* use the words *more* and *most* to form their comparatives and superlatives.

The adverb *far* has two comparative and superlative forms.

far → further → furthest
(refers to physical distance)

far → farther → farthest
(refers to distance in time and space)

Watch Out!

Adverbs like *sometimes, never, here, there, now, then, first, again, yesterday,* and *daily* do not have the comparative form.

F Complete the sentences using the correct form of the given adverbs.

1. That building stands __________ (tall) than any other building in the city.
2. She picked up the new born baby __________ (carefully)
3. I reached __________ (early) than usual.
4. Airplanes can fly __________ (high) than birds.
5. Could you please write __________? (clearly)
6. Rajat is working __________ (hard) than his brother.
7. The man ate his lunch __________, (hungrily) as he had missed breakfast.
8. This is the __________ (far) I have ever come from home.
9. She spoke __________ (little) in class than she did in the playground.
10. They are running as __________ (fast) as our school team.

11 Prepositions

Let's Get Started

Read the passage and identify the prepositions.

Suddenly Alice came upon a little three-legged table, all made of solid glass. There was nothing on it except a tiny golden key, and her first thought was that it might belong to one of the doors of the hall, but alas! Either the locks were too large, or the key was too small, but at any rate it would not open any of them. However, the second time round, she came upon a low curtain she had not noticed before. Behind it was a little door about fifteen inches high. She tried the little golden key in the lock.

Prepositions are words placed before a noun or a pronoun. They show the relationship of the noun with the other parts of a sentence.

Examples: *The principal commented **on** the performance of the students.*
*The bridge **across** the river was destroyed **by** an earthquake last year.*

Types of Prepositions

Based on the functions they perform, prepositions can be of several types.

Prepositions of time give information about the time when the action in the sentence takes place.

Examples: *We are going to Rajkot for a family trip **on** Friday.*
*The team plans to complete the project **in** a month.*

Look at these common prepositions of time and their usage.

Prepositions	Usage
in	To refer to a particular time of day, month or year **Examples**: ***in** the morning, **in** January, **in** 1968* To refer to the time within which an action will happen in the future **Examples**: ***in** an hour, **in** a year*
on	To refer to a particular day or date **Examples**: ***on** 16 June, **on** Tuesday*
at	To indicate a specific time of the day **Examples**: ***at** 4.30 p.m., **at** noon*
from	To indicate the starting time of an action **Examples**: ***from** morning, **from** 2011*

Grammar Bytes

On time refers to the exact time of an action.

*We reached the station **on time**.*

In time suggests that something happened at the time or before the deadline.

*She reached the school **in time** to attend dance practice before class.*

for	To indicate the period of time for which an action continues **Examples**: ***for*** *eleven hours*, ***for*** *six months*
since	To indicate the starting time of an action that has continued till the present moment **Examples**: ***since*** *9 o'clock*, ***since*** *last night*

Some other common prepositions of time are *during, before, after, till, by* and *within*.

Prepositions of place show the position of the person, place, animal or thing referred to by the noun.

Examples: *Our uncle has been living* ***in*** *California for the last ten years.*
Have you looked ***behind*** *the table for your book?*

This table lists some prepositions of place and their usage.

Prepositions	Usage
in	To refer to large areas. **Examples**: ***in*** *India*, ***in*** *the world* To indicate something contained within a space. **Examples**: ***in*** *the lobby*, ***in*** *the cupboard*
on	To indicate the surface of something. **Examples**: ***on*** *the table*, ***on*** *the wall*
at	To refer to small areas. **Examples**: ***at*** *Bandra*, ***at*** *Laxmi Nagar* To refer to a specific place. **Examples**: ***at*** *the entrance*, ***at*** *the hotel*

Some other common prepositions of place are *over, under, above, below, opposite, near, behind, between* and *beside*.

Prepositions of movement and direction show the movement to and from a place or the direction which is to be taken.

Examples: *We decided to climb* ***up*** *the stairs instead of taking the lift.*
This river flows ***down*** *the hill and joins a stream.*

This table lists some prepositions of movement and direction and their usage.

Prepositions	Usage
across	To indicate movement from one end of something to the other. **Examples**: ***across*** *the road*, ***across*** *the river*
into	To indicate movement from outside to inside. **Examples**: ***into*** *the pool*, ***into*** *the tunnel*
through	To indicate movement within a space. **Examples**: ***through*** *the jungle*, ***through*** *the leaves*
towards	To indicate movement in the direction of something. **Examples**: ***towards*** *the post office*, ***towards*** *the school*
along	To indicate movement from one point to another. **Examples**: ***along*** *the beach*, ***along*** *the road*

Grammar Byte

Look at the way the prepositions of movement *by* and *on* are used.

He goes to school ***by*** *bus.*
The prince travelled ***on*** *horseback.*

Similarly, we say, *by car*, *by air* and *by train*. But we say *on foot* and *on a bike*.

A Fill in the blanks with the correct prepositions.

1. The price ________ (for, of, about) each shirt is different.
2. These bangles are made ________ (from, with, of) gold.
3. He goes to school ________ (by, on, with) foot.
4. The dress I bought is very similar ________ (to, from, with) the one that you bought.
5. The principal stressed ________ (for, on, with) the importance ________ (for, of, on) being punctual.
6. Let me congratulate you ________ (for, on, about) winning the inter-school dance competition.
7. The two brothers are very different ________ (from, to, with) each other.
8. Vineet is known ________ (about, for, in) his many talents, such as drawing, skating and swimming.
9. I have no idea ________ (into, about, for) the time ________ (of, for, at) their arrival.
10. If you want to work ________ (with, about, of) us, you should adhere ________ (from, for, to) our policies.
11. I'm not interested ________ (about, in, for) what you are going to tell me.
12. She is quite pleased ________ (about, with, of) my performance.

B Fill in the blanks with suitable prepositions of time from the box.

in	within	for	during	since	before	around	at	by	after	about

1. It's only 5.30 p.m. now; the film begins ________ 6 p.m. We have reached the theatre ________ time for the show.
2. Check your answers once ________ you submit the answer script to the invigilator.
3. This song is ________ a brave explorer.
4. It has been raining ________ three hours; and it looks like it is not going to stop anytime soon.
5. I walked ________ the house ________ the river.
6. The breaking news was broadcast ________ the regular programme.
7. The new session will begin ________ 7 June 2017.
8. I will be back from my trip ________ two weeks.
9. The teacher has been correcting the answer scripts ________ 2 o'clock.

C Fill in the blanks with suitable prepositions.

1. Are you ready? We must leave ________ ten minutes.
2. I'm sorry, I forgot all ________ it.
3. Beauty lies ________ the beholder's eye.
4. There is no shortcut ________ success.
5. Have patience; I can't do everything ________ one go!
6. The grass is always greener ________ the other side.

7. I'm fascinated ________ these new gadgets.
8. Birds ________ a feather flock together.
9. None of the competitors are deserving ________ this award.
10. Your house is far ________ my house; it will take at least an hour ________ me ________ reach.
11. You have performed very well ________ the exams. I'm really proud ________ you.
12. Don't spend your money ________ that bag; it's way too expensive. Go ________ something cheaper.
13. Don't judge a book ________ its cover.
14. The fabric of these trousers is ________ excellent quality.
15. A journey ________ a thousand miles begins ________ a single step.

Common Errors

Look at these common errors made in the use of prepositions.

1. We discussed *about* the matter. (incorrect)
   We discussed the matter. (correct)
2. We ordered *for* some food. (incorrect)
   We ordered some food. (correct)
3. She entered *into* the room. (incorrect)
   She entered the room. (correct)
4. What is the time *in* your watch? (incorrect)
   What is the time *by* your watch? (correct)
5. She was trembling *in* fear. (incorrect)
   She was trembling *with* fear. (correct)
6. Did you watch this programme *in* the TV? (incorrect)
   Did you watch this programme *on* TV? (correct)
7. The last ten kilometres of the pilgrimage site can be travelled only *by* foot. (incorrect)
   The last ten kilometres of the pilgrimage site can be travelled only *on* foot. (correct)
8. Sit *besides* Sita. (incorrect) ('besides' means in addition to)
   Sit *beside* Sita. (correct) ('beside' means by the side of)

D Rewrite the sentences after correcting the errors in prepositions.

1. Of what colour is your new dress? I am planning of buying it.
2. The dog was not allowed to enter in the house. It trembled in fear at the sight of other dogs.
3. According to the time in my watch, it is approaching to 5 p.m. I think I will go to home.
4. The old gentleman covered the short distance by foot.

5. I sat besides Prema and discussed about the upcoming Diwali celebrations. We wanted to draw a rangoli design which we had seen in the TV. 'Let us meet on next Friday and decide what we will do,' said Prema.
6. My teacher advised to me to take part in the play.

Don't Forget!

1. A preposition shows the relationship between a noun and other parts of the sentence.
2. Some common types of prepositions are prepositions of place, prepositions of time and prepositions of movement and direction.

Let Us Write

Your friend is coming to your house for the first time. Give him or her directions to your house. Note the prepositions you use and state their types.

12 Conjunctions

Let's Get Started

Read these sentences and underline the joining words. Then, circle the words, phrases or clauses they join.

1. She is a rare combination of wealth and humility.
2. We may visit you in the morning or in the evening.
3. I liked the film very much, so I watched it twice.
4. I went home early because I was tired.

Conjunctions are words which join words, phrases or clauses.

Conjunctions are of three types: coordinating conjunctions, subordinating conjunctions and correlative conjunctions.

Coordinating Conjunctions

Single-word conjunctions that connect two or more independent clauses or words of equal importance are called **coordinating conjunctions**. Some of the common coordinating conjunctions are *for, and, nor, but, or, yet, still, neither* and *so*.

Examples: *What would you like, milkshake **or** ice cream?*
*She refuses to meet me, **nor** will she talk to me on the phone.*
*The sky was filled with clouds, **still** it didn't rain.*

A Fill in the blanks using suitable coordinating conjunctions.

1. We have planned a week-long trip in May; shall I book the tickets for the first week ________ (for, or, and) the second?
2. I'd prefer to go on holiday only in the third week ________ (and, so, but) are you free?
3. You have submitted the assignment pretty late, ________ (but, and, or) I'll accept it this time.
4. We listened to him, ________ (so, for, and) he was wise.
5. She does not want to have lunch, ________ (nor, but, or) does she want anything to drink.
6. They were hungry, ________ (yet, so, but) they decided to have an early dinner.
7. Her two favourite pastimes are trekking ________ (for, or, and) reading.

Subordinating Conjunctions

Conjunctions that connect an independent clause with a dependent clause are called **subordinating conjunctions**. Some common subordinating conjunctions are *while, as, because, since, until, although, even though, as soon as* and *so that.*

Examples: *We started early* ***so that*** *we could avoid the rush hour traffic.*
I could not write my exams ***since*** *I fell ill.*
She browsed through the magazines ***while*** *I got ready.*

Subordinating conjunctions can be of different types based on the dependent clauses following them.

a. Subordinating conjunctions introducing noun clauses

Examples: *He said* ***that*** *he was not interested in meeting her.*
The children asked the teacher ***if*** *they could go the library.*

b. Subordinating conjunctions introducing adverb clauses

The table lists some subordinating conjunctions that can be used to introduce various types of adverb clauses.

Grammar Bytes

A subordinate clause is a group of words which has a finite verb and a subject and needs the help of the main clause to make complete sense.

A noun clause acts as a noun in the sentence, while an adverb clause acts as an adverb.

Type of clause	Subordinating conjunctions
Adverb clause of time	*when, whenever, before, after, till, since, as, while, as soon as* **Examples:** *We will inform you* ***when*** *we receive the books.* *I called her* ***as soon as*** *I got to know the result.*
Adverb clause of place	*where, wherever* **Examples:** *He bought the shirt from a shop* ***where*** *there was a sale.* *You will find people of Indian origin* ***wherever*** *you go in the world.*
Adverb clause of purpose	*so that, that, lest* **Examples:** *She made the travel arrangements early* ***so that*** *they did not face problems later.* *Don't get wet in the rain* ***lest*** *you catch a cold.*
Adverb clause of condition	*if, unless* **Examples:** *You can chat with us* ***if*** *you have the time.* *Your assignment will not be graded* ***unless*** *you submit it on time.*
Adverb clause of manner	*as, as if* **Examples:** *You should do* ***as*** *you are told.* *She looked at me* ***as if*** *I were a stranger.*
Adverb clause of comparison	*as ... as, than* **Examples:** *Sunil is* ***as*** *tall* ***as*** *Rahman.* *Mary is more hardworking* ***than*** *Ritu.*
Adverb clause of concession or contrast	*though, although, even if* **Examples:** *You will not find a more generous person than Manish* ***even if*** *you search the whole world.* ***Although*** *it was late, I stayed up to finish my homework.*

Type of clause	Subordinating conjunctions
Adverb clause of cause or reason	*because, since, as* **Examples:** *He reached home late* ***because*** *the traffic was bad.* ***Since*** *he is unwell, he cannot meet you now.*
Adverb clause of result or consequence	*so ... that, such ... that* **Examples:** *It rained* ***so*** *heavily* ***that*** *we had to postpone our trip.* *It was* ***such*** *a hot day* ***that*** *we could not step out of the house.*

Correlative Conjunctions

Correlative Conjunctions are paired conjunctions that connect two or more statements or words of equal importance. Some common correlative conjunctions are *neither ... nor, either ... or, not only ... but also, although ... yet, no sooner... than, hardly ... when* and *whether ... or.*

Examples: *I have not decided* ***whether*** *to take up painting* ***or*** *pottery.*
You can pay ***either*** *by cheque* ***or*** *credit card.*
Hardly *had he finished cooking* ***when*** *the guests arrived.*
He ***neither*** *came,* ***nor*** *did he send a message.*
Not only *is he a great player* ***but*** *he is* ***also*** *a humble person.*
Although *she started early,* ***yet*** *she reached late because of the heavy rain.*
Whether *you want to join our team* ***or*** *theirs is your decision.*

B Fill in the blanks with appropriate conjunctions.

1. ________ you can meet me on Tuesday, I will give you the book.
2. We bought our new books ________ our uniforms.
3. He got very good grades ________ he is unhappy.
4. You can choose to buy the red ________ the green purse; both are of the same price.
5. Why don't you read a book ________ waiting for your friends to arrive?
6. I can wait ________ you finish.
7. He will forgive you ________ he is a kind man.
8. Do not go out ________ the rain stops.
9. Eat your carrots and peas; ________ you will not get the ice cream.

C Fill in the blanks with the most suitable conjunctions.

1. She has not spoken to me ________ (for, since, when) she left the colony.
2. The lights went off ________ (as soon as, as well as, whenever) the thunder struck.
3. You cannot interview the painter for the school magazine ________ (unless, if, although) you meet him in person.
4. You can come ________ (after, before, when) you are free.
5. Keep trying ________ (while, until, after) you succeed.
6. You will have to book the ticket now, ________ (but, else, unless) the seat will go to someone else.

7. You cannot understand our problems ________ (though, while, because) you have never lived here.
8. I did not realise that I had made a mistake ________ (when, until, unless) you told me.
9. It is terribly hot today; ________ (if, but, unless) it is necessary, don't go out.
10. Scarcely had I reached home ________ (when, than, before) it started raining.

D Rewrite the sentences using the given conjunctions.

1. She was very upset but she did not cry. (Although)
   Although she was very upset, she did not cry.
2. Unless you speak up, we can't hear you. (if)
3. Both Ramesh and Suresh attended the interview. (as well as)
4. We are both tired and hungry. (not only ... but also)
5. You won't find the books if you don't search properly. (unless)
6. I read a book and waited for him. (while)
7. I don't know their phone number, so I cannot call them. (for)

Conjunctions are used to join clauses to form different types of sentences.
Coordinating and correlative conjunctions are used to join independent clauses to form compound sentences.
Subordinating conjunctions are used to join an independent clause with dependent clauses to form complex sentences.
This is covered in greater detail in the chapter 'Transformation and Synthesis of Sentences'.

Don't Forget!

1. Conjunctions are of three types: coordinating, subordinating and correlative.
2. Coordinating conjunctions join statements or words of equal importance.
3. Subordinating conjunctions join a main clause with one or more dependent clauses.
4. Correlative conjunctions are paired conjunctions that join statements or clauses of equal importance.

Let Us Write

You are working on a group project with two friends. You can submit it on time only if another person joins your group. Write a letter to explain the situation to your teacher. Note the conjunctions that you use and state their types.

13 Determiners and Quantifiers

Let's Get Started

Read this recipe for mango sherbet. Underline all the words used before the nouns that indicate quantity or number.

Take two raw mangoes. Steam them in a pressure pan. Peel the mangoes. Take out the pulp. Add three glasses of water, a hundred grams of jaggery and a teaspoon of salt. Blend these ingredients in a mixer. Garnish with a few mint leaves. Serve the sherbet chilled.

The words that you underlined tell us *how many, how much* or *which one* in relation to a noun. In the first sentence, the word *two* answers the question *how many* in relation to the noun *mangoes*.

Determiners are words used before nouns to indicate which nouns are being referred to. They are either specific or general in meaning.

These are the most common types of determiners.

Types	Determiners
Articles	*a, an, the*
Demonstratives	*this, these, that, those*
Possessives	*my, our, your, his, her, its, their*
Cardinal and ordinal numbers	*one, two, ten, first, second, tenth*, etc.
Quantifiers	*many, few, several, all, some, more, most, none*
Distributives	*each, every, neither, either*
Interrogatives	*which, whose, what*

Examples: *I should add **a little** salt to the curry.*
__This__ decision to postpone the match is fine by me.
*There was **much** confusion over the outcome of the election.*
*I met **my** English teacher yesterday in the market.*
*There are a **few** things I wanted to ask you.*

A **Underline the determiners in these sentences and state their types.**

1. The old fort on the big hill has several interesting secrets.
2. My uncle has two houses in Mumbai.
3. A hundred people have applied for the two vacancies that we have.
4. The brave soldiers saved the country from many attacks by the enemy.
5. Mary has bought these apples. She is distributing a dozen of them among the poor children.

6. This list names the top ten tourist attractions in the city of Paris.
7. To make this delicious cake, you need four eggs, half a kilo of sugar, an ounce of chocolate and two cups of flour.
8. My ninety-year-old grandmother is quite healthy and has full control of all her faculties.
9. The recipe needs red grapes.
10. That lovely dog is my friend.
11. Some children always seem happy.
12. This watermelon tastes sweet.
13. All six stories are quite interesting.
14. My grandfather lives in that house.
15. That house has a huge red roof.
16. I painted the walls of my room green.

Difference between Adjectives and Determiners

Both adjectives and determiners provide more information about nouns. However, adjectives describe or modify the quality of nouns. They can be placed before or after the noun. Adjectives do not get affected by the gender and number of the noun.

Examples: *The **blue** flowers are arranged beautifully on the table.*
*The **tall** man is my neighbour.*

Determiners specify the nouns or point out the positions of nouns. They can only be placed before the noun. They change form depending on the gender and number of the noun.

Example: ***Those** blue flowers are arranged beautifully on the table.*

Articles

The **articles** *a*, *an* and *the* are used as determiners. They are the most commonly used determiners.

Examples: *I need **a** glass of water.*
*That is **an** intelligent answer!*
*Pass me **the** salt, please.*

B Fill in the blanks using appropriate articles.

1. When I woke up in ________ morning, I was surprised to see ________ envelope near my pillow.
2. In ________ kingdom of Crete, there lived ________ cruel king.
3. If you want ________ answer to your question, you have to ask Trisha yourself.
4. Iqbal is often seen as ________ ideal student. He is ________ good student, ________ fine sportsman and takes part in all ________ extra-curricular activities.
5. There is ________ girl who sells seashells by ________ seashore. Have you seen ________ seashells she sells?
6. Roger Federer is commonly regarded as ________ greatest tennis player in ________ world. He has already won ________ championship this year.
7. ________ difficult problem can often be solved by ________ simple answer. ________ intelligent answer is not always a complex one.
8. Bob Dylan won ________ Nobel Prize in Literature in ________ year 2016.
9. Do you know ________ name of ________ current President of India?
10. Tarun is ________ university student and ________ state-level badminton player.

Demonstratives

The words *this*, *that*, *these* and *those* are used as **demonstratives**. *This* and *that* are used with singular nouns, while *these* and *those* are used with plural nouns.

Examples: ***This*** *egg has not been boiled properly.*
That *blue house near the park belongs to my aunt.*
These *term papers were submitted by the students last week.*
Those *students have registered for the course.*

C Complete the sentences using appropriate demonstratives.

1. Look at ________ birds flying in the sky. Aren't they beautiful?
2. I wanted to buy ________ jersey; however, ________ blue ones are nice as well.
3. ________ mango tree was planted by my grandfather. ________ mangoes are from ________ tree.
4. The country from where ________ coffee is imported is in South America.
5. Can you please take ________ flowers and put them in the vase?
6. ________ students who have not submitted their projects should do so by tomorrow.
7. ________ days, I leave for school early.
8. ________ trees on the other side of the fence were planted by my father when he was young.

Possessives

Possessives help show ownership. Words like *my, your, our, his, her, their* and *its* are used as possessives.

Examples: *Wahida is **my** best friend.*
*We are travelling in **our** car.*

D **Complete the passage using appropriate possessives.**

One evening after tea, my mother, father and ________ younger brother, Revanth, sat around the dining table to plan ________ holiday trip. ________ brother pointed out that we had never gone on a road trip before. ________ father was uncertain whether our car would be able to survive a long trip because ________ engine kept failing. So, I suggested that this year ________ family could travel by train through south India. ________ best friend's mother worked in the Indian Railways and she could help us select a tour package. ________ parents thought that it was a good plan, but Revanth had a different idea. He suggested that we rent a car at each of ________ destinations and explore the places by car.

Cardinals and Ordinals

Cardinals specify the number of countable nouns. **Ordinals** indicate a series or a sequence.

Examples: *She bought **six** oranges.* (cardinal number)
*This is my **second** trip to Lucknow.* (ordinal number)

Quantifiers

Quantifiers specify the quantity or amount of the nouns.

This table lists some common quantifiers and their usage.

Quantifiers	Meaning and Usage	Examples
few	means 'almost none' used with countable nouns	*There are **few** people in the auditorium.*
little	means 'hardly any' used with uncountable nouns	*There is **little** light in the room.*
all	means 'everything and everyone' used with both countable and uncountable nouns	***All** the passengers have boarded the plane.* ***All** the money is spent.*
much	used with uncountable nouns	*There is not **much** sugar in the coffee.*
many	used with countable nouns	***Many** kids have registered for the summer camp.*

Quantifiers	Meaning and Usage	Examples
some	used to refer to an unspecified number or amount used with both countable and uncountable nouns	*There is **some** bread in the fridge.* *There are **some** guests waiting for you.*
any	used to refer to a specified number or amount used with a negative verb used in interrogatives	*She does not have **any** apples.* *He does not have **any** spare time.* *Do you have **any** suggestions?*

E Fill in the blanks with appropriate quantifiers.

1. He has ________ good news for you. (much, some, any)
2. I don't have ________ hope of getting the job. (some, any, few)
3. Even though I made a ________ mistakes, I think I sang well. (some, any, few)
4. Could you buy me a pencil? I can't find ________ in my pencil box. (much, some, any)
5. I think ________ of our students will pass with flying colours. (much, many, any)
6. Bengaluru roads always have too ________ traffic. (many, much, few)
7. There are ________ cards left over from last Christmas. (all, little, some)
8. The new mayor has received ________ support from the citizens. (all, little, few)
9. ________ the paintings have been sold! The sale was a success! (All, Little, Some)

Distributives

Distributives refer to each one of a group. They are *each, every, neither* and *either*.

Examples: ***Each** of the two boys has won a prize.*
***Every** child is unique.*
*I can stay at **either** hotel.*
***Neither** of the children wanted to go home.*

Watch Out!

The determiner *every* cannot be used with plural nouns.

Every morning Jaya goes jogging.

Interrogatives

Interrogatives are used in questions to gather more information about the noun. There are three interrogative determiners: *what, which* and *whose.*

Examples: ***What** spice have you added to the biryani?*
***Which** book do you want to read?*

F Fill in the blanks with *each, every, either* or *neither*.

1. ________ (every/either) child in the class participated enthusiastically.
2. The teacher spoke to ________ (neither/each) student separately after the exam.
3. ________ (every/neither) problem has a solution. You just have to search for it.
4. ________ (each/every) of their answers was correct.
5. Mr Simon gave ________ (either/each) of his students a gift on Children's Day.
6. The security guard needs to check ________ (every/either) car.
7. There are two chairs here. You can take ________ (either/every) of them.
8. ________ (neither/either) of the books by the new author is very interesting.
9. I gave ________ (each/either) patient a 'get well soon' card.
10. Sometimes ________ (either/each) of us wants a day off to do as we like.
11. I have helped you in ________ (every/each) way.
12. My uncle wanted his two sons to become doctors but ________ (either/neither) wanted to study medicine.

G Fill in the blanks with the given determiners.

third	any	all	neither	few	my	our

1. We are going to sell ________ old car.
2. This is the ________ time that the bell has rung.
3. She didn't have ________ money in her purse.
4. There were ________ people in the restaurant.
5. ________ grandfather's day starts with some brisk morning exercise.
6. ________ of the designs pleased Mrs Chand.
7. ________ the workers went on strike.

H Underline the errors in these sentences and rewrite them correctly. More than one answer is possible for some of the sentences.

1. There is few water in the jug.
2. They bought an car recently.
3. The teacher said that little students have applied for the scholarship.
4. Every of the workers received bonus for the festival.
5. There is a few milk in this tea.
6. There are much students waiting near the principal's office.
7. Do you have much advice for us?
8. I've got a little toffees for your friends in the kitchen.

I Fill in the blanks with appropriate determiners. More than one answer may be possible for some sentences.

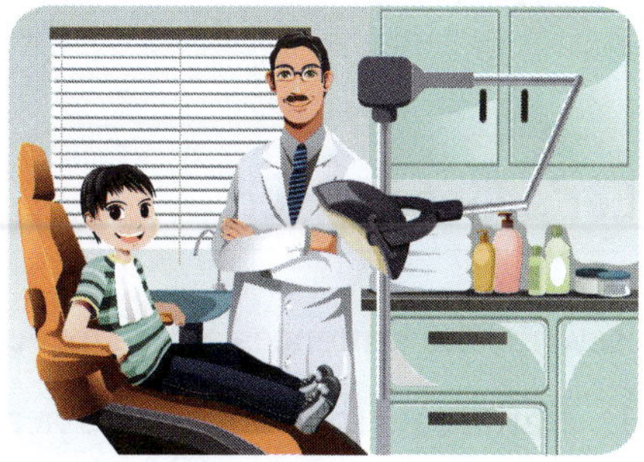

1. There are ________ books in the library.
2. I found ________ dog lying under the bed.
3. ________ brother is a dentist.
4. In ________ countries, you have to pay for the medical treatment.
5. ________ people think that development is the same as modernisation.
6. Only ________ houses were spared by the earthquake.
7. My father has repaired ________ old air conditioner.
8. Is there ________ water in the bucket?
9. ________ table in the restaurant do you want to sit at?
10. ________ colour was the cover of the book we bought yesterday?

Don't Forget!

1. Determiners are used before nouns and indicate whether a noun refers to something specific or general. They also indicate quantity.
2. They include articles, demonstratives, possessives, cardinal and ordinal numbers, quantifiers, distributives and interrogatives.

Let Us Write

Write a short paragraph about your trip to a national park. Underline the determiners and identify their types.

You can write about:

- how many animals and birds you saw
- the different types of birds
- what they were doing
- conservation efforts at the park
- anything you did not like about the trip
- any animal or bird that you found particularly interesting

14 Articles

Let's Get Started

Rewrite the sentences after correcting the errors.

1. Ratna said she had the bad headache.
2. Tarun bought an new camera.
3. It takes about a hour to get to the museum.
4. Binodini lives on a third floor of the 'Presidium' building.
5. You need to buy an dictionary.

The words you just wrote are articles.

Articles are words that tell us whether we are referring to a particular person or thing or a general one.

There are two types of articles: definite article (*the*) and indefinite articles (*a, an*).

Indefinite Articles

A and *an* are the **indefinite articles**. They are used with singular countable nouns. They refer to a single person or thing of a general kind.

Examples: *There is **a** crack in this wall.*
*We have been waiting for them for **an** hour.*

Use of the Indefinite Articles

The indefinite article *a* is used for the following.

1. Before a word beginning with a consonant.
   Examples: ***a*** *chair,* ***a*** *cap,* ***a*** *yolk,* ***a*** *yard*
2. Before a word beginning with a vowel that has a consonant sound.
   Examples: ***a*** *European,* ***a*** *union*
3. Before a singular countable noun when it is used for the first time.
   Examples: *There is* ***a*** *mouse on the shelf.*
   She won ***a*** *medal in sports.*
4. Before a proper noun when it refers to an unfamiliar person.
   Examples: ***A*** *Ms Mehra has come to see you.*
   I met ***a*** *Mr Mehta in the train.*

5. Before expressions of quantity and numbers.
   Examples: ***a*** *lot of noise,* ***a*** *great deal of care,* ***a*** *hundred million dollars,* ***a*** *thousand people*
6. Before nouns in exclamations.
   Examples: *What* ***a*** *shame!*
   Such ***a*** *nuisance!*

The indefinite article *an* is used for the following.

1. Before a word beginning with a vowel sound.
   Examples: ***an*** *eagle,* ***an*** *apple*
2. Before a word beginning with a consonant but which has a vowel sound.
   Examples: ***an*** *MP,* ***an*** *MLA*
3. Before a word beginning with a silent *h*.
   Examples: ***an*** *hour,* ***an*** *honour*

A Complete the sentences using *a* or *an*.

1. My sister has two colleagues in her team; one is _____ American while the other is _____ European.
2. My brother studies in _____ university. He recently got _____ excellent internship offer to work in _____ well-known company abroad.
3. Shall we watch _____ film tonight? There is _____ adventure film showing in the theatre nearby.
4. Do not hesitate to make _____ call if there is _____ emergency.
5. The house was in such _____ mess that it took me _____ entire day to clean it up.
6. What do you prefer, _____ orange or _____ banana? There is _____ piece of cake too.
7. You may win _____ argument, but lose _____ friend in the process.
8. There was _____ lot of traffic; it took us nearly _____ hour and _____ half to reach the place.
9. Although he is _____ famous writer, Mr Mehta is _____ humble man.
10. She has _____ appointment with the doctor but he is busy with _____ emergency case. So she will be late to office by _____ few hours.

Definite Article

The is the **definite article**. It is used to indicate a specific person or thing. It can be used with countable and uncountable nouns as well as plural nouns.

Use of the Definite Article

The is used for the following.

1. Before a noun which has already been mentioned once.
   Examples: *He bought a car;* ***the*** *car was silver grey in colour.*
   She made a cake; ***the*** *cake was delicious.*

2. Before a noun referring to a particular person or thing.
   Examples: *This is* ***the*** *man who helped you.*
   This is ***the*** *film that won the national award.*

3. Before an adjective that acts like a noun.
   Examples: ***The*** *rich are not always generous.*
   You must help ***the*** *needy.*

4. Before a singular noun that represents a whole class.
   Examples: ***The*** *cat is a comfort-loving animal.*
   The *sparrow is a tiny bird.*

5. Before ordinal numbers when they are used as adjectives and with words like *last, next, previous, following, only* and *same.* **Examples:** *This is* ***the*** *first thing that you should do.*
   He is ***the*** *last person who would harm you.*
   My flat is of ***the*** *same size as yours.*

6. Before superlatives. **Examples:** *New Zealand is one of* ***the*** *least polluted countries in the world.*
   Meghna is ***the*** *most intelligent student in Class VII.*

7. Before some nouns such as *earth, moon, sun* and *sky.*
   Examples: ***The*** *sky is cloudy today.*
   The *moon is shining in the sky.*
   The *Earth revolves round* ***the*** *sun.*

8. Before names of rivers, mountain ranges, seas, groups of islands, universities, holy books, newspapers, well-known buildings, directions and entire families.
   Examples: ***the*** *Godavari,* ***the*** *Alps,* ***the*** *Indian Ocean,* ***the*** *Andamans,* ***the*** *Nalanda University,* ***the*** *Bible,* ***the*** *Hindustan Times,* ***the*** *Eiffel Tower,* ***the*** *south,* ***the*** *Deys*

Omission of the Definite Article

The definite article *the* is not used in the following situations.

1. Before proper nouns, material nouns, abstract nouns and nouns representing general categories.
   Examples: *Saumya is an expert in judo.* (not *the Saumya*)
   Gold is a precious metal. (not *the gold*)
   Honesty is the best policy. (not *the honesty*)
   Dogs are faithful animals. (not *the dogs*)

2. Before plural nouns when we refer to a category of nouns rather than specific objects in that category.
   Examples: *Oranges are rich in vitamin C.* (not *the oranges*)
   Necessity is the mother of invention. (not *the necessity* and *the invention*)

3. Before days of the week and dates.
   Examples: *The meeting is scheduled for 7 June 2017.* (not *the 7 June 2017*)
   She was married on Tuesday. (not *the Tuesday*)

Watch Out!

Some names of places include the definite article.

They are relocating to ***the*** *United States of America.*

We use *the* with proper nouns when we want to make a special reference.

He is not ***the*** *Surya that you are looking for.*

The *Hyderabad that you see today is very different from what it was three decades ago.*

The is not repeated if two nouns refer to the same person.

The *Dean and Principal is on leave.* (The same person holds two positions.)

4. Before names of seasons, languages, subjects and games.
   Examples: *Summer is my least favourite season.* (not *the summer*)
   English is his favourite subject. (not *the English*)
   Football requires a lot of stamina. (not *the football*)
5. Before names of countries, states, regions and cities.
   Examples: *India is a multi-lingual country.* (not *the India*)
   Telangana is located in the south of India. (not *the Telangana*)
6. Before titles indicating professions.
   Examples: *Meet Dr Joshi.* (not *the Dr Joshi*)
   They wrote a letter to Professor Shankar. (not *the Professor Shankar*)

Repetition of the Definite Article

The definite article *the* is repeated in the following situations.

1. When we refer to two different people in a sentence.
   Example: ***The*** *Dean and* ***the*** *Principal are on leave.*
2. In some double comparisons.
   Example: ***The*** *higher you climb,* ***the*** *colder it gets.*
   The *more,* ***the*** *merrier.*

B Fill in the blanks with the definite article where necessary. Put a cross where no article is needed.

1. _____ curiosity is a great trait; _____ more curious you are, _____ better you will learn.
2. _____ eye is _____ most sensitive organ in _____ human body.
3. I love _____ cats; but I don't like _____ cat my friend Vinnie owns since it scratches people.
4. _____ children of today are _____ citizens of tomorrow.
5. _____ honesty is _____ best policy; but _____ honest are not often respected or rewarded.
6. _____ Chairman is busy for _____ next three months; you cannot hope to get an appointment in _____ near future.
7. She contested for _____ post of _____ General Secretary but she did not win _____ election.
8. I play _____ piano; my brother plays _____ guitar; my mother plays _____ sitar. All of us are _____ lovers of _____ music at _____ home.
9. _____ sooner you learn, _____ better for you!
10. This is _____ best deal that I can offer you.
11. I love _____ chocolate ice cream, especially _____ one that you get in _____ mall near my house.
12. Don't let _____ failure demotivate you; _____ failures are _____ stepping stones to _____ success.
13. _____ pen is mightier than _____ sword.
14. _____ more Raghav earns, _____ less he spends, though usually, it is _____ opposite.

C **Fill in the blanks with suitable articles. Put a cross where an article is not necessary.**

1. I have _____ uncle who loves to travel by _____ train. He can never take _____ flights because he gets _____ earache.
2. There was _____ cyclone last night. The train met with _____ accident. All _____ nearby hospitals are full with _____ people who are injured.
3. May we have _____ answer to _____ question, please? _____ audience is eagerly waiting.
4. All _____ roads are dug up; they are laying _____ telephone cables.
5. You look sad; is there _____ problem? Do you need _____ help?
6. I'm living in _____ hostel for the first time. _____ life in _____ hostel is good. I have _____ friends and I like _____ place.
7. Yesterday, I had _____ funny experience. I went to _____ store. I needed to buy _____ few things. I finished _____ shopping and when I went to pay _____ bill, I realised that I had not carried my wallet which had _____ money.
8. This film won _____ award but I don't understand how; it was _____ extremely silly film!
9. When I went to Taiwan _____ last year, I thought I'd face _____ problems since I did not know _____ Chinese. Fortunately, _____ hotel I stayed in treated _____ customers with utmost care; _____ management offered _____ help whenever I needed it.

D **Rewrite the passage using articles where necessary.**

In small town where Mansi lived, there was old lady who could see future of anyone who went to her. old lady told Mansi's friend, Nishant, that he would become pilot one day. Nishant did not take prediction seriously. After they left school, small advertisement in daily newspaper caught Nishant's eye. It asked young men and women to join Indian Air Force. On a whim, Nishant applied and after few weeks, received letter, asking him to appear for examination. Nishant appeared for exam. Imagine his surprise when he got selected and joined Air Force. The old lady had been right all along!

Don't Forget!

1. *A*, *an* and *the* are articles.
2. *A* and *an* are the indefinite articles.
3. *The* is the definite article.
4. *A* and *an* are used with singular, countable nouns.
5. *The* is used with singular as well as plural nouns.

15

Active and Passive Voice

Let's Get Started

Identify the sentences in which the subjects perform the action.

1. The dog was chasing the postman down the road.
2. The ball was hit hard by the batsman.
3. This story was written by one of my favourite authors.
4. Shut the door.

The sentences which you identified are in the active voice.

Read these sentences.

Zakir Hussain plays the tabla.

The tabla is played by Zakir Hussain.

In the first sentence, the subject *Zakir Hussain* is performing the action, *plays*. It is in the active voice.

In the second sentence, the subject *tabla* is receiving the action, *is played*. The object in the first sentence is the subject in the second. The sentence is in the passive voice.

When the doer of the action is the subject, the sentence is in the **active voice.**

When the recipient of the action of the verb is the subject, the sentence is in the **passive voice.**

When a sentence is rewritten in the passive voice, the object of the sentence becomes the subject. We add *by* before the doer of the action, which was the subject earlier.

Uses of the Passive Voice

We use the passive voice in the following situations.

When the agent is implied, understood, unknown, or not to be revealed.

Examples: *The match has been suspended.*
Rumours have been spread.

When the recipient of the action is the focus of the sentence.

Examples: *Oxygen is released by plants during photosynthesis.*
My notebook was chewed up by my dog.

When we want to use an authoritative tone.

Examples: *Smoking is strictly prohibited.*
The children must not be left alone.

Voice and Verbs

Only transitive verbs have a passive form because they can take objects. Sentences with intransitive verbs cannot have a passive form since there is no object.

Examples: *Medha* ***installed*** *the software on her computer.* (*installed:* transitive verb in the active voice; *software*: object)

The software ***was installed*** *by Medha on her computer.* (*was installed:* transitive verb in the passive voice; *software:* subject)

Remember to change the verb to agree with the passive subject.

Examples: *How* ***did*** *you solve those sums?* (active) → *How* ***were*** *those sums solved by you?* (passive)
(*did:* singular verb, agrees with the singular subject, *you*) (*were:* plural verb, agrees with the plural subject, *sums*)

Which subjects ***does*** *Anu like?* (active) → *Which subjects* ***are*** *liked by Anu?* (passive)
(*does:* singular verb, agrees with the singular subject, *Anu*) (*are:* plural verb, agrees with the plural subject, *subjects*)

A State whether the sentences are in the active or passive voice.

1. Let's donate some money to charity.
2. The meal was prepared by the chef.
3. The decimal system was invented by the Mesopotamians.
4. Bill Gates co-founded Microsoft.
5. Fortune favours the brave.
6. Bluetooth was invented by Dr Jaap Haartsen.
7. The board members elected a new chairman yesterday.
8. India's first individual Olympic gold medal was won by Abhinav Bindra.
9. With whose permission have you entered the staff room?
10. The winning runs were scored by Vikas Joshi, playing his first international match.

Changing Voice in the Various Tenses

While changing sentences from the active to the passive voice, the main verb is changed to *be* + past participle form of the verb. Look at this table for the changes in verb form for each tense.

Tense	Present	Past	Future
Simple *Active* *Passive*	She *studies* physics. Physics *is studied* by her.	She *studied* physics. Physics *was studied* by her.	She *will study* physics. Physics *will be studied* by her.
Continuous *Active* *Passive*	She *is studying* physics. Physics *is being studied* by her.	She *was studying* physics. Physics *was being studied* by her.	She *will be studying* physics. No passive

Perfect *Active* *Passive*	She *has studied* physics. Physics *has been studied* by her.	She *had studied* physics. Physics *had been studied* by her.	She *will have studied* physics. Physics *will have been studied* by her.

The perfect continuous tense does not have a passive form.

B **Change the sentences from active voice to passive voice.**

1. Her behaviour annoys me!
2. She asked me to come again.
3. They liked her performance.
4. The museum guide always answers the visitors' questions.
5. The two Presidents are signing the climate change treaty.
6. My father irons and folds our school uniforms every night.
7. The party planner is booking the auditorium.
8. Sally has to bake fifty cookies for the birthday party.
9. Who drank the last bottle of mango juice?
10. The commanding officer will give the cadets instructions.

Passive Voice with Modal Auxiliaries

You know that modal auxiliaries include *can, could, may, might, should, would, must* and *ought to*.

While changing a sentence with modal auxiliaries from active to passive, we use the following structure: modal auxiliary + *be* + past participle of the verb. The modals themselves do not change form.

Examples: *He **ought** to finish his homework.* (active)
*His homework **ought** to be finished.* (passive)
*We **might** visit our grandparents this weekend.* (active)
*Our grandparents **might** be visited by us this weekend.* (passive)

Changing Verbs with Two Objects to Passive Voice

When a verb has more than one object, we can change it into passive voice in two ways.

By using the indirect object as the subject.
Examples: *Arun gave the iPad to **Varun**.* (active)
***Varun** was given the iPad by Arun.* (passive)
*Ms Gundersson taught **Kaushik** German.* (active)
***Kaushik** was taught German by Ms Gundersson.* (passive)

By using the direct object as the subject.
Examples: *Rhea baked a **cake** for Mala.* (active)
*A **cake** was baked by Rhea for Mala.* (passive)
*I gave my brother **pocket money**.* (active)
***Pocket money** was given to my brother by me.* (passive)

Grammar Byte

While rewriting a sentence with a phrasal verb (verb + preposition) in passive voice, remember that the preposition will follow the verb in passive voice too.

*I **looked at** the options. (active)*
*The options were **looked at** by me. (passive)*
*The teacher will **look into** the matter. (active)*
*The matter will be **looked into** by the teacher. (passive)*

Personal Pronouns

Personal pronouns change their forms when written in the passive voice. This table shows the changes.

Active	Passive
I	*me*
we	*us*
he, she	*him, her*
they	*them*

Passive Voice in Interrogative Sentences

Interrogative sentences retain their 'question' form in the passive voice. Sometimes the interrogative words also remain the same.

Examples: ***Why*** *does he write such long answers?* (active)
Why *are such long answers written by him?* (passive)
Where *did you buy your book?* (active)
Where *was your book bought?* (passive)
Do *you know the answer to this question?* (active)
Is *the answer to this question known by you?* (passive)

Grammar Byte

The interrogative word *who* in the active voice becomes *whom* in the passive and is often used with a preposition.
Who rang the bell? (active)
By whom was the bell rung? (passive)
Who won the tournament? (active)
By whom was the tournament won? (passive)

C Change the sentences from active voice to passive voice.

1. Do you know her?
2. Who broke the window of my car?
3. How many stoles did you buy?
4. Have they paid the rent?
5. What kind of books do you like?
6. Where can I buy good shoes?
7. Who started the Chipko movement?
8. When did they book the tickets?
9. Have you submitted the papers for scrutiny?
10. Are you not watering the plants regularly?
11. Who will carry out all these instructions?
12. Where can I find dried dates in this market?

Passive Voice in Imperative Sentences

In imperative sentences, the subject is often understood and not mentioned. These sentences often begin with verbs like *let, may, do*.

Examples: *May you find success.* (active) → *May success be found by you.* (passive)
Do not litter the streets. (active) → *The streets should not be littered.* (passive)
Let him take the car. (passive) → *Let the car be taken by him.* (passive)

When changing an imperative sentence to passive voice, we can sometimes begin the sentence with *you + requested to/ordered to.*

Example: *Please hurry up.* (active) → *You are requested to hurry up.* (passive)

D Change the sentences from active voice to passive voice.

1. Drive the car slowly.
2. Walk to the left.
3. Do it as soon as you reach home.
4. Open the door for your mother.

5. Please take the leftovers.
6. Do not wash the car here.
7. Please pay the bill on time.
8. Learn the song.
9. Do not touch the icing on the cake.
10. Practise for two hours.

E Change the verbs to the passive form and fill in the blanks.

1. The teacher *was impressed* by my science project. (impress, past tense)
2. The *Harry Potter* series ________ by J. K. Rowling. (write, past tense)
3. Rohit's cap ________ away by the wind. (blow, past tense)
4. Our team ________ loudly by the entire school. (cheer, past tense)
5. In future, advice on the project ________ by the project manager. (provide, future tense)
6. The students ________ by the teacher to write neatly. (instruct, past tense)
7. William Wordsworth's poem 'The Solitary Reaper' ________ by everyone. (enjoy, present tense)
8. The assignment ____________ by tomorrow. (submit, future tense)
9. Water vapour ____________________ by the process of evaporation. (form, present tense)
10. Independence Day ______________ on 15 August in India. (celebrate, present tense)

F Change the sentences from active voice to passive voice.

1. Geeta cares for stray animals.
2. We are running the marathon tomorrow.
3. What have you done?
4. Aastha told Tara the truth.
5. I await your response.
6. Consuming contaminated water causes jaundice.
7. The floods damaged many houses and left hundreds of people stranded.

8. Have you spoken to your mother about the party?
9. The rules forbid us from bringing anything apart from a pen into the exam hall.
10. Priya designs the artwork while Maria edits the school magazine.

G Change the sentences from passive to active voice. Insert the subject where necessary.

1. The bone was being chewed by the dog.
2. The earthquake was followed by a tsunami.
3. We will be congratulated by everyone.
4. By whom were you taught to swim?
5. Money was owed to him by Aakash.
6. This pickle was made by my grandmother.
7. The details are to be remembered.
8. My course will have been completed by December.

9. A new photo-sharing app was developed by my sister Laila.
10. When will your room be cleared?
11. Has the mail been delivered by the mailman?
12. Will the rule be changed by the committee?
13. Many interesting stories about the monument's history were told to us by the guide.
14. The roads have been cleared by the authorities in an effort to reduce traffic jams.
15. The cat was almost run over by speeding cars before it was saved by Hina.

Don't Forget!

1. In the active voice, the subject is the doer of the action. In the passive voice, it is the recipient of the action. We add *by* before the new subject to indicate it.
2. The object of a sentence in the active voice becomes the subject in the passive voice.
3. The main verb in the active voice changes to *be* + past participle form of the verb in the passive.
4. Only sentences with transitive verbs have a passive form.

Let Us Write

Change the following sentences from active to passive voice, once with the direct object and then with the indirect object.

1. She sent me a bouquet.
2. My father bought my brother a laptop.
3. They paid her many compliments.
4. The teacher gave the question papers to the students.
5. My sister brings me chocolates every Sunday.
6. My mother cooked a delicious meal for all my friends.
7. Radhika gave the train tickets to her teacher.

16 Direct and Indirect Speech

Let's Get Started

Sumit made some mistakes while reporting his father's words to his brother. Write Sumit's words correctly.

Mr Sen: Sumit, ask your brother to finish his maths homework in an hour. He has a maths test tomorrow.

Sumit *(to his brother)***:** Father asked you to finish your maths homework in an hour. He said that you had a maths test the day before.

Rohan: I have my maths test tomorrow. I didn't have it the day before!

When we refer to the exact words of the speaker in a sentence, it is said to be in **direct speech**.

Examples: *The teacher said to the students, 'You can leave the exam hall if you have finished writing.'*
Simon said to Asha, 'Did you attend the 2016 Rio Olympics?'

When we report what somebody said or thought in our own words, we use **indirect speech**.

Examples: *The teacher told the students that they could leave the exam hall if they had finished writing.*
Simon asked Asha if she had attended the 2016 Rio Olympics.

Rules of changing Direct to Indirect Speech

When we change a sentence from direct to indirect speech, we change the following.

1. The tense of the verb
2. The reporting verb *(said → told, asked)*
3. Personal pronouns, possessive pronouns and possessive adjectives
4. Punctuation marks used
5. Expressions of time and place

Tenses

When the main verb in the sentence being reported is in the present tense, it is changed to past tense in indirect speech. When the main verb is in the simple past tense, it is changed to past perfect tense.

Examples: *Afsar said to Rohan, 'We **are going** to Ocean Park this Sunday.'* (direct speech)
*Afsar said to Rohan that they **were going** to Ocean Park that Sunday.* (indirect speech)
*Jasmine said to Minu, 'You **gave** me all the documents for processing your visa.'* (direct speech)
*Jasmine told Minu that she **had given** her all the documents for processing her visa.* (indirect speech)

This table shows the change in tenses.

Direct Speech	Indirect Speech
is/am/are	*was/were*
was/were	*had been*
do	*did*
did	*had done*
has/have	*had*

Watch Out!

The tense of the main verb remains in the present tense if it expresses a universal truth.

Example: *The teacher said, 'An empty vessel **makes** much noise.'*
*The teacher said that an empty vessel **makes** much noise.*

The tense of the main verb does not change if it describes an action which still holds true at the time of reporting.

Example: *She said, 'My son **wants** to study engineering.'*
*She said that her son **wants** to study engineering.*

If the main verb in the sentence is in the simple future tense, it changes to *would* + verb in indirect speech.

Example: *Tanya said, 'I **will go** swimming in the evening.'* (direct speech)
*Tanya said that she **would go** swimming in the evening.* (indirect speech)

If the reporting verb in the sentence is in the simple present or the simple future tense, the tense of the reporting verb in indirect speech remains the same.

Example: *Manish **says**, 'I will not be able to attend the wedding.'* (direct speech)
*Manish **says** that he will not be able to attend the wedding.* (indirect speech)

Personal Pronouns, Possessive Pronouns and Possessive Adjectives

The pronouns and possessive adjectives in indirect speech change depending on the subject of the reporting verb. Look at these sentences.

You said, '**I** want to change the address in **my** passport.'
You said that **you** wanted to change the address in **your** passport.

Seema said, 'The board game is **mine**.'
Seema said that the board game was **hers**.

Charu said, '**We** want to go for a movie.'
Charu said that **they** wanted to go for a movie.

Gemma said to Ronald, '**You** were very good in today's football match.'
Gemma said to Ronald that **he** was very good in that day's football match.

Meenal said to me, 'Your friends have come to meet **you**.'
Meenal told me that my friends had come to meet **me**.

The teacher told the students, 'The headmaster wants to see **you**.'
The teacher told the students that the headmaster wanted to see **them**.

Grammar Byte

Personal pronouns change in the following way in indirect speech.

I → *he, she, you*
you → *he, she, they, me, them* (if plural)
we → *they*
us → *them*
my → *his, her, your, its*
our → *their*

Punctuation

In a sentence in direct speech, the words of the speaker always begin with a capital letter and are placed within inverted commas. The reporting verb is followed by a comma.

In indirect speech, the comma following the reporting verb is replaced by *that*. Inverted commas are not used. Question marks and exclamation marks are replaced by full stops (.).

Examples: *She said to me, 'What a skilful tailor he is!'*
She exclaimed that he was a very skilful tailor.
Unni said to Shivam, 'How will you go home?'
Unni asked Shivam how he would go home.

Expressions of Time and Place

You have learnt that we change the tense of the sentence from present to past in indirect speech. When the reporting verb is in the past tense, the expressions of time and place change in the following way.

Direct Speech	Indirect Speech
this/these	*that/those*
here	*there*
now	*then* (often omitted)
ago	*before*
today	*that day*
yesterday	*the day before/the previous day*
tomorrow	*the next day/the following day*
next week/month/year	*the following week/month/year*
last week/month/year	*the week/month/year before*

Examples: *Pritam said, 'I was planning to go home **yesterday**, but I will go home **tomorrow**.'* (direct speech)
*Pritam said that he was planning to go home **the day before**, but would go home **the next day**.* (indirect speech)
*'I checked **these** pipes **last week**,' Samarth said.* (direct speech)
*Samarth said that he had checked **those** pipes the week **before**.* (indirect speech)

We follow different rules to change the various types of sentences from the direct speech to the indirect.

Assertive Sentences

When we rewrite an assertive sentence in indirect speech, we change the reporting verb *said* to *told* if the verb is followed by an object. We also use verbs like *remark, promise, answer, explain, object, argue, assure* and *explain*.

Watch Out!

We use the reporting verb *told* only if there is an object. Otherwise, we use *said*.

Ella told me that she was going to the USA. [✓]

Ella said that she was going to the USA. [✓]

Ella told she was going to the USA. [✗]

Examples: *Nisha* ***said*** *to me, 'I am going for a run in the evening.'* (direct speech)
Nisha ***told*** *me that she was going for a run in the evening.* (indirect speech)

Ved ***said****, 'Summer is going to be terrible.'*
Ved ***remarked*** *that summer was going to be terrible.*

A Rewrite these sentences in indirect speech.

1. Mohit said, 'I have been invited to the inauguration ceremony tomorrow.'
2. Lina said to me, 'I will meet you next week.'
3. Rohit said to his father, 'I'm working on my project now.'
4. Smriti said, 'I always drink milk in the morning.'
5. Pranati explained to me, 'My cousins spent the weekend with me.'
6. Mrs Patil said, 'I've visited six countries in the last month.'
7. Linda complained, 'I just cleaned the entire kitchen!'
8. Kavitha said, 'I've been practising with the band for a week.'
9. Sunil said, 'I will be done with my exams next Monday.'
10. They told me, 'We are staying in the hotel down the street.'
11. She said, 'I'll be tutoring my neighbour's children next week.'
12. Vivek said to Surya, 'I have watched the film twice already.'

Interrogative Sentences

Interrogative sentences are written in indirect speech as statements, using reporting verbs like *asked*, *enquired* or *demanded*.

In indirect speech, the 'verb + object' order of words in questions is reversed.

In questions with *did, do, does*, these verbs are omitted in indirect speech.

Example: *Mary asked Venu, 'How much* ***did you*** *pay for the trip?'*
Mary asked Venu how much ***he had*** *paid for the trip.*

In *wh-* questions, the verb comes at the end.

Example: *Sudama said, 'Where is the painting by Picasso kept?'*
Sudama asked where the painting by Picasso was kept.

For *yes/no* questions and questions beginning with *do*, *does* or *did*, the conjunctions *if* and *whether* are used to introduce the reported words.

Examples: *The teacher said to me, 'Are you contesting the Student Council elections next month?'*
The teacher asked me ***if*** *I was contesting the Student Council elections the following month.*

The traveller said to a passer-by, 'Do you know the way to Dehra?'
The traveller asked a passer-by ***if*** *he knew the way to Dehra.*

Jeevan said, 'Can I come a little late to office tomorrow?'
Jeevan asked ***whether*** *he could come a little late to office the next day.*

Watch Out!

We don't use *that* while converting questions to indirect speech.

Sohail said, 'What time does the play start?'
Sohail asked that what time the play would start. [✗]
Sohail asked at what time the play would start. [✓]

We don't use *to* after verbs like *asked*.

Suman asked Rama, 'Who is the new English teacher?'
Suman asked to Rama who the new English teacher was. [✗]
Suman asked Rama who the new English teacher was. [✓]

B Rewrite the sentences in indirect speech.

1. The teacher said to the students, 'How many of you can come for the special class this Sunday?'
2. The airhostess said, 'May I request the passengers to remain seated till the aircraft halts?'
3. Nikhil said, 'Do you like the new generation smartphones?'
4. My mother said, 'Will Robin come for the party tomorrow?'
5. I said to him, 'Are you being able to cope with the new syllabus?'
6. Raj said to me, 'Are you left-handed or right-handed?'
7. Mr Krishnan said to me, 'What is the name of the boy sitting next to you?'
8. Elwin said to John, 'Do you have a laptop?'
9. Hima said to him, 'Why did you take so long to reach?'
10. Krishna said to the event manager, 'When will the caterers arrive?'
11. She said to the boy, 'Why are you making so much noise?'
12. The student asked the teacher, 'May I help you carry the books?'

Reporting Question Tags

We use question tags to confirm an opinion or a piece of information. While rewriting a question tag in indirect speech, we expand the tag to a full question. The question mark is dropped.

Examples: *Revathi said to me, 'The principal has confirmed the date of the parent-teacher meeting, hasn't she?'*
Revathi asked me if the principal had confirmed the date of the parent-teacher meeting.

Vinay said to Veena, 'The last date for submitting the scholarship applications hasn't passed, has it?'
Vinay asked Veena if the last date for submitting the scholarship applications had passed.

C Change these sentences to indirect speech.

1. Mohit said to the shopkeeper, 'We can pay through credit card, can't we?'
2. She said to the students, 'You have understood the sum, haven't you?'
3. She said to me, 'Sindhu has gone home, hasn't she?'
4. Lydia whispered to me, 'She can't be 12 years old, can she?'
5. Justin asked Priyank, 'Your father works in the railways, doesn't he?'
6. Fred asked Molly, 'The Thomases never go out on a Sunday, do they?'
7. Gina said to Supriya, 'I'm right about the play, aren't I?'
8. Saba said to Jasmine, 'Close the door, will you?'
9. Fiona said to Chand, 'Your parents have four dogs, don't they?'
10. Sunil said to his mother, 'Grandmother goes to sleep quite early, doesn't she?'

Imperative Sentences

While rewriting imperative sentences in indirect speech, the verb is changed into the infinitive form.

Example: *The teacher said, 'Maintain silence!'*
The teacher asked them ***to maintain*** *silence.*

Look at this table for the usage of various reporting verbs with different types of imperative sentences.

Type of imperative sentence	Reporting verb	Examples
Commands and orders	*told, asked, ordered, warned, commanded*	*'Stay where you are until further orders!' the captain told the soldiers.* *The captain commanded the soldiers to stay where they were until further orders.*
Requests	*requested, begged, pleaded, invited*	*'Please switch off the lights,' said Deepak to his colleague.* *Deepak requested his colleague to switch off the lights..*
Advice or suggestions	*advised, suggested, warned, reminded, forbade*	*Kirti said to her son, 'Check your answer script before you submit it.'* *Kirti advised her son to check his answer script before he submitted it.*
Imperatives with *let*	*urged, suggested, proposed* (Sometimes, the infinitive *should* is added.)	*He said, 'Let people learn from their mistakes.'* *He said that people should learn from their mistakes.* *She said, 'Let's do this together.'* *She suggested that they do it together.*

When a person is addressed in an imperative sentence, that person becomes the object of the reporting verb in indirect speech.

Examples: *He said, 'Don't blame me for everything, Madhur.'*
He asked Madhur not to blame him for everything.

Swayam said, 'Neha, please lend me your pen.'
Swayam requested Neha to lend him her pen.

Watch Out!

Verbs of command, request, invitation and advice are not usually followed by *to*.

D Rewrite these sentences in indirect speech.

1. He said to Prashant, 'Please help Vivek with his work.'
2. Michelle said to Luke, 'You should think of taking up music classes.'
3. They said to him sternly, 'Don't lie about what you did.'
4. Mr Laxman said to his assistant, 'Arrange the files in alphabetical order in the cabinet.'
5. Simi said to Vineet, 'Don't blame the bus driver for your delay!'
6. The teacher told the students, 'Don't waste time during your study leave.'
7. The shopkeeper said, 'Everyone, please leave the shop right now. There is a fire in the storeroom.'
8. Rithu said to Harsha, 'Let me help you with your bags.'

Exclamatory Sentences

Exclamatory sentences are written in indirect speech as statements, using reporting verbs like *exclaimed*, *cried*, *apologized*, *wished* and *thanked*.

Interjections like *alas*, *hurrah* and *oh* are written using phrases like *exclaimed sadly*, *exclaimed with happiness*, and *exclaimed joyfully*.

Examples: *Aneesh said, 'Hurrah! I have got a GPA of 10.' His mother said, 'Congratulations!'*
Aneesh exclaimed with joy that he had got a GPA of 10. His mother congratulated him.
Reema said, 'What a nuisance these mosquitoes are! We have to buy a mosquito repellent.'
Reema exclaimed angrily that the mosquitoes were a great nuisance. She added that they would have to buy a mosquito repellent.

E **Change the sentences to indirect speech.**

1. 'How I wish we could go for a vacation after the exams!' Mona said.
2. 'Alas! Nelson Mandela is no more,' my grandfather said sadly. 'He was our hero when we were young.'
3. Rosa said, wiping her forehead, 'What a hot day it is! I can't believe that today's temperature is 48 degrees Celsius!'
4. Rajan said, 'Hurrah! We won the match, and I got the Man of the Match award too!'
5. Jo cried, 'Oh, come and see, Mother! The cat has spilled the milk again!'
6. Shabina said, 'How handsome the actor looks even though he is 70 years old!'

Let Us Write

Rewrite these dialogues in indirect speech.

1. 'I'm going to play cricket,' said Manu. 'I can't study all day.'
'You have an examination tomorrow!' exclaimed his mother.
'I've almost finished studying,' said Manu, 'Can I please take a break for half an hour?'
'You can take an hour off,' said his mother, 'but only after you have finished studying.'
'But it will get dark soon!' said Manu.

2. 'Excuse me,' said the man. 'Can you tell me how to get to the railway station?'
'Take a left at this junction, and you will see the station on the right side,' replied Geeta.
'I haven't got my watch with me,' the man said, 'Could you please tell me the time?'
Geeta looked at her watch and replied, 'It's a quarter to six.'
'Thank you,' said the man, and hurried on his way.

Test 2

A Underline the adverbs in the following sentences and identify their types.

1. I am terribly hungry.
2. Sit inside.
3. I have spoken to him already.
4. Mary always wanted to be a teacher.
5. The little girl eagerly waited for the results of her test.
6. The girls searched for the keys everywhere.
7. Abhijit never comes late to work.
8. I watched a very interesting film last weekend.

B Fill in the blanks with suitable prepositions.

1. People who live ________________ glass houses should not throw stones at others.
2. They increase the house rent ________________ 10 per cent every year.
3. The twins look so similar ________________ each other that you cannot tell them apart.
4. He pushed his way ________________ the crowd of people to meet the superstar.
5. He is addicted ________________ playing video games.
6. He wears a sweater ________________ his shirt even in summer.
7. The teacher congratulated Niraj ________________ getting a scholarship.
8. You cannot enter the classroom ________________ 9 a.m. as the gates do not open until then.

C Fill in the blanks with the most suitable conjunctions.

1. You will not get the 'no dues' certificate ________________ (when, if, unless) you clear the canteen bill.
2. She was extremely happy ________________ (when, while, yet) she bagged the prestigious award.
3. The function began ________________ (as soon as, as well as, whenever) the chief guest arrived.
4. Everybody likes him ________________ (because, yet, and) he is kind and helpful.
5. ________________ (Yet, If, Although) she was very ill, she decided to sit for the exam.
6. I think I know ________________ (where, what, why) he left early.

D Fill in the blanks with appropriate determiners and quantifiers.

1. Don't you have ________________ (much, some, any) manners?
2. We have very ________________ (little, few, much) hope of winning the match.

3. There are __________ (some, any, few) cookies still left in the tin. You can have them if you want.
4. We were told that __________ (all, few, some) the participants would get prizes. We were thrilled.
5. We bought __________ (few, some, all) eggs to make omelettes for everyone.
6. Since she did not add too __________ (little, much, few) salt, the dish tasted delicious.
7. __________ (All, Some, Few) the students, except a __________ (all, few, some) will participate in the competition.

E Fill in the blanks with appropriate articles.

1. We started late in __________ afternoon.
2. Mumbai is __________ largest cotton textile centre in __________ country.
3. ______ Ganga is one of India's longest rivers.
4. Ram has come to school without ______ umbrella.
5. I bought ____ house, ______ ox and ______ buffalo.
6. Who is ______ girl sitting there?

F Change the sentences in active voice to passive and vice versa.

1. Keep your room clean.
2. You ought to pay the fees on time.
3. The money is deposited in the bank.
4. By whom were the flower pots decorated?
5. They are building an amphitheatre at the institute.
6. The library books have been returned.
7. She knitted mittens for her grandson.
8. The principal gifted all the teachers beautiful stoles.

G Rewrite the following sentences in indirect speech.

1. Megha said, 'I have not studied well for today's test.'
2. Joel said to Monisha, 'Have you shifted to your new flat?'
3. The teacher said to the students, 'Where shall we go for the picnic this month?'
4. Aryan said to Kavya, 'Can you help me solve this puzzle?'
5. John said, 'I have bought a car for my wife.'
6. He said to me, 'Have you read the book?'
7. Suman said to Preeti, 'Do you know anything about him?'
8. They said, 'We want to go to Mysore.'
9. The astronomer asked the students, 'Who knows what the Perseids meteor shower is?'
10. Leela said, 'Let's start a photography club.'

17 Finite and Non-Finite Verbs

Let's Get Started

Complete the sentences with verbs of your choice.

This summer, I will learn to ________________

When the baby is hungry, it ________________

The 'to + verb' structure in the first sentence does not change its form with the number and person of the subject. The verb in the second one does.

There are two types of verbs: finite and non-finite.

Finite Verbs

Finite verbs are those that change their form according to the number and person of the subject of the sentence. They have present, past and future forms.

Examples: *I **am planning** to visit my grandparents this summer.*
*Sara and Kumar **play** the synthesizer.*
*Fatima **spoke** in German when she **met** her German colleagues.*

Finite verbs indicate the tense of the verb and the person and number of the subject. They must agree with the subject and can be in the active or passive voice.

Non-Finite Verbs

Non-finite verbs are those that do not change their form according to the number and person of the subject of the sentence. They do not indicate tense and function as nouns and adjectives.

Examples: *They attempted **to find** the snake.*
***Crawling** is the hardest exercise I had to do in physical education class.*
*There is a **Laughing** Club in my colony.*

In these sentences, the verbs *to find* and *crawling* do not change their forms in relation to the person and number of the subject. They do not indicate the time of the action done by the verb. Even if the tense of the sentences and the number and person of the subject were changed, the form of the non-finite verbs would remain the same.

Examples: *He is attempting **to find** the snake.*
***Crawling** was the hardest exercise they had to do in physical education class.*

A Identify the verbs in these sentences. Circle the finite verbs and underline the non-finite verbs.

1. They were looking at the painting curiously.

2. Looking is allowed, but touching the exhibits is prohibited.
3. Plucking flowers should be discouraged.
4. Jane's younger sister wants to be a pilot.
5. The students couldn't solve the math problem.
6. The nurse is attending to the patients in the ICU.
7. The soldier's mission was to cross the enemy lines without getting caught.
8. Benjamin practised hard in order to pass the piano examination.
9. His grandparents always encouraged him to pursue his dreams.
10. The cat began to purr to express its affection.

Types of Non-Finite Verbs

There are three kinds of non-finite verbs.

Non-finite verb	Form	Examples
The infinitive	*to* + verb	*I forgot* ***to clean*** *the stove this morning.*
The participle	verb + *-ing* verb + *-ed/-en/-d/-t/-n*	*The lady left the room with the* ***crying*** *child.* *The* ***injured*** *animal was taken to the vet.*
The gerund	verb + *-ing*	*I like* ***camping*** *in the woods.*

The Infinitive

The **infinitive** is the base form of a verb. It is usually preceded by *to*. Infinitives often function as nouns in a sentence, acting as the subject or object.

Examples: *She remembered* ***to greet*** *me on my birthday.*
To err *is human.*

An infinitive without the preceding *to* is called a **bare infinitive**.

Examples: *I made her* ***consult*** *a doctor about her headaches.*
My coach let me ***stay*** *an hour longer in the swimming pool.*

Uses of the Bare Infinitive

The bare infinitive is used in the following ways.

1. As the main verb after modal auxiliaries. **Example:** *I can* ***walk*** *ten miles at a stretch.*
2. With verbs such as *let, need, make* and *bid*. **Example:** *You need not* ***call*** *me again.*
3. With verbs like *hear, see, watch, know* and *feel*. **Example:** *I heard them* ***say*** *that he will be here soon.*
4. With the phrases *had better, would rather, would sooner than* and *rather than*.
Example: *You had better* ***book*** *the tickets now.*
5. With *than* and *but* when they mean 'except'.
Example: *They did nothing but* ***complain***.

B Fill in the blanks with infinitives.

1. Let us __________ (go) for a walk.
2. How dare you __________ (talk) back to me!
3. Do we dare __________ (disturb) her now?
4. The teacher wanted __________ (meet) the parents.
5. She hopes __________ (find) a suitable house for her parents.
6. Let the guard __________ the car. (check)
7. My younger sister likes __________ (help) out at an old age home.
8. My mother demanded __________ (know) what was bothering me.
9. I love __________ (dance).
10. The twins can ______ (speak) both English and French.

Watch Out!

When we use the infinitive with *dare* and *need*, the *to* + verb form is used in affirmative sentences, while the bare infinitive is used in negative sentences.

*I dared **to disagree** with her.*
*I dared not **disagree** with her.*

*You need **to come** again.*
*You need not **come** again.*

The Participle

Participles are words that are used as adjectives. They qualify the nouns that follow them.

Examples: *The doctor tried to calm down the **crying** mother.*
*The **lost** gold chain was found in the garbage bin.*
*The **wounded** soldiers were treated by the doctors.*

Participles are of three types: present, past and perfect.

Grammar Byte

Participles can denote an ongoing action/state or a completed action/state.

Present participles are formed by adding *-ing* to the base form of the verb. They denote incomplete actions or states of being.

Examples: *I watched the **sleeping** baby in its mother's lap.*
***Seeing** her grandchildren after many years, Mrs Subaiya was overjoyed.*

Past participles are formed by adding *-ed, -en, -d, -t* or *-n* to the base form of the verbs. They denote actions that have been completed in the past but whose effects are still present.

Examples: *The **broken** cell phone needs to be repaired.*
***Tired** after a long day, Tina lay down on the bed.*

Participles with the form *having + past participle of the verb* are called **perfect participles**. They denote actions completed in the past.

Example: ***Having made up** my mind to leave the place, I took up a job in another city.*

C **Underline the participles in these sentences and state their types.**

1. The talking parrot mimicked an old pirate.
2. Having lost all his belongings on the way, he felt miserable.
3. We found a broken vase in the living room.
4. His neglected talent as a footballer always made him sad.
5. The planning committee for the annual function meets every week.
6. Having risen late, we hurriedly set out on our journey.
7. Everyone went on a walking tour of the city.
8. The people saw a floating car in the middle of the river.

Placement of Participles

The meaning of a sentence can change completely depending on where the participle is placed. Read this sentence.

He gave food to the children packed in aluminum foil.

The sentence means that the children were packed in aluminum foil. It should be:

He gave food wrapped in aluminum foil to the children.

D **Rewrite these sentences after placing the participles in the correct positions. Add other necessary words.**

1. Sitting on the gate, a snake bit him.
2. Crossing the road, the car hit the old woman.
3. Returning from Dubai, his luggage was lost.
4. Hissing loudly, she was scratched by a cat.
5. Copying slyly, the invigilator caught the student.
6. Raging with choppy waters, the fishermen were warned not to go into the sea.
7. I gifted a book to my friend bound in leather on his birthday.
8. I saw the tiger clearly wearing my prescription glasses.
9. She bought coffee mugs from the mall made of porcelain.

The Gerund

Gerunds are words that look like verbs but function like nouns. They function as the subject of a sentence or the object of a verb or preposition.

Examples: ***Eating*** *junk food is not good for health.*
Playing *chess is her hobby.*

E **Identify the gerunds and the present participles in these sentences.**

1. Barking dogs seldom bite.
2. I saw the thief running across the street.

3. Collecting stamps is an interesting hobby.
4. Flying kites is a fun activity associated with Makar Sankranti.
5. Eating cold watermelon on a hot day is a good way to keep cool.
6. Sangeeta has annoying neighbours who play loud music all the time.
7. Arriving early, Minisha sat in the first row.
8. John, feeling tired after basketball practice, slept on the sofa.
9. Putting too many clothes in the washing machine may cause it to stop working.

Watch Out!

The present participle and the gerund both have the *-ing* form. However, the participle functions as an adjective, while the gerund functions as a noun.

Laughing *is good for one's health. (gerund)*

His ***laughing*** *eyes expressed his happiness.* (present participle)

Gerunds and Infinitives

Gerunds and infinitives both function as nouns and can replace each other in sentences.

Examples: ***To forgive*** *someone is divine.* (infinitive)
Forgiving *someone is divine.* (gerund)

Playing *for the national team is her dream.* (gerund)
To play *for the national team is her dream.* (infinitive)

F Rewrite the sentences using gerunds in place of infinitives. You may have to change some words.

1. The state encourages us to recycle. *The state encourages recycling.*
2. I like to jog. It's my hobby.
3. Some people prefer to get up early in the morning.
4. To find my car keys in this mess is a challenge.
5. To travel around the world requires a lot of money.
6. Will you continue to work after relocating to the new city?
7. Mr Kumar likes to invite people for dinner.
8. To help people in times of need is noble.

G Fill in the blanks with the correct forms of the given words. State whether they are being used as gerunds or participles.

1. She is happy with her daughter for __________ selected for the job. (get)
2. My mother insisted on my __________ German classes in the evenings. (join)
3. There is no chance of the film __________ on time. (start)
4. Can you imagine her __________ us? (cheat)
5. I'm annoyed by the __________ bird outside the window. (chirp)
6. The doctor objects to his __________ junk food. (eat)
7. __________ to forward the link to me was helpful on her part. (agree)
8. We got to know the time by the __________ of the clock. (chime)

Don't Forget!

1. Finite verbs are those that change their form according to the number and person of the subject of the sentence. They have present, past and future forms.
2. Non-finite verbs are those that do not change their form according to the number and person of the subject of the sentence. They do not indicate tense and function as nouns and adjectives. There are three kinds of non-finite verbs.
3. The infinitive is the base form of a verb. It is usually preceded by *to*. Infinitives often function as nouns in a sentence, acting as the subject or object.
4. Participles are words that are used as adjectives. They qualify the nouns that follow them. They are of three types: present, past and perfect.
5. Gerunds are words that look like verbs but function like nouns. They function as the subject of a sentence or the object of a verb or preposition.

18 Phrases

Let's Get Started

Complete these sentences in your own words.

1. A box of gold ______________
2. ______________ a man of honour.
3. ______________ blue in colour.
4. At that time ______________
5. ______________ at this place.
6. The marble staircase ______________

Did you notice that the given groups of words do not have a verb? But they give additional information about the rest of the sentence. They are phrases.

Read these sentences.

The peacock danced **with grace**.
The man **in the black coat** is a detective.
The sudden weather change is causing viral fever.

In each sentence, the group of words in bold give additional information about the sentence. These are phrases.

> A **phrase** is a group of words which conveys some meaning but does not make complete sense. A phrase does not have a finite verb or a subject of its own.

A phrase needs to be a part of a sentence for it to make complete sense.

Examples: *We went out for tea* ***in the afternoon.***
The principal spoke with the students' parents ***at the meeting****.*

A Identify the phrases in these sentences.

1. They returned home late at night.
2. The festival was celebrated with a lot of fun and merriment.
3. There is a discount sale in the supermarket throughout this week.
4. Lata is a woman of principles.
5. Our neighbour was an old man with many funny stories to tell.
6. Smita couldn't stop worrying about her teammates' performance during the debate.
7. Yousuf wants to visit Italy, a city known for its art and culture.
8. Very few families could rent a house in the heart of the city.

Types of Phrases

Phrases can be of three types depending on the function they perform in a sentence: adjective, adverb and noun. Read these sentences.

Mrs Tandon has a necklace **made of pearls**.
He looked at us **in a meaningful way**.
George's indecisive nature is landing him in trouble.

In the first sentence, the phrase *made of pearls* describes the noun *necklace.* In the second sentence, the phrase *in a meaningful way* modifies the verb *looked.* In the third sentence, the phrase *George's indecisive nature* acts as the subject of the sentence. They are adjective, adverb and noun phrases, respectively.

Adjective Phrase

Read these sentences.

Parthiv is a <u>batsman</u> **with skill**.
Kalidasa was a <u>poet</u> **of great renown**.
Rachel wore a **quarter-sleeved** <u>dress</u> **of red colour**.

In all three sentences, the phrases describe the underlined nouns. They act as adjectives and are adjective phrases.

An **adjective phrase** is a group of words that performs the function of an adjective in a sentence.

B **Identify the adjective phrases in these sentences.**

1. The sprinter at the head of the race was the world champion.
2. Are the shoes under the chair yours?
3. The film playing now is my favourite.
4. You can buy freshly-caught fish from the beach in Puri.
5. Mikado has a bushy tail with a pointed tip.
6. Pauline bought a dark brown jacket on her way to the party.
7. This craftsmanship is of the highest quality.
8. The book in my bag is written by Neil Gaiman.
9. The cat that Natasha got on her birthday has fur as soft as velvet.

Look at these sentences.

The student made **silly** mistakes. (adjective)
The student made mistakes **of a silly nature**. (adjective phrase)

Both the sentences mean the same. However, the adjective in the first sentence has been replaced by an adjective phrase in the second sentence.

This table has some adjectives and their corresponding adjective phrases.

Adjectives	Adjective phrases
gold bangles	bangles made of gold
a friendly neighbour	a neighbour of a friendly nature
Japanese bikes	bikes made in Japan
a wise decision	a decision made with wisdom

C Rewrite the sentences replacing the adjectives in italics with adjective phrases.

1. Soumen is an *intelligent* man.
2. She poured the soup into *glass* bowls.
3. Please buy *fresh* vegetables.
4. Mr Singh is an *honourable* man.
5. Usha took a bouquet of *pink* roses for her teacher.
6. The mobile phone is *useless* as it keeps switching off.
7. Nobody likes to have a *short-tempered* roommate.
8. Simran carefully polished the *wooden* floor.

D Underline the adjective phrases in these sentences. Then rewrite the sentences by replacing the adjective phrases with adjectives.

1. Megha is a student capable of hard work.
   Megha is a hardworking student.
2. Shakespeare was a dramatist of great talent.
3. Mithali Raj is a cricketer by profession.
4. The nawab was a man of great wealth.
5. I know why the bird in the cage sings.
6. Every piece of jewellery is made by hand.
7. He led a life of great adventure.
8. We spent a day filled with enjoyment at the amusement park.

Adverb Phrase

Read these sentences.

The driver was driving **in a dangerous way**. (manner)
I am staying **at the hotel**. (place)
I wrote the letter **in the morning**. (time)

The phrases in bold modify the verbs *was driving*, *am staying* and *wrote*. Since they do the work of an adverb, they are adverb phrases.

The phrase *in a dangerous way* tells us *how* the driver drove. The phrase *at the hotel* tells us *where* someone is staying. The phrase *in the morning* tells us *when* the letter was written.

An **adverb phrase** is a group of words that acts as an adverb in a sentence.

E Underline the adverb phrases in these sentences.

1. The lion growled in a ferocious way at the bear.
2. He explained the matter to me with patience.
3. Let us meet outside the school at 4 p.m.
4. Sam was waiting for his parents in the auditorium.
5. Tanima waited for the train on the platform.
6. The match was contested in a fierce manner.
7. The candidate made her presentation with confidence.
8. The arrow flew with great swiftness.

Look at these sentences.

She spoke **angrily**.
She spoke **in an angry way**.

Both the sentences mean the same. In the second sentence, the adverb is replaced with an adverb phrase.

This table lists some adverbs and their corresponding adverb phrases.

Adverbs	Adverb phrases
beautifully	in a beautiful manner
fortnightly	every fourteen days
confidently	with confidence
occasionally	now and then

Adverbs	Adverb phrases
early	at an early hour
inarguably	without any argument
now	at this moment
eventually	in the long run

F Rewrite the sentences replacing the italicized adverbs with adverb phrases.

1. The hotel staff behaved *courteously*.
2. The chef carved the fruit *skilfully*.
3. Respond to the mail *briefly*.
4. The doctor is busy *now*.
5. She always speaks *politely*.
6. The soldiers fought *bravely*.
7. She acted *strangely* around Sayani.
8. Suneet is *always* on the phone.
9. Jeevan will be home *soon*.

G **Rewrite the sentences replacing the italicized adverb phrases with adverbs.**

1. He visits this place *quite often*.
2. Radha and her daughter unpacked the boxes *with a lot of patience*.
3. I wish you good luck *with all my heart*.
4. It was *at this spot* that I met the famous musician.
5. *With great regret*, I inform you that I am unable to take up your offer.
6. We walked to the gate *in silence*.
7. *At that moment*, the teacher entered the room.
8. He said that he would win everyone's hearts *in the long run*.
9. You can find this advertisement *at all places*.
10. *In former times*, this building was a school.
11. Come to my room *at this moment*.
12. He did his homework *in a sloppy manner*.

Noun Phrase

Read these sentences.

Walking in the rain is enjoyable.

The teacher found **her lost book**.

In the first sentence, the phrase *walking in the rain* acts as the subject of the sentence. In the second sentence, the phrase *her lost book* acts as the object of the verb *found*.

> A **noun phrase** is a group of words that acts as a noun in a sentence. It can function as a subject or an object.

H **Underline the noun phrases in these sentences.**

1. To lie to others is wrong.
2. The lawyer demanded a fair trial.
3. Rushing into decisions is not a good idea.
4. Living without friends makes one feel lonely.
5. Grandmother found the old family album.
6. To live honestly is the best policy.
7. I bought a loaf of bread for dinner.
8. The white snow covered the field.

I **Complete the sentences with suitable noun phrases.**

1. ____________________ is a great skill.
2. Do you mind ____________________?
3. ____________________ is an interesting hobby.
4. ____________________ were dancing.
5. ____________________ said he would do it.
6. My aunt bakes ____________________
7. ____________________ covered the lawn.
8. Should I buy ____________________?

J **Identify the italicized words as noun, adjective or adverb phrases.**

1. *To keep your cool at all times* is not a joke.
2. All the students waited *with a lot of eagerness* to welcome the chief guest.
3. I can only drive a car *without gears*.
4. The thief was a man *of few morals*.
5. The horse galloped *with swiftness*.
6. *Being able to swim* is a necessary skill for survival.
7. Thomas has to leave *in half an hour*.
8. I want to buy the car *with the best mileage*.
9. They spoke *for a while*.
10. *Learning a musical instrument* improves concentration.
11. She wrestled against her opponent *with all her might*.
12. He sings *without restraint*.

Don't Forget!

1. A phrase is a group of words giving additional information about a sentence.
2. A phrase does not have a finite verb or a subject.
3. An adjective phrase acts as an adjective in a sentence.
4. An adverb phrase acts as an adverb in a sentence. It can tell us where, when and how an action took place.
5. A noun phrase acts as a noun in a sentence.

Let Us Write

You are contesting the elections for school captain. Make a list of things you will do if you are elected. Then identify the phrases you used and write their types.

You can include these points.

- improving the students' library
- more instruments for the music room
- better sports facilities
- increased participation in inter-school competitions

19 Clauses

Let's Get Started

Complete the sentences according to the instructions.

1. I like chocolate ______________________________ (use *because*)
2. Rahul will do his homework ______________________________ (use *when*)
3. Diwali is the time ______________________________ (use *when*)
4. I have a friend ______________________________ (use *who*)
5. I started going to the school ______________________________ (use *which*)

The parts of the sentences you have written have subjects and finite verbs of their own. They are clauses.

A **clause** is a group of words that contains a subject and a finite verb. A clause can be a part of the sentence or a sentence by itself.

Examples: *The girl* ***who is standing there*** *is my friend.* (part of a sentence)
The boy is eating a vegetable sandwich. (sentence by itself)

A clause has the following characteristics.

- It has a subject and a finite verb.
- It can be a sentence by itself or be a part of a sentence.
- It can stand on its own and make complete sense, but not always.

A Write whether the italicized words are phrases (P) or clauses (C).

1. The boss invited all the employees for lunch *on Saturday*. ______
2. The tiger was hungry *because it had not eaten in days*. ______
3. Rohan could not attend the party *because of his ill health*. ______
4. All schools will be closed on Wednesday *due to heavy rains*. ______
5. *Opening the gate*, John let the visitors into the compound. ______
6. It's sad that *our security guard has to retire next year*. ______
7. Riding *through the waves* seems like a lot of fun. ______
8. *Until you try new food*, you can't say whether you like it or not. ______

Grammar Byte

Remember that a phrase does not give complete meaning. It is part of the predicate of a sentence. It may have a subject but not a finite verb.

Main Clause and Subordinate Clause

Look at these sentences.

Vivek loves chips *if they are crisp*.
Susan likes hot and sour soup *when she goes out for dinner*.
I know the doctor *who lives in Besant Nagar*.

The underlined words in each sentence have subjects and finite verbs and make complete sense by themselves. They are main clauses. The italicized sections have subjects and finite verbs of their own. However, they depend on the rest of the sentence to make complete sense. They are subordinate clauses.

A **main clause** has a subject and a finite verb and makes complete sense by itself.

A **subordinate clause** has a finite verb and a subject but does not make complete sense on its own. It depends on the main clause for its meaning.

B Underline the subordinate clauses and circle the main clauses in these sentences.

1. We have twenty new students who have joined our class this year.
2. The man who called didn't leave a message.
3. Sanjana's mother refused to buy the shoes since they were expensive.
4. Vineet likes to read stories which are humorous.
5. As she was not at home, I couldn't invite her for the party.
6. I waited for him until he finished his piano lessons.
7. I don't know if she'll be a good team player.
8. If you eat too much ice cream, you may fall sick.

Grammar Byte

Subordinate clauses can be identified by the words they begin with, including relative pronouns like *who*, *which*, *that*, and subordinating conjunctions like *because*, *when*, *where*, *although* and *if*.

Types of Subordinate Clauses

A subordinate clause can be an adjective clause, an adverb clause or a noun clause.

Examples: *She is looking for a teacher* ***who can teach mathematics well***. (adjective clause)
You can meet me ***as soon as you arrive***. (adverb clause)
He claims ***that he submitted his assignment last week***. (noun clause)

In the first sentence, the clause acts as an adjective. It gives additional information about the noun *teacher*.

In the second sentence, the clause gives additional information about the verb *meet*. It is an adverb clause.

In the third sentence, the clause acts as the object of the verb *claims*. It is a noun clause.

Let us look at each of the three types in detail.

Adjective Clause

Look at these sentences.

Sushma likes films *with a happy ending.*
Sushma likes films *which have a happy ending.*

In both the sentences, the words in italics describe the word *films*. They perform the function of an adjective.
In sentence 1, the words *with a happy ending* do not have a subject and a finite verb. It is an adjective phrase.
In sentence 2, the group of words *which have a happy ending* has a subject, *which*, and a finite verb, *have*. It is an adjective clause.

> An **adjective clause** describes, qualifies or defines a noun or a pronoun. An adjective clause answers the questions *who?* or *which?* in relation to the noun it qualifies.

Examples: *People* ***who pamper their children*** *harm them in the long run.*
I like films ***which were made in the 80s****.*

An adjective clause has the following characteristics.

1. It describes a noun or a pronoun. **Example:** *The man* ***who has a limp*** *is a sailor.* (The clause describes the noun, *man*.)
2. It is introduced by the words *who*, *whom* or *whose* (for living beings), *which* (for non-living things and animals), *that* (for both) and sometimes, by *where* and *when*.
   Examples: *The girl* ***who won the prize*** *is his niece.*
   The cat ***which has a ginger-coloured coat*** *is from Persia.*
   The box ***that you gave me*** *is in my closet.*
   The country ***where I was born*** *lies across the river.*
3. It sometimes omits the introductory pronoun. **Example:** *This is the book I wanted to buy.* (which omitted)
4. It is always placed close to the noun it describes. The meaning of the sentence changes depending on where the clause is placed. **Example:** *The passenger will have to pay the man who bought her the ticket.* [✓]
   The passenger who bought her the ticket will have to pay the man. [✗]

C Underline the adjective clause in each sentence and circle the noun it qualifies.

1. He is the man who met with an accident last night.
2. These days it is hard to find people who are honest and sincere.
3. The girl who played the last song is my neighbour.
4. The route which we took was scenic.
5. My aunt who lives nearby took me shopping.
6. This is the same advertisement which has been playing on TV since I was a child.
7. The city in which I grew up is huge.
8. Maria has a cat which follows her everywhere.

A sentence can be written using an adjective phrase or an adjective clause without changing its meaning.

Example: *This is the house* ***with the red door***. (adjective phrase)
This is the house ***which has a red door***. (adjective clause)

D Rewrite the sentences by changing the italicized adjective phrases into adjective clauses. Use *who, which* or *that*.

1. Hampi is an ancient city *of great historical importance*.
2. All teachers appreciate *intelligent and obedient students*.
3. *The man talking to* Manyata is her father.
4. *The umbrella with the broken handle* is mine.
5. Mrs Kumar was *the only teacher in-charge of the nursery students*.
6. This is a large class *consisting of over 40 students*.
7. Mr Nicholas, *our physics teacher*, lives near the school.
8. *The lost papers* are not really needed for the project.

E Complete the sentences with suitable adjective clauses. Use *who, which* or *that*.

1. The bus ____________________ has already left.
2. Anil, ____________________ could not take the interview.
3. Moni gets angry with people ____________________
4. The peacock unfurled its tail ____________________ as it walked towards the peahen.
5. The little girl ____________________ is my friend's sister.
6. Sunny Pawar is the boy ____________________
7. A magazine ____________________ arrived yesterday evening.
8. Mrs Jalal is the lady ____________________

Adverb Clause

Look at these sentences.

Praneet could not write the exams *because of his illness*.
Praneet could not write the exams *because he was ill*.

In sentence 1, the words *because of his illness* do not have a subject and a finite verb. It modifies the verb *could not write*. It is an adverb phrase.

In sentence 2, the words *because he was ill* have a subject, *he*, and a finite verb, *was*. It modifies the verb *could not write*. It is an adverb clause.

An **adverb clause** provides additional information about the verb in the main clause.

Examples: *People panicked* ***when they heard about the strike.***
Although he was angry with his friends, Amit did not shout at them.

Kinds of Adverb Clauses

An adverb clause is classified into various types. It may describe the action in terms of when it took place (time), where it took place (place), why it took place (reason), how it took place (manner), the reason it took place (purpose) and the result of the action (consequence).

Adverb Clause of Time: It indicates *when* the action was carried out by the verb. To identify the adverb clause of time, find the main verb in the sentence and ask the question, *when?* in relation to the verb.

Example: *He will have dinner* ***after he finishes your work***. (Ask: *When* will he have dinner?)

Adverb Clause of Place: It shows the *place* where the action was carried out by the verb. To identify the adverb clause of place, find the main verb in the sentence and ask the question *where?* in relation to the verb.

Example: *The arrow fell* ***where the giant was sleeping***. (Ask: *Where* did the arrow fall?)

Adverb Clause of Reason/Purpose: It shows the *reason* why the action indicated in the verb is carried out. To identify the adverb clause, ask the question *why?* in relation to the verb.

Example: *We eat* ***so that we may live***. (Ask: *Why* do we eat?)

Adverb Clause of Manner: It shows *how* the action indicated by the verb is carried out. To identify the clause, ask the question *how?* in relation to the verb.

Example: *She spoke* ***as if she knew everything about the incident.*** (Ask: *How* did she speak?)

Adverb Clause of Condition: It shows the *condition* under which the action indicated by the verb can be done or completed. **Example:** *You will not reach the station in time* ***unless you start now***.

Adverb Clause of Comparison: These can show *comparison* in degree or manner. It begins with the conjunction *than* or the adverb *as*.

Examples: *He is older* ***than he looks.***

He is more intelligent ***than you think he is!***

Adverb Clause of Result: It shows the *result* of the action of the verb.

Example: *Anita reached school early* ***so that her friends would not have to wait for her.***

This table lists the words that come before different types of adverb clauses.

Adverb Clause	Introductory Words
time	*when, whenever, before, after, till, since, as soon as, while*
place	*where, wherever*
reason	*because, since, as, so that, that, lest*
manner	*as, as if*
condition	*if, unless, whether, provided that, so long as*
comparison	*as ... as, than*
result	*so ... that, such ... that*

F **Underline the adverb clause in each sentence and mention what type it is.**

1. You can sit here till you finish your work.
2. You should finish all your work, even if you are tired.
3. Can you tell me where I can buy sports shoes?
4. I haven't exercised for the last two weeks because I'm lazy.
5. Even though she was tired, she went for her son's concert.
6. If you don't finish your food, you won't get any dessert.
7. Varun can reach the book rack because he is taller than Minty.
8. While you were out, I did your chores for you.

G **Rewrite the sentences replacing the italicized adverb phrases with adverb clauses.**

1. *On seeing the teacher approach the class*, the students fell silent.
2. *While driving to the park*, Jimmy saw a homeless man on the road.
3. *After buying the potted plant*, Samantha felt like buying two more.
4. *Before the beginning of the school year*, John and his sister went to visit their grandparents.
5. *Since moving to Hyderabad*, Harsha has begun to enjoy Irani tea.
6. *Having exercised for two hours*, I felt fit.
7. *Being early*, Shruti got the best seats in the theatre.
8. *Before stepping onto the stage*, Srinivas said a prayer.

Noun Clause

Look at these sentences.

We expect *them to win*.

We expect *that they will win*.

In sentence 1, the words *to win* do not have a subject and a finite verb. It is a noun phrase.

In sentence 2, the words *that they will win* have a subject, *they*, and a finite verb, *will win*. They answer the question, *We expect what?* They act like the subject of the sentence and form a noun clause.

> A **noun clause** acts like a noun in a sentence. It can be the subject, the object or the complement of the verb. It is introduced by the word *that*, the question words *why*, *what*, *how*, and *if* and *whether*.

Examples: *I cannot understand* ***why you are always late***. (object of the verb *understand*)

That we are late is no surprise. (subject of the verb *is*)

Noun clauses have the following characteristics:

1. They begin with words such as *how, that, what, whatever, when, where, whether, which, whichever, who, whoever, whom, whomever*, and *why*. **Examples:** *Do you know* ***what you have done***?
   Who you go on holiday with *is up to you.*
2. They can act as the subject of a sentence, as direct or indirect objects and as complements.
   Examples: ***Where he lives*** *is a mystery.* (subject)
   Give the money to ***whoever needs it***. (indirect object)

H Underline the noun clauses in these sentences.

1. We should realize that it is never too late to correct our mistakes.
2. It is true that he always treats his staff courteously.
3. Lauren told me that she would pick up the snacks.
4. Please tell me who sent the email to the whole class.
5. Whoever is the first one to come to class must open the windows.
6. What the judges said made the contestant cry.
7. Their excuse was that they didn't receive the notice.
8. I am not sure whether we should leave the forest guest house after dark.

I Rewrite the sentences after changing the italicized noun phrases into noun clauses.

1. The zoo director fully understood *the need for additional staff.*
2. My friend always lays stress on *the importance of physical exercise*.
3. No one can guess *the size of her shoe*.
4. I know *Michael to be a loyal man.*
5. Kohli is confident of *winning the series.*
6. Kindly show him *where to put his bags.*
7. Hima and Raj should find out *what to do first.*
8. Do you know *what to buy?*

J Underline the clauses in the sentences and identify what type they are.

1. The house that I live in belongs to my father.
2. The boy who is sitting near me is my cousin.
3. I am sure that I will get a good rank.
4. I thought that it would be a fine day.
5. Ram, who worked very hard in class, has won a scholarship.
6. I will give you a map so that you can find your way.
7. Shreya speaks better than she writes.
8. Don't make noise while she is singing.

Watch Out!

The type of the clause is not determined only by the word introducing it. Recognize the function it performs in the sentence to identify the clause.

*I do not know **when I can meet you**.* (noun clause)

*You can meet me **when you are free**.* (adverb clause)

*Is this the time **when you go to sleep**?* (adjective clause)

K Identify the type of the underlined clause in each sentence. Then, change the clause to its corresponding phrase and rewrite the sentences.

1. He remembers the year when there was a devastating flood.
2. The soldiers believed that their commander was courageous.
3. Whoever is the owner of this book should take it from the staff room.
4. He was unhappy because he had failed to keep the promise.
5. I hired the taxi which was waiting on the kerb.
6. Come to our house at any time you want.
7. They behaved as responsible people do during the difficult situation.
8. Everyone had to knock on the door because the doorbell was malfunctioning.

Don't Forget!

1. A clause is a group of words that includes a subject and a verb.
2. The main clause can express a complete thought. A subordinate clause needs the help of the main clause to complete its meaning.
3. Subordinate clauses are of three types: adjective clause, adverb clause and noun clause. They do the work of an adjective, adverb and noun, respectively.

20 Kinds of Sentences: Meaning

Let's Get Started

Correct the punctuation mark at the end of each sentence. Then, write whether it is a statement, question, exclamation, order or request.

1. The problem for the students was too difficult to solve? ________
2. Leave now? ________
3. Will you wait here! ________
4. What a wonderful writer Michael Morpurgo is? ________
5. Please explain this lesson to me! ________

Parts of a Sentence

We know that a sentence is a group of words arranged in a particular order and expressing complete meaning. A sentence has two parts: the subject and the predicate.

> The **subject** of a sentence is the part which indicates what the sentence is about.
> The **predicate** is the part of the sentence which says something about the subject. It always includes the verb.

Example: ***Many people*** *gathered at the store to avail of the discounts*.

The subject is usually placed at the beginning of the sentence but it can also come in the middle or at the end.

Example: *Deep inside the sea live* ***dangerous sharks***.

A Circle the subjects and underline the predicates in these sentences.

1. All living organisms require food to survive.
2. Association of two different organisms in which both are benefitted is called symbiosis.
3. There are four types of teeth in our mouth – incisors, canines, premolars and molars.
4. Tucked neatly under the pile of clothes in the cupboard are the letters written by my mother to my father thirty years ago.
5. The process of removing wool from the body of an animal is called shearing.
6. Many people have come from faraway places to pray at the Medak Church on Easter day.

Grammar Bytes

A sentence always has at least one finite verb. Sometimes, a single finite verb can form a sentence, in which the subject is implied.

(You) go.

When a sentence begins with *there*, it is never the subject. To find the subject, we ask '*who/what* + verb'.

There is ***an underwater railway link*** *being built here.*

7. The Belcher Sea Snake is the most poisonous snake in the world.
8. The blue whale's heart is as big as a small car!
9. Three of the world's biggest animals – the ostrich, the elephant and the giraffe – live in Africa.
10. A sand sculptor uses only water and sand to make sand sculptures.

Based on their meaning, sentences can be divided into four types.

1. Assertive (statement)
2. Interrogative (question)
3. Imperative (order, request, instruction, advice)
4. Exclamatory (conveying strong feelings)

Assertive Sentence

An **assertive sentence** states something or provides some information. The statement can be positive (to affirm something) or negative (to negate something).

Examples: *Mary made a delicious cake for her daughter on her birthday.* (affirmative)
I did not go to the beach yesterday. (negative)

Interrogative Sentence

An **interrogative sentence** asks questions. These can be *wh-* questions or *yes/no* questions.

Examples: *Why are you so anxious? (wh- question)*
Are we leaving now? (yes/no question)

Wh- questions begin with a question word. The question words can be:

a. interrogative pronouns (*what, who, whose, which* and *whom*)
b. interrogative adverbs (*when, why, where, how*)
c. interrogative adjectives (*which* book, *whose* pen, *what* cuisine)

Grammar Byte

A *wh-* question can only be answered using an assertive sentence.

Yes/no questions can be answered with a *yes* or a *no*. These questions begin with an auxiliary verb like *can, may* and *should*.

Examples: ***Can** we leave in another ten minutes?*
***May** I leave a message with you?*
***Should** we buy this book by Charles Dickens?*

Question Tags

Interrogative sentences can also be formed by adding a question tag to an assertive sentence.

A question tag consists of an auxiliary verb and a pronoun. The pronoun must be of the same gender, number and person as the subject of the sentence.

Watch Out!

If the subject is *I*, the verb in the question tag is *are*, not *am*.

I am wrong, am not I? [✗]

I am wrong, aren't I? [✓]

Examples: *The peacock is a beautiful bird,* ***isn't it****?*
Malini is an expert chef, ***isn't she****?*
You are not left-handed, ***are you****?*

If the assertive part of the sentence is affirmative, the question tag is negative. If the assertive sentence is negative, the question tag is positive.

Examples: *He is an honest man,* ***isn't he****?*
We are not running late, ***are we****?*

Imperative Sentence

An **imperative sentence** gives a command, an instruction, a piece of advice, or makes a request.

Examples: *Submit the assignment this evening.* (command)
Switch on the fan, please. (request)
Fry the onions till they are golden brown. (instruction)
Pay attention to the lessons in class. (advice)

Exclamatory Sentence

An **exclamatory sentence** expresses strong emotions or feelings of excitement, joy, surprise, anger or sadness.

Examples: *How wonderful the performance is!* (joy)
I can't believe it! (surprise)
How dare you do that! (anger)
Alas! He is no more. (sadness)

B Identify the type of sentences and write A for assertive, I for interrogative, E for exclamatory and IM for imperative.

1. The jaguar is the largest member of the American cat family.
2. Tony had lunch before he left, didn't he?
3. What an amazing fish the Pirarucu is!
4. Have you ever read an ebook?
5. Do as you are told.
6. One should exercise at least five days a week.
7. Antarctica has some of the coldest places on the earth.
8. How hot it is here, isn't it?
9. Name two animals that live in the seas around Antarctica.
10. Do you like the *Harry Potter* series of books?
11. Check if you have taken everything before you leave.
12. Where on earth did you keep the notes?

C **Arrange the given words to make the type of sentence mentioned. Add the necessary punctuation marks.**

1. the obtaining process food of called get to energy is nutrition (assertive)
2. you tell can me way the to the post office please (interrogative)
3. to left the keep (imperative)
4. annoying his how behaviour is (exclamatory)
5. the are of modes transfer heat of different what (interrogative)
6. device a the measure anemometer to wind of speed is the (assertive)
7. times in carry a passport foreign while country your with at you all (imperative)
8. messy is it what room a (exclamatory)

Let Us Write

Neha and Nihal are discussing what breakfast they like. Read the conversation and write the sentence type for each.

Neha: What is your favourite breakfast, Nihal?

Nihal: I like idli with coconut chutney.

Neha: Really! I don't like idli at all.

Nihal: But why? It's a healthy breakfast dish.

Neha: I don't like the taste. I like dosa. Do you also like it?

Nihal: Yes, I do.

Neha: What delicious dosas my mother makes! Please come home one day for breakfast.

Nihal: How nice of you to invite me, Neha! I shall surely come.

21 Types of Sentences: Structure

Let's Get Started

Read these sentences. Identify the main and the subordinate clauses in each.

1. Mary has a little brother.
2. Mary has a little brother and he looks very cute.
3. Mary has a little brother who looks very cute.
4. Mary has a little brother and he looks very cute, especially when he smiles.

Sentences can be of different types depending on their structure.

Simple Sentences

A **simple sentence** is one which contains only one finite verb and one independent clause.

Examples: *I love samosas.*
Ashni kicked the football.

A simple sentence may have two subjects or two objects (direct and indirect). It may also contain phrases.

Examples: ***The children** and **their mother** are returning from the market.* (two subjects)
*She sent **me** a **bouquet**.* (two objects: direct object, *bouquet*; indirect object, *me*)
*The girl **with the long plait** is my next-door neighbour.* (with phrase)

Watch Out!

A simple sentence is not always short in length.

The baby, happy in its own world of innocence, is sleeping with a smile on its face.

Compound Sentences

A **compound sentence** is one which contains at least two independent clauses. These clauses are joined by a coordinating conjunction or a semicolon.

Examples: *Anirudh kicked the ball and it hit Aditya.*
The duck quacked; the horses neighed.

In the first sentence, *Anirudh kicked the ball* and *it hit Aditya* are two independent clauses. They are joined by the coordinating conjunction *and*.

In the second sentence, the two independent clauses are connected by a semicolon.

When a compound sentence consists of two clauses and the subject of both the clauses is the same person or thing, the subject is often omitted in the second clause.

Example: *Vinay turns thirteen this December and plans to celebrate his birthday grandly.* (The pronoun *he* is omitted.)

Complex Sentences

A **complex sentence** is one which contains one main clause and one or more subordinate clauses. The clauses are joined using subordinating conjunctions or relative pronouns.

Examples: *If everyone agrees, we will postpone the celebrations.*

We will postpone the celebrations is the main clause since it expresses complete meaning by itself and can stand on its own.

If everyone agrees is the subordinate clause since it does not make complete sense and therefore, cannot stand on its own.

Grammar Bytes

In a complex sentence, the subordinate clause may be a noun clause, an adverb clause or an adjective clause.

Some common subordinating conjunctions are *while, as, since, until, although, even though* and *as soon as*.

Who, whom, which and *that* are the most-often used relative pronouns.

A Identify the sentences as S (simple), C (compound) or CM (complex).

1. I will be back by Monday and we can discuss the arrangements for the exhibition anytime afterwards.
2. Despite several warnings, he does not change his mischievous ways.
3. They had promised to deliver the books before mid-April so that we could inaugurate the shop.
4. You must submit the assignment on Thursday if you want it to be graded.
5. Ronnie ate too much ice cream at the buffet and felt sick.
6. Raj's mother asked him a question in Hindi; he replied in English.
7. Mrs Das, who taught us history, retired last April.
8. After Emma had been to the market, she joined her friends for lunch.
9. Although twenty school children protested against the construction of a factory near their school, the newspapers did not cover it.
10. Neeta wanted to buy a rare coin for her coin collection, but she did not have enough money.
11. I looked for Bindu and Kanika at the station.
12. After Sanvi and Kashish left on the metro, they realised that their friend Rani was not with them.
13. While Abhinay reads novels, Tamanna reads comics.
14. I wrote a story and sent it to a publisher last week.
15. The leaves of the curry tree glistened after the rain.

Don't Forget!

1. A simple sentence is one which contains only one finite verb and one independent clause.
2. A compound sentence is one which contains at least two independent clauses. These clauses are joined by a coordinating conjunction or a semicolon.
3. A complex sentence is one which contains one main clause and one or more subordinate clauses. The clauses are joined using subordinate conjunctions or relative pronouns.
4. In a complex sentence, the subordinate clause may be a noun clause, an adverb clause or an adjective clause.

22 Transformation and Synthesis

Let's Get Started

Match the sentences with their types.

Sentences	Types
1. Rita baked a cake and gave it to her neighbour.	a. complex sentence
2. Sangeeta likes to sculpt.	b. simple sentence
3. Unless Nitin works hard, he cannot join the basketball team.	c. compound sentence

Transformation of Sentences

We know that sentences can be of different types depending on their meaning and structure.

They can be classified as affirmative, negative, imperative, interrogative, assertive and exclamatory, based on their meaning.

We can change one type of a sentence to another without changing its meaning.

Examples: *Ahmed is hardworking.* (assertive affirmative)
Ahmed is not lazy. (assertive negative)
Is Ahmed not hardworking? (interrogative)
How hardworking Ahmed is! (exclamatory)

Sentences can also be classified into simple, compound and complex depending on their structure. Look at these sentences. They all express the same meaning, but are of different kinds.

In spite of working hard, he failed in the exam. (simple)
He worked hard but failed in the exam. (compound)
Although he worked hard, he failed in the exam. (complex)

Transformation of Assertive, Exclamatory and Interrogative Sentences

We can change an exclamatory sentence to an assertive sentence and vice versa.

Examples: *How hot it is in Hyderabad!* (exclamatory)
It is very hot in Hyderabad. (assertive)
She made a terrible mistake. (assertive)
What a terrible mistake she made! (exclamatory)

We can also change an interrogative sentence to assertive and vice versa.

Examples: *Does she have a new job as a shop assistant?* (interrogative)
She has a new job as a shop assistant. (assertive)
Is it a good idea to stay up late tonight? (interrogative)
It isn't a good idea to stay up late tonight. (assertive)

A **Transform the exclamatory sentences into assertive sentences and the assertive sentences into exclamatory sentences.**

1. How irritating these mosquitoes are!
2. Mother made a delicious vegetable stew.
3. Anil told me an interesting story.
4. What a thumping majority he got in the student body elections!
5. They are very upset about your decision.
6. The bird is patiently building its nest.
7. What a shame it is to lose the match like that!
8. What an intelligent person you are!
9. Children are curious about everything they come across.
10. How annoyingly slow the train is!

Grammar Bytes

The word *ever* in an interrogative sentence becomes *never* in the assertive sentence.

*Has Suresh **ever** gone to the zoo?*

*Suresh has **never** gone to the zoo.*

B **Transform the sentences as instructed.**

1. The man with the bowler hat is a famous painter. (change to interrogative)
2. Isn't there going to be a cultural programme during Durga Puja? (change to assertive)
3. The old man could never forget the day when a young man saved him from a road accident. (change to exclamatory)
4. He has no way of getting out of the situation. (change to interrogative)
5. Could Jacob think of a new way to make money after his business fell through? (change to assertive)
6. You have never cooked a complete meal by yourself. (change to interrogative)

Transformation of Affirmative and Negative Sentences

An affirmative sentence makes a positive statement; a negative sentence makes a negative statement. We can change an affirmative sentence to a negative sentence by using an antonym for the adjective, adverb or verb and adding a negative word.

Examples: *She **always** speaks the truth.* (affirmative)

*She **never** tells lies.* (negative)

*It is not **easy** to speak the truth at all times.* (negative)

*It is **difficult** to speak the truth at all times.* (affirmative)

C **Transform the affirmative sentences into negative sentences. Make sure that the meaning remains the same.**

1. She is a bold person.
2. The king is known for his kindness.
3. They strongly disagree with us.
4. This is very unfair.

5. The two sisters behave in very dissimilar ways.
6. It is unlikely that we will win the match this time.
7. They are a happy couple.
8. This is an unexpected surprise.
9. We will be late for lunch.
10. The soldier was very brave.

D **Transform the negative sentences into affirmative sentences.**

1. This is not a suitable size for the baby.
2. It is not easy to convince her.
3. This is not acceptable to them.
4. The food is not spicy.
5. No one disagrees that he is a hardworking man.
6. You must not leave without my permission.
7. Do not take foolish decisions.
8. The film is not boring.
9. We may not reach before six o'clock.
10. The hotel is not expensive.

Transformation of Simple and Compound Sentences

We know that a simple sentence consists of one subject and one predicate.

A compound sentence consists of two or more coordinate clauses, each of which has its own subject and predicate.

Simple sentences can be transformed into compound sentences by using coordinating conjunctions like *and, but, for, nor, or, yet* and *so*.

Examples: *The film being boring, we decided to leave the theatre midway.* (simple)
The film was boring, ***so*** *we decided to leave the theatre midway.* (compound)

You must eat a good breakfast to feel energetic through the day. (simple)
You must eat a good breakfast, ***or*** *you will not feel energetic through the day.* (compound)

Knowing that she would get hungry, she packed an extra sandwich. (simple)
She knew that she would get hungry ***and*** *packed an extra sandwich.* (compound)

Transformation of Simple and Complex Sentences

Simple sentences can be transformed into complex sentences by expanding a word or phrase into a subordinate clause. This subordinate clause can be a noun clause, an adjective clause or an adverb clause.

Examples: *The man standing across the street is a famous painter.* (simple sentence)
The man who is standing across the street is a famous painter. (complex sentence)

We were shocked to hear about the flood in Chennai. (simple sentence)
We were shocked to hear that a flood had hit Chennai. (complex sentence)

E **Change these simple sentences to compound sentences.**

1. In spite of being poor, they are always happy.
2. Being considerate, she helped him.
3. Proven guilty, the criminal was given punishment.
4. You must eat well to avoid falling ill.
5. In spite of being intelligent, Rebecca makes silly mistakes in the exam.
6. Being very tired, we slept early.
7. I don't remember the route to the market despite going there several times.
8. Teena sang in the choir in spite of being ill.
9. The injured player had to leave the field for treatment.
10. Wanting a job soon, he decided to study engineering.

F **Rewrite these simple sentences as complex sentences as instructed.**

1. The satellite exploring the planet Mars returned to Earth last month. (Use *that*)
2. Sir Edmund Hillary, the first person to climb Mount Everest, was a beekeeper. (Use *who*)
3. This country is investing in clean energy to develop its industries further. (Use *so that*)
4. Pluto, the most distant member of the solar system, is considered a dwarf planet. (Use *which*)
5. In spite of coming from a humble background, Suhas has achieved a lot in life. (Use *although*)
6. The news of India winning the match made us very happy. (Use *that*)
7. Meera's brother gave her a box decorated with precious stones. (Use *which*)

Synthesis of Sentences

Read these sentences.

The accused was guilty. He admitted it in court.
The accused admitted in court that he was guilty.

The first two sentences have been joined to form a single sentence without changing the meaning.

Synthesis of sentences refers to the joining of two or more sentences into a new sentence without changing the meaning. The new sentence can be a simple sentence, a compound sentence or a complex sentence.

In this chapter, we will focus on joining simple sentences to form simple, compound and complex sentences.

Joining Simple Sentences to form another Simple Sentence

Two simple sentences can be joined to form another simple sentence in the following ways.

Using a Non-finite Verb

We know that non-finite verbs include infinitives, gerunds and participles. These can be used to join two simple sentences.

Examples: *She met her childhood friend at the party. She was very happy.*
She was very happy ***to meet*** *her childhood friend at the party.* (infinitive)

Tom opened the can of juice. He took a gulp.
***Opening** the can of juice, Tom took a gulp.* (present participle)

Manu was tired of playing. He sat down to rest.
***Tired** of playing, Manu sat down to rest.* (past participle)

I swim in the morning. It keeps me fresh.
***Swimming** in the morning keeps me fresh.* (gerund)

Using a Noun or a Noun Phrase in Apposition

Sentences can be joined by changing one sentence into a noun phrase or a noun, in apposition. When something is in apposition, it is placed next to the thing it refers to.

Examples: *I saw a large bird swooping down on the chicks. It was an eagle.*
*I saw a large bird, **an eagle**, swooping down on the chicks.*
Marlowe was a playwright of great talent. He wrote a play called Dr Faustus.
*Marlowe, **a playwright of great talent**, wrote a play called* Dr Faustus.

Using an Adverb or an Adverb Phrase

Sentences can be joined by changing one sentence into an adverb or an adverb phrase.

Examples: *Udit was praised. The principal praised him highly.*
*Udit was **highly** praised by the principal.* (adverb)

He was walking. He had a stealthy way of doing so.
*He was walking **in a stealthy way**.* (adverb phrase)

Using *Too ... to* and *Enough*

Examples: *It was very hot. We could not play outside.*
*It was **too** hot for us **to** play outside.*

She is kind. She can understand your problem.
*She is kind **enough** to understand your problem.*

Watch Out!

Be careful while using a present participle to join sentences.

It was a hot day. I stayed inside.
Being a hot day, I stayed inside. [✗] (*I* is not *a hot day*.)
It being a hot day, I stayed inside. [✓]
She was going out. A knock on the door stopped her.
Going out, a knock on the door stopped her. [✗]
(*She*, and not *A knock on the door*, was going out.)
She was going out, when a knock on the door stopped her. [✓]

G Join these sentences to form simple sentences using infinitives, participles or gerunds.

1. She went to Shimla. She wanted to attend her cousin's wedding.
2. People queued up early in the morning at the bank. They wanted to withdraw money.
3. Samantha didn't even have Rs 10 with her. She could not buy a bottle of water.
4. China and Germany are conducting talks. They want to do a joint space expedition.
5. The cat was lost in the woods. It could not find its way out.
6. We have two tests today. We are very nervous.
7. Rohit hadn't seen Gautam in ages. Rohit didn't recognize him.
8. She was talking to her friend sitting next to her. She forgot she was in science class.
9. Meera is a vegan. She does not drink milk.
10. Chitra was cleaning her room. She found some old books.

H **Join each pair of simple sentences to form another simple sentence.**

1. She is busy. She cannot take the call.
2. I am going to the railway station. I have to pick up my cousin.
3. Venu is intelligent. He can solve the puzzle.
4. Carol wants to support her parents. She wants to find a job.
5. This is Karunya's brother. His name is Kiran.
6. Malala Yousafzai is the youngest Nobel Peace Prize recipient. She has honorary Canadian citizenship.
7. Zeenat is tall. She can reach the top shelf.
8. Robin was frustrated with his roommate. He tried to move out of hostel.
9. Theresa saw Mr Singh's dog. It was chasing a cat.
10. The students completed their examination. They went home.
11. The baby is sleepy. She cannot keep her eyes open.
12. The rain stopped. We set out on our regular walk.

Joining Simple Sentences to form Complex Sentences

Two simple sentences can be joined to form a complex sentence in the following ways.

Using subordinating conjunctions

Examples: *They are poor. They are too proud to ask for money.*
***Though** they are poor, they are too proud to ask for money.*

I started dance classes last week. I have no time in the evening.
***Since** I started dance classes last week, I have no time in the evening.*

To join two simple sentences, we can also convert one of them into a subordinate clause, while the other is used as the main clause in the sentence.

Using a Noun Clause

Example: *He is innocent. Everyone knows that.*
*Everyone knows **that he is innocent**.*

Using an Adjective Clause with a Relative Pronoun

The relative pronouns are *who, whom, whose, that* and *which*.

Examples: *She sold her house. The house had eight rooms.*
*She sold her house **which had eight rooms**.*

This is the gentleman. He helped my brother.
*This is the gentleman **who helped my brother**.*

Using an Adverb Clause

Example: *We entered the theatre. The film started.*
***As soon as we entered the theatre**, the film started.*

I Join the pairs of simple sentences to form complex sentences with the given subordinating conjunctions.

1. Dr Sarkar was on leave. He went to the hospital on an emergency. (although)
2. You need not worry about the interview. You have prepared well. (since)
3. She should give correct measurements. She wants her jacket to be stitched well. (if)
4. Rohit cleaned his room. Rohit went to play cricket. (after)
5. The refugees were driven out of their motherland. The refugees sought to make Canada their home. (as)
6. She knew about my visit. She left for Chennai. (although)
7. The students are seriously ill. The students cannot miss their examinations. (unless)
8. The baby cried all night. The neighbours did not complain. (even though)
9. My mother goes to the supermarket. She takes her own cloth bags. (whenever)
10. We did not take our umbrellas. There were no clouds in the sky. (because)

J These complex sentences have more than one conjunction. Underline the conjunction that is not required.

1. Since I reached the school early, then I had time to play before everyone arrived.
2. Although you lost the opportunity now, and there is always a next time!
3. They are willing to contribute some money and if you need it.
4. Though it seemed like an impossible task, John still learnt to ride a unicycle.
5. Until I started exercising regularly, since I did not lose weight.
6. Even though it is raining outside, and the students did not stop playing football.
7. If the business succeeds, so Mr Dutt wants a share of the profits.
8. As Tejas won the lottery last week, because he doesn't work here anymore.
9. Since the new car has a lot of power but it uses lots of fuel.
10. Whenever there is a cricket match and I usually have an examination.

Joining Simple Sentences to Form Compound Sentences

Simple sentences can be joined by using coordinating as well as correlative conjunctions to form compound sentences.

Examples: *I had guests at home. I did not go to the gym yesterday.*
I had guests at home, ***so*** *I did not go to the gym yesterday.*

They have packed the luggage. They are ready to leave.
They have packed the luggage ***and*** *are ready to leave.*

It is not hot. It is not cold.
Neither *is it hot* ***nor*** *is it cold.*

Eva tried to convince Lata. Lata did not listen to Eva.
Eva tried to convince Lata, ***but*** *she did not listen to her.*

He is kind. He is generous.
Not only *is he kind,* ***but*** *he is* ***also*** *generous.*

You can have pasta. You can have dosa.
You can ***either*** *have pasta* ***or*** *you can have dosa.*

K **Change the pairs of simple sentences into compound sentences using the given conjunctions.**

or yet whenever but while still so else either ... or neither ... nor not only ... but also both ... and

1. You can submit an online application. You can submit a hard copy.
2. The two brothers fight like cats and dogs. They love each other very much.
3. I was very sleepy. I finished the assignment before sleeping.
4. You can have chocolate ice cream. You can have vanilla ice cream.
5. The drought has affected the urban population. The drought has affected the rural population.
6. Mr Kona will not buy a dog. Mr Kona will not buy a cat.
7. Sunil missed his swimming class. He was unhappy.
8. Sleep early tonight. You will not wake up early tomorrow.
9. Manu is young. Manu is mature for his age.
10. You can sleep in the bedroom. You can sleep in the drawing room.
11. I chatted with my mother. She was cutting the vegetables.
12. You are ready with the report. You can call me.

L **Join the sentences in column A with the sentences in column B to form compound or complex sentences using appropriate conjunctions. Then, mention whether the new sentence is complex or compound.**

Column A	Column B	New Sentence
1. You must tell me what is bothering you.	a. I cannot help you.	
2. They moved into the new flat.	b. They invited many guests.	
3. You can send me an email.	c. You can send me a WhatsApp message.	
4. She came here.	d. She saw me.	
5. Virat practised hard.	e. He didn't succeed.	
6. Swati danced beautifully.	f. The dance instructor praised her.	
7. She is popular.	g. She cannot be considered a great poet.	
8. The old man was thrown into prison.	h. He was heavily fined.	
9. Bindu had a pleasant manner.	i. She became popular in school.	

Column A	Column B	New Sentence
10. These shoes are not mine.	j. They are too big.	
11. You want to lose weight.	k. You must give up fast food.	
12. You must drink plenty of water.	l. It is summer.	

M Convert the following simple sentences into compound sentences.

1. Atish fled for fear of being robbed.
2. Rishi sat in a corner, brooding.
3. Being innocent, Ashima never thought of running away.
4. Besides being handsome, Kavish is clever.
5. Being lazy, Dominic failed.
6. In spite of her illness, she attended the class.
7. Besides being hardworking, Avinash was also punctual.

Let Us Write

Renu is a seventh grade student. Her father got transferred from Trivandrum to Delhi. Renu is describing her first day in the new school. Help her join the sentences in each pair into one.

1. It was my first day in the new school. I was very nervous.
2. I walked into a classroom full of students. I didn't know a single person.
3. I sat in an empty chair. I was afraid to talk to anyone.
4. Two girls came up to me. They were smiling.
5. They introduced themselves as Neeta and Swati. They were twins.
6. They asked my name and where I was from. I replied timidly.
7. Other students also began to introduce themselves. I began to feel less scared.
8. Finally, the teacher entered the classroom. Everyone was silent.
9. I went towards her to introduce myself. The teacher smiled. I lost all my fear then.

23 Punctuation

Let's Get Started

Look at these sentences.

1. Let's eat grandma.
2. Rachel Ray finds inspiration in cooking her family and her dog.
3. Most of the time travellers worry about their luggage.
4. We're going to learn to cut and paste kids.
5. 'Thank you! Your donation just helped someone. Get a job.'

Did you notice that the sentences sound strange? There are missing and misplaced punctuation marks that change the meaning of the sentences.

Now rewrite the sentences with proper punctuation.
Did you notice how the meaning changed completely?

Punctuation marks are essential to convey meaning clearly. They allow us to separate sentences, showing us where to pause and where to place emphasis on particular words.

Full Stop

A **full stop** (.) is used to show a long pause. We use it when we want to end a statement or a command.

Examples: *The school will reopen on 7 June.*
Close the door.

We also use a full stop to show abbreviations.
Examples: *I.I.T. (Indian Institute of Technology)*
W.H.O. (World Health Organization)

Comma

A **comma** (,) is used to show a very short pause.

We use the comma for the following.

1. To separate words in a sequence.
   Examples: *My boss is friendly, helpful and understanding.*
   The place where we stayed is neat, safe and cheap too.

2. To separate phrases in a sequence.
Examples: *Festivals or ordinary days, weekdays or weekends, she is always elegantly dressed.*
Soups or salads, fruits or vegetables, anything healthy will do for me.

3. To separate short clauses in a sequence.
Examples: *He has no idea about who he should consult, where he should stay, or what he should carry with him.*
We all love you, care for you and miss you!

4. To separate the term used to address someone, from the rest of the sentence.
Examples: *Sir, will you please grant me leave tomorrow?*
Will you please grant me leave tomorrow, sir?

5. To separate the parts of the date and any word following the date.
Examples: *On 15 August, 1947, India became independent.*
On 11 January, 2005, they shifted to Malaysia.

6. To separate words like *yes, no, oh,* and *well* from the other words in a sentence.
Examples: *Well, you can call her but she may not respond.*
Oh, I'm sorry. I did not know that.

7. To separate expressions which refer to the same person.
Examples: *Our Vice Chancellor, a highly able administrator, runs the university efficiently.*
Mr Solomon, our new maths teacher, teaches excellently.

8. To separate question tags from statements.
Examples: *You locked the door, didn't you?*
They have left, haven't they?

9. To separate reported speech from the rest of the sentence.
Examples: *The lawyer said, 'We do not have enough evidence.'*
She said, 'I'm not the culprit.'

A Rewrite the sentences using commas and full stops where required.

1. Come what may I'm going to finish this today
2. May I call you in the morning madam?
3. Swayam brings you clean hygienic and wholesome products
4. We are impressed by her performance by her behaviour and by her attitude
5. He started preparations for his trip on Monday 26 May on a hot afternoon
6. In our company we ensure high standards of food safety while cleaning sorting and packaging all products
7. Brother will you take me with you?
8. They never called you back did they?

Semicolon

A **semicolon** (;) is a longer pause than a comma but a shorter pause than a full stop.

We use the semicolon for the following.

1. To separate two independent clauses which are not connected by a conjunction.
   Examples: *Children are eager to please the teacher**;** they have short attention spans.*
   *I might be late**;** I have a meeting to attend.*

2. Before expressions like *however, then, moreover, nevertheless, hence, thus, for instance, consequently, that is*, and *therefore* if they come between independent clauses not connected by a conjunction.
   Examples: *In summer, prices of vegetables always go up**;** moreover, we don't often get fresh vegetables.*
   *You have submitted the assignment late**;** hence, it will not be graded.*

Colon

A **colon** (:) is a longer pause than a semicolon but a shorter pause than a full stop. The colon acts as a pause which introduces related information.

The colon is used for the following.

1. Between two main clauses when the second clause explains the first clause.
   Examples: *That is the problem with Surya**:** he always makes silly mistakes and loses marks.*
   *The trip wasn't a pleasure**:** we missed the flight and had to wait for the next one for a long time.*
2. To introduce lists.
   Examples: *Here is what you need to get from the market**:** a loaf of bread, a packet of cheese, and a dozen bananas.*
   *There are many places of tourist interest in Hyderabad**:** the Golconda Fort, the Salar Jung Museum, Nehru Zoological Park and Ramoji Film City.*
3. Before quotations, and sometimes before direct speech.
   Examples: *The headlines read: 'Oil prices go up again.'*
   The people cried: 'Long live the king!'

B Rewrite the sentences inserting semicolons, colons and commas where needed.

1. While in Himachal Pradesh we plan to visit three people my brother who works in Shimla my aunt who lives near Solan and my friend Sheela who is studying at the Central University of Himachal Pradesh.
2. It was the poet Ella Wheeler Wilcox who wrote 'Laugh and the world laughs with you weep and you weep alone.'

Question Mark

A **question mark** (?) is used at the end of an interrogative sentence.

Examples: *How many people are there?*
Why are you late?

Exclamation Mark

An **exclamation mark** (!) is used at the end of a sentence which shows strong feelings such as happiness, sadness and anger.

Examples: *How sweet of you to do that!*
What a beautiful picture!
Alas! We lost the match.

> **Watch Out!**
>
> 1. A full stop, and not a question mark, is used at the end of an indirect question.
>
>   *She asked me where I bought my shoes from.*
>   *He told me why he had to resign from his job.*
>
> 2. Do not use the apostrophe with the possessives *ours*, *yours*, *hers*, *its*, *theirs* and *whose*.

Apostrophe

The apostrophe is mainly used for the following.

1. To form possessives. **Examples:** *Mary's pen, teachers' meeting, men's salon*
2. To form contractions. **Examples:** *I will → I'll* *She is → She's*
3. To show the duration of time, area of space or amount of money.

Examples: *one month's vacation, a penny's worth*

Inverted Commas

Inverted commas or **quotation marks** (') are used to report someone else's exact words.

Examples: *She said, 'I'm very pleased with your performance.'*
They said, 'What a wonderful house you own!'

Capital Letters

Capital letters are used for the following.

1. With the first word in a sentence. **Example:** ***M****y plane leaves at two o'clock.*
2. For the first word of a reported speech. **Example:** *Sarla asked, '****W****here did you get that book from?'*
3. With the pronoun *I*. **Example:** *You and* ***I*** *can go the market together.*
4. With the first letter of all the words in a title, except prepositions and conjunctions.
   Example: *I saw* **G**one with the **W**ind *recently.*
5. With proper nouns and titles. **Example:** *That's* ***D****r* ***D****ogra and his son,* ***S****unny.*
6. With names of nationalities and languages. **Examples:** ***I****ndian,* ***S****wiss,* ***G****erman*
7. With geographical names and regions (but not directions). **Example:** *You can see the* ***H****imalayas from* ***N****orth* ***S****ikkim.*
8. With words indicating an address. **Example:** *My house is at the corner of* ***A****maltas* ***M****arg on* ***D. L. R****oy* ***R****oad.*
9. With days, months, and holidays. **Example:** *Today is* ***T****hursday, 23* ***A****ugust.*
10. With names of organizations, companies and brand names. **Example:** *The* ***U****nited* ***N****ations was founded in 1945.*

C Rewrite the sentences using appropriate punctuation marks.

1. are you not coming with us
2. the audience shouted what a catch
3. you need a lot of things to be a winner in sports patience hard work perseverance stamina
4. will you give me a weeks break
5. now that it is festival time its raining discounts
6. you did not fill the application form correctly therefore you cannot come for the interview
7. ms meenakshi our new project head is a stickler for punctuality
8. she asked me where I had gone for my vacation

Let Us Write

Rewrite this passage from the story 'The Gift of the Magi' by O. Henry using correct punctuation.

Jim, she cried dont look at me that way I had my hair cut off and sold because I couldnt have lived through Christmas without giving you a present itll grow out again you wont mind will you I just had to do it My hair grows awfully fast Say Merry Christmas Jim and let's be happy You dont know what a nice what a beautiful nice gift Ive got for you

Youve cut off your hair asked Jim as if he had not arrived at that fact yet even after the hardest mental effort

Cut it off and sold it said Della dont you like me just as well anyhow Im me without my hair am I not

Test 3

A **In the following sentences, replace the italicized adverb or adjective with a corresponding adverb or adjective phrase.**

1. The chief lived in a *stone* house.
2. She spoke *confidently* at the meeting.
3. You will receive a *fortnightly* report on the performance of your ward.
4. I like to see a *smiling* face.
5. We used to meet *occasionally* at family functions.
6. He wore a *blue* turban.

B **Underline the clauses in these sentences and mention what type each is.**

1. I do not know why she is always unhappy.
2. You must understand that it is too late now to apologize.
3. I remember the house where I was born.
4. It is the long road that has no turning.
5. You may sit wherever you like.
6. It was so dark that you could not see your hand.
7. He is the florist who changed the entire look of the auditorium.
8. She wanted to find out if they were selling their three-bedroom flat.
9. I cannot imagine how he completed the assignment against all odds.
10. That you will do well in your exams is certain.
11. We should agree that this is the best solution to the problem right now.

C **Identify the non-finite verbs in these sentences. Mention whether they are gerunds, participles or infinitives.**

1. I won't let you go.
2. Having recovered from my illness, I reported back to duty today.
3. Cooking for a hundred people is child's play for Sita and her team.
4. Being very annoyed with their behaviour, she left the meeting in a huff.
5. Collecting vintage cars is this man's hobby.
6. At the fair, I saw a little girl crying for her parents.
7. I would like to meet your friends today.
8. Singing along to the song playing on the radio, Shweta went about her day.
9. Dancing is her way to relax at the end of a long day.

D **Identify whether these sentences are assertive, interrogative, imperative or exclamatory.**

1. What a terrible mistake I made!
2. Don't quarrel with your brother.
3. Blue whales occasionally swim in groups but usually alone or in pairs.
4. Where did you hide the chips packet?
5. How silly her jokes are!
6. How many times should I tell you not to talk loudly?
7. Vinod got a job as the project head in an IT company in Lucknow.

E **Transform these simple sentences into complex sentences.**

1. My boss is kind and patient. Everyone likes her.
2. We worked day and night. We could not finish the project on time.
3. You may leave now. You have to come back after lunch.
4. Our train tickets did not get confirmed. We travelled by bus.
5. The judge found the accused guilty. He sentenced him to prison.
6. She has travelled to all seven continents. I did not know that.
7. It rained heavily the whole morning. The match got cancelled.
8. My mother is very old. She insists on doing things herself.

F **From the pairs of simple sentences, first make a compound sentence and then a complex sentence.**

1. This place is too small. We can't hold the meeting here.
2. Mary was hungry. She ate the cake all by herself.
3. We went to watch a movie. We met our old friends.
4. Mamta is a costume designer. She is a hairstylist too.
5. Drive slowly. Reach safely.
6. Hari met him several times. Hari could not trust him at all.
7. I had known him earlier. I could not recognize him at first.
8. The bells chimed loudly. They called the faithful to prayer.
9. You should hurry. You will miss the bus.
10. Reema will visit the doctor. Reema will finish her work.

H **Rewrite the passage using the correct punctuation marks.**

Renu have you seen my earrings asked mother anxiously no mummy I haven't replied renu I had kept them on the bedside table last night but I can't find them dont worry Ill look for them do you remember seeing them in the morning no I don't do you think they are lost lets search properly first here they are under the pile of saris in the wardrobe thank God they have been found God bless you renu.

24 Grammar on the Go

Correct Use of Adjectives

The following series of adjectives are often confused. Learn how to use them correctly.

Later and *Latter*

The adjective *later* refers to a time subsequent to a given time.

Examples: *The test will take place at a* ***later*** *date.*
In his ***later*** *years, Mr Das took up astronomy as a hobby.*

The adjective *latter* refers to the second of two things.

Examples: *They had the option of selling their old house or renovating it. They chose the* ***latter*** *option.*
Of the two parts in the essay, the ***latter*** *part is more important.*

Late, Latest and *Last*

The adjective *late* refers to something taking place after the usual time. *Latest* refers to the most recent thing, while *last* refers to something which comes after all the others in time or order.

Examples: *The train is* ***late*** *by two hours.*
I will be ***late*** *today; don't wait for me.*
This is the ***latest*** *news about the earthquake in Indonesia.*
Have you watched the ***latest*** *film in the Harry Potter series?*
She was the ***last*** *person to get the tickets.*
We caught the ***last*** *train back home.*

Nearest and *Next*

The adjective *nearest* refers to something located a short distance away. *Next* refers to something which comes immediately after the present one in order, rank, or space.

Examples: *Do not make this mistake* ***next*** *time.*
I will wait for you in the ***next*** *room.*
Which is the ***nearest*** *bus stop?*

Few, A Few and *The Few*

These are used with countable nouns.

Few indicates a very small number; almost none.

Example: *There being a transport strike,* ***few*** *students came to class today.*

A few indicates a small number; however, this number is important.

Example: ***A few*** *of us waited at the entrance to receive the chief guest.*

The few indicates a small number of something but all that is there of it.

Example: ***The few*** *who were waiting also left a little later.*

A Fill in the blanks with the correct options.

1. The ________ (nearest, next) stationery shop within this locality is half a kilometre away.
2. She is the ________ (late, later, last) person to put the blame on you!
3. It's a bit too ________ (late, latest, later) to change your options.
4. My father offered me a choice between getting bored at home and going with him to his office. I chose the ________ (later, late, latter) option.
5. Have you read the ________ (late, last, latest) novel by Dan Brown?
6. You are always ________ (last, late, later) to class.
7. Despite being in her ________ (last, latter, late) fifties, Revathi is fit and regularly attends karate classes.
8. There are ________ (few, a few, little) tickets left. You can get one if you try right now.
9. There was a strike at the college. ________ (Few, Little, The few) students who had come left after a while.
10. The ________ (latest, last, later) time I heard from him was three years ago!
11. The ________ (latest, last, late) news is that we will get an extra week of summer holidays.
12. She always presents her ideas in a convincing manner. ________ (A few, Few, The few) people disagree with her.
13. You could take the online test or the pen and paper test. I advise you to choose the ________ (later, latter, latest) option.
14. The ________ (nearest, next) person in the queue should be ready with all the papers.
15. I'll meet you ________ (late, later, latter) in the afternoon.

Question Tags

Look at these sentences.

You have not done your homework yet, **have you**?
You will help me, **won't you**?
We must go shopping soon, **mustn't we**?
We shall go shopping this weekend, **shan't we**?

These sentences all have a statement and a short question attached to them. These are question tags.

A **question tag** confirms the information or opinion expressed in the main statement. They are often used in informal, spoken English.

A positive statement has a negative question tag. A negative statement has a positive question tag. The question tag usually uses the same verb as the verb in the main sentence, but may also use other verbs.

Examples: *Let us **play** a game of chess, **shall** we?*
*You **like** bitter gourd, **don't** you?*
*Raghav never **misses** a match played by the Indian cricket team, **does** he?*
*Jose **plays** the sitar well, **doesn't** he?*

Grammar Byte

The question tag must agree with the subject and the tense of the verb in the statement.

They visited the museum, isn't it? (✗)
They visited the museum, didn't they? (✓)

B Add suitable question tags to these statements.

1. Gautam won the first prize at the concert, __________?
2. Oil painting is Manu's hobby, __________?
3. Don't shout so much, __________?
4. Let us go for a walk, __________?
5. They have repaired the water connection, __________?
6. The children love animals, __________?
7. He walks to his office, __________?
8. Let us ask for some discount, __________?
9. Don't stay up late into the night, __________?
10. Clean your room now, __________?

C Add suitable statements to the question tags.

1. ______________________________, won't you?
2. ______________________________, do they?
3. ______________________________, have you?
4. ______________________________, will you?
5. ______________________________, shall we?
6. ______________________________, doesn't it?
7. ______________________________, has she?
8. ______________________________, won't you?
9. ______________________________, shall we?
10. ______________________________, aren't you?

25 Words: A Mixed Bag

This chapter discusses various vocabulary concepts that have enriched the English language.

Idioms

Idioms are groups of words which help us convey our ideas and feelings in a forceful way. Their meanings are often established by usage.

Examples: *Mohan is someone who **calls a spade a spade**.* (Mohan is a straightforward person.)

*The handbag that Neetu bought at the airport **cost** her **an arm and a leg**.* (The bag was very expensive.)

Look at these commonly used idioms.

add insult to injury: make an unfair or difficult situation worse

Example: ***To add insult to injury**, Mohan's bitter rival won the competition.*

the ball is in your court: It is up to you now to take a decision.

Example: *You know my final offer; **the ball is now in your court**.*

beat about the bush: talk about something for a long time without coming to the main point

Example: *I know this is not a casual call. So why don't you tell me the real reason for your visit instead of **beating about the bush**?*

bite off more than one can chew: to take up more things than one can handle

Example: *Deciding to pursue degrees in two streams, Rishav realised he had **bitten off more than he could chew**.*

burn the midnight oil: to work late into the night

Example: *The exams are just round the corner. Every student is **burning the midnight oil**, preparing for the tests.*

judge a book by its cover: judge someone/something based on appearance

Example: *Tania may look young, but she is a good lawyer. **Don't judge a book by its cover**.*

cry over spilt milk: feel bad about something that cannot be changed/repaired

Example: *We should figure out how we lost the match instead of **crying over spilt milk**.*

to play the devil's advocate: to present an opposing or unpopular view, often for the sake of argument

Example: *The professor decided **to play the devil's advocate** to encourage the discussion between the students.*

to count one's chickens before they are hatched: to make plans for something that might not happen

Example: *The match is not over yet.* ***Do not count your chickens before they hatch****.*

give someone the benefit of the doubt: to accept that someone has told the truth or not done something wrong because there is no proof against it

Example: *Since you have always been honest in your dealings with me, I am giving you* ***the benefit of the doubt*** *this time.*

straight from the horse's mouth: to hear something from an authentic source

Example: *There is a parent-teacher meeting next week. I have heard it* ***straight from the horse's mouth****.*

keep someone/something at bay: to keep an enemy or something bad away

Example: *Shipra has been trying to* ***keep*** *her financial worries* ***at bay*** *for quite some time now.*

A Match the idioms with their meanings.

Idioms	Meanings
1. at the drop of a hat	a. looking in the wrong place
2. far cry from	b. have all the advantages
3. hit the sack	c. to hear rumours about someone
4. hear it on the grapevine	d. final problem
5. barking up the wrong tree	e. instantly
6. last straw	f. very different from
7. best of both worlds	g. go to bed

B Fill in the blanks with suitable idioms.

1. Wait for the results of the lottery before planning what you will do with the money.
   ____
2. Rajat ____________________ that his company was going to set up two new offices in another city.
3. Tina has been ____________________ to complete the syllabus before her exams.
4. Despite a previous complaint, the manager decided to give the employee
   ____
5. I was not given a part in the play; then ____________________, I was asked to train the other actors auditioning for the role!
6. Don't ____________________. He may not be smartly dressed, but he is one of the greatest scientists in the country.

Phrasal Verbs

Phrasal verbs are phrases consisting of a main verb and a preposition or an adverb. The meaning of a phrasal verb might be completely different from that of the main verb.

Examples: *Don't* ***rule out*** *the possibility of Bangladesh winning the match.* (think that something is not possible)
Sudhir ***owned up*** *to breaking the torch.* (admit)

Look at these commonly used phrasal verbs.

1. **add up:** make sense
2. **blow up:** explode, get angry
3. **break in:** enter forcefully
4. **bring up:** raise a topic in a conversation, raise a child
5. **call off:** cancel
6. **clamp down on:** act in a strict manner to prevent something
7. **cut back on:** consume lesser amounts
8. **ease off:** become less severe
9. **fall through:** fail
10. **set out:** start a journey

C **Match the phrasal verbs in column A with their meanings in column B.**

Phrasal Verbs	Meanings
1. look forward to	a. search
2. look for	b. investigate
3. look after	c. think happily about something that is about to happen
4. look into	d. treat with disrespect
5. look down upon	e. take care of
6. get along (with)	f. manage to survive
7. get back at (someone)	g. avoid doing something
8. get by	h. recover from (illness, disappointment)
9. get over	i. work well with
10. get out of	j. get revenge on someone

Words Followed by Prepositions

We often use particular prepositions after certain words.

Examples: *She is* ***bent on*** *getting that job.*
I ***apologize for*** *not informing you earlier.*
She ***agreed to*** *what I was saying.*
She ***agreed with*** *me.*
We both ***agree on*** *this point.*
They are ***annoyed with*** *him for not responding to their mail.*
They are ***annoyed at*** *his indifference.*
She is ***good at*** *painting.*
He is ***fond of*** *ice creams.*
She knows his ***fondness for*** *ice creams.*

D Fill in the blanks with appropriate prepositions.

Sunil was cross __________ Sunitha because she broke his mobile phone. She is never happy __________ what she has, he thought. That's why she took his things. Sunitha knew that her brother was annoyed __________ her. She wanted to apologize __________ her misdeeds and was anxious __________ make Sunil smile again. She appealed __________ her father __________ help. Her father was upset __________ her carelessness. She apologized __________ her mistake and asked if she could borrow some money __________ him. Without Sunil's knowledge, Sunitha took his phone and got it repaired. When Sunil saw the repaired phone, he was very happy.

Homophones and Homonyms

Homophones are words that have the same pronunciation but different spelling and meaning.

Example: *aloud (in a spoken voice)* *allowed (permitted)*

Homonyms are words that have the same pronunciation and the same spelling but different meanings.

Example: *party (a celebratory event)* *party (a group formed by people with common goals and ideas)*

E Fill in the blanks with the correct words.

1. Option 'c' is the __________ (right, write) answer for this question.
2. I would like some __________ (plane, plain) water.
3. She's in her __________ (forth, fourth) year of college.
4. Tea and biscuits __________ (complement, compliment) each other.
5. I'm worried that there might be __________ (lead, led) in our water supply.
6. I was offered a __________ (peace, piece) of cake.
7. I hope I don't __________ (bore, boar) you with my tale.
8. To become a professional pianist, you must __________ (practice, practise) very hard.
9. This crime novel is about a __________ (serial, cereal) killer.
10. You need 200 grams of __________ (flower, flour) to make the cake.
11. There is __________ (peace, piece) and harmony in the kingdom.
12. May his __________ (sole, soul) rest in peace.
13. They booked a special __________ (sweet, suite) for the President.

F Choose the correct meanings of the homonyms in each pair.

1. The dog's loud bark woke us up.
   The bark of some trees have medicinal properties.
   a. the sound a dog makes b. outer covering of a tree
2. You should read the newspaper regularly to be up-to-date with current affairs.
   Don't step into the water. The river's current is very swift.
   a. movement of water in a sea or river b. happening now

3. I bought this scarf in London. It cost me £10.
   The pounding of the rain on the tin roof kept the children awake.
   a. the unit of money in the UK b. hitting something or someone hard
4. Every evening, the forest was filled with the noise of crickets chirping.
   Cricket is said to be a gentleman's game.
   a. a game played with a bat and ball and eleven players b. an insect
5. This spring, I will attend an aeronautics camp.
   The children spring to their feet when they see the ice cream man.
   a. the season between winter and summer b. jump up

Synonyms

Synonyms are words with similar meanings.

G **Rewrite the sentences with the synonyms of the underlined words.**

untrue response prepared lost smart feeble shut lean anxious risky

1. Shraddha is <u>intelligent</u> for her age.
2. Playing with fire is <u>dangerous</u>.
3. Don't think that Jordan is <u>weak</u>. He just looks so.
4. Though Tanvi is <u>slim</u>, she is strong.
5. I was <u>nervous</u> when I went on stage for the first time.
6. Are you <u>ready</u> to play against your brother?
7. The pharmacy is <u>closed</u>. We'll have to come tomorrow.
8. Please don't give the manager <u>false</u> reasons for not coming to office.
9. I waited at the door for a while but there was no <u>answer</u>.
10. My new, red purse is <u>missing</u>.

H **Match the words in column A with their synonyms in column B.**

Words	Synonyms
1. brave	a. twisted
2. end	b. impartial
3. funny	c. finish
4. happy	d. assist
5. important	e. tidy
6. crooked	f. silent
7. help	g. essential
8. fair	h. fearless
9. neat	i. comical
10. quiet	j. joyful

Antonyms

Antonyms are words with opposite meanings. Adjectives, nouns and verbs all have antonyms.

Examples:

abundant – scarce
bold – meek, timid
captive – free
courteous – rude
rare – common
sow – reap
strict – lenient
transparent – opaque
admit – deny
ally – enemy
enter – exit
victory – defeat

Prefixes

Prefixes are letters added before another word to form a new word. We often form antonyms by using prefixes.

Look at these antonyms formed with prefixes.

un: ***un**important, **un**interested, **un**believable*
in: ***in**ability, **in**accurate, **in**visible*
im: ***im**mature, **im**possible, **im**mobile*
il: ***il**legible, **il**legal, **il**literate*
ir: ***ir**regular, **ir**relevant, **ir**replaceable*
dis: ***dis**comfort, **dis**satisfied, **dis**advantage*

I Rewrite the sentences by using the antonyms of the underlined words.

1. The tall tower had a broad staircase.
   *The tall tower had a **narrow** staircase.*
2. We descended the flight of steps together.
3. I may look weak, but I am not.
4. She has seen great poverty in her childhood.
5. I thought the bottle would float in the river.
6. The water was too shallow for us to swim in.
7. I finished the difficult part of the question.
8. The man lost his wallet in the city.

J Fill in the blanks with the antonyms of the given words. Use prefixes to form the antonyms.

responsible honest possible believable kind agree legal accurate regular understand

1. This result is wrong. It is ________
2. I think she's making excuses. Her stories are ________
3. Hacking a person's email account is ________
4. It's ________ to find a needle in a hay stack.
5. We ________ with your views.
6. Sunil often does not come to class. He is very ________
7. Don't let people ________ you.
8. Mr Bumble was often ________ to Oliver Twist and did not give him enough to eat.
9. That man is very ________. He has been known to accept bribes.
10. John shouldn't be the leader of the team, he is very ________

Words Often Confused

Some words sound almost similar but mean quite different things.
Read these commonly confused words.

older (to be of a greater age than someone or something else): *This church is **older** than the one we visited yesterday.*
elder (the older of two members in a family): *Surya is the **elder** of the two brothers.*

complement (something which completes something else): *A good pair of shoes **complements** any kind of clothing.*
compliment (to appreciate someone on something): *She **complimented** me on the success of the event.*

uninterested (not showing interest): *She sat quietly in a corner, **uninterested** in the goings-on around her.*
disinterested (impartial, neutral): *The doctor gave his **disinterested** diagnosis.*

lay (put something down): *The minister **laid** the foundation stone for the new building.*
lie (falsehood): *That you returned the money I had lent you is a **lie**.*

discover (to be the first person to find out that something exists): *Marie Curie **discovered** radium.*
invent (to create a new thing): *Thomas Alva Edison **invented** the electric bulb.*

ensure (make sure): ***Ensure** that someone comes to the station to pick you up.*
insure (to buy insurance): *Have you **insured** your newly bought car yet?*

sympathy (feeling of pity and sorrow for someone else's misfortune): *The minister expressed **sympathy** for the people who lost their lives in the accident.*
empathy (ability to understand the feelings of others): *I can **empathize** with your situation. We too were stuck in a flood with no electricity last year.*

stationary (without movement): *The train stayed **stationary** till all the goods were unloaded.*
stationery (items like paper, pens): *There is a **stationery** shop near my house.*

loose (not firmly fixed or fitted): *These shoes are a little **loose** for me.*
lose (be unable to find something): *Keep the money safely, or you will **lose** it.*

K **Fill in the blanks with the correct options.**

1. Captain Cook is said to have __________ Hawaii. One wonders how different things would have been if mobile phones had been __________ in that period. (invented, discovered)
2. Don't __________ me to __________ your silly proposal! (accept, expect)
3. After reading the __________ of the book, I walked __________ to meet the author. (forward, foreword)
4. The __________ bear that was terrorizing the town caused many pets to die a __________ death. (grizzly, grisly)
5. A __________ of animals wanted to raid the forest dwellers' __________ of food, but the people scared them off. (horde, hoard)
6. Take the loudspeaker off the __________ after the __________ are over. (polls, pole)
7. You should __________ that you __________ your new house against any kind of calamity. (insure, ensure)
8. The __________ began in the twelfth __________ of this building. (storey, story)
9. He took a walk __________ the trees that stood __________ the two cottages. (between, among)
10. The __________ of parents and teachers gave the students __________ (counsel, council) on how to deal with the problem.

26 What Katy Did

Read the passage carefully.

In the morning, Katy asked Miss Marsh, 'How is Miss Jane today?'

'About the same. She is not dangerously ill, but she coughs a lot and has some fever.'

'Is anybody sitting with her?'

'Oh, no! there's no need of anyone. Susan answers the bell, and she has her medicine on the table within reach.'

It sounded forlorn enough. Katy had lived in a sickroom long herself to know how dreary it is for an invalid to be left alone with 'medicine within reach,' and someone to answer a bell. She felt sorry for Miss Jane and went and tapped at her door.

The 'Come in!' sounded very faint.

Miss Jane looked weak and quite unlike the sharp person whom the girls feared so much. She was amazed at the sight of Katy, and made a feeble attempt to speak as usual.

'What is it, Miss Carr?'

'I only came to see how you are,' said Katy, shocked at her own daring, 'Isn't there something I could do for you?'

'Thank you,' said Miss Jane, 'you are very kind. You might put another stick of wood on the fire.'

Katy did so, and seeing that the iron cup on top of the stove was empty, she poured some water into it. Around the room, books and papers were scattered over the table, clean clothes from the wash lay on the chairs, nothing was in its place. Katy, who knew how particular Miss Jane was, guessed the discomfort this untidy state of affairs must have caused her.

'Wouldn't you like me to put these away?' she asked, touching the pile of clothes.

Miss Jane sighed impatiently. Katy, taking silence for agreement, laid the clothes inside the drawers, making as little bustle as possible. Next, she sorted and arranged the papers, piled up the books, and put the pens and pencils in a small tray. When she began to dust the table with her pocket handkerchief, Miss Jane said, 'Don't. There is a duster in the cupboard.'

Katy could not help smiling. She found the duster and continued to work, laying a fresh towel over the bedside table, arranging watch, medicine and spoon within reach.

Miss Jane watched her.

Sick people often agree to things because they feel too weak to object. After all, it was comfortable to have someone come in and straighten the things.

Lastly, smoothing the quilt, Katy asked if Miss Jane wouldn't like to have her pillow shaken up?

'I don't care,' was the answer.

But Katy boldly picked it up, beat, smoothed and put it again in place. Then she left the room as noiselessly as she could.

Rose Red and Clover could hardly believe their ears when she told them where she had been. They stared at her as if she had come out of the lion's den.

'My stars!' exclaimed Rose, drawing a long breath. 'And she didn't say anything!'

'Not a bit,' said Katy, laughing. 'What's more, I'm going again.'

A Write whether the following sentences are true (T) or false (F). Correct the false statements.

1. Miss Marsh was seriously ill. ☐
2. Susan answered Miss Jane's bell. ☐
3. Miss Jane asked Katy to add a stick of wood on the fire. ☐
4. Miss Jane liked to have her things neatly arranged. ☐
5. Katy was asked to dust the table with her pocket handkerchief. ☐
6. Katy smoothed the quilt and the pillow for Miss Jane. ☐
7. Miss Jane was angry with Katy for making a mess of the things in her room. ☐

B Answer these questions in your own words.

1. What was Miss Jane suffering from?
2. Why did Katy decide to visit Miss Jane?
3. What made Katy guess that Miss Jane was in discomfort?
4. What did Katy do to clean up Miss Jane's room?
5. Why do you think Rose Red and Clover were surprised to know where Katy had been?

C Find words from the passage which have the following meanings.

1. dull and boring
2. sick person
3. weak
4. courage
5. spread over an area
6. noise

D Which words will you choose to describe Miss Jane and Katy? Circle the ones which you think are suitable.

Miss Jane: affectionate, proud, kind, sick, short-tempered, angry, active, lively, silly, lonely

Katy: kind, understanding, affectionate, scared, bold, organized, timid, funny, friendly, energetic

E **Underline the adverbs and circle the word the adverb modifies in these sentences. Write whether the modified word is a verb, an adjective or an adverb.**

1. Miss Jane sighed impatiently.
2. She was not dangerously ill.
3. Katy left the room noiselessly.
4. It sounded very forlorn.
5. The girls could hardly believe their ears.
6. Books and papers were scattered everywhere.
7. Katy will again check on Miss Jane.

27 Leaving Japan

Read the passage carefully.

The next morning, a tired and starving Passepartout decided that he must get something to eat at any cost. He could have sold his watch, but he would have starved first. He decided to sing.

He had a strong, if not melodious voice. He knew several French and English songs, and decided to try them upon the Japanese, who must be lovers of music, since they were forever beating their various drums.

It was rather early in the morning to start a concert, though. If the audience were awakened from their sleep by his singing, they might not pay their entertainer. Then he realised that he was rather too well dressed for a wandering artist. He decided to exchange his clothes for poorer fare and some money.

After a long search, Passepartout discovered a local dealer in old clothes. The man liked his European clothing, and soon Passepartout left his shop dressed in an old Japanese coat and a sort of faded, one-sided turban. A few pieces of silver jingled in his pocket.

After a hearty meal at a modest tea house, he thought, 'Enough spending. I can't sell this costume again for one still more Japanese. I must find a way to leave this country as quickly as possible.'

His eyes fell upon an immense placard that was being carried by a clown. This placard, in English, was an advertisement for the last performance by the 'acrobatic Japanese troupe' run by the 'Honourable William Batulcar' before their departure for the United States.

'The United States!' said Passepartout, 'that's just what I want!'

He followed the clown, and a quarter of an hour later, stopped before a large cabin adorned with clusters of streamers.

It was William Batulcar's office. That gentleman was the director of a troupe of tricksters, jugglers, clowns, acrobats and gymnasts.

'What do you want?' Mr Batulcar said to Passepartout, whom he took for a native.

'Would you like a servant, sir?' asked Passepartout.

'A servant!' cried Mr Batulcar, caressing his thick grey beard. 'I already have two who are obedient and faithful, and here they are,' he added, holding out his two robust arms.

'So I can be of no use to you? But I should so like to cross the Pacific with you!'

'Ah!' said Batulcar. 'You are no Japanese! Why are you dressed like one?'

'A man dresses as he can.'

'You are a Frenchman, aren't you?'

'Yes, a Parisian of Paris.'

'Then you must know how to make faces?'

'Why,' replied Passepartout, annoyed, 'we Frenchmen know how to make faces, but not any better than Americans.'

'Well, I can take you with me as a clown. You see, in France they exhibit foreign clowns, and in foreign parts, French clowns. You are pretty strong, eh?'

'Especially after a good meal.'

'Can you sing?'

'Yes,' returned Passepartout, who once sang in the streets.

'But can you sing standing on your head, with a top spinning on your left foot, and a sword balanced on your right?'

'Humph! I think so,' replied Passepartout, recalling the exercises of his younger days.

'Well, that's enough,' said Batulcar.

Passepartout had found a job. He was going to act in the Japanese troupe. It was not a very dignified position, but within a week he would be on his way to San Francisco.

A Choose the correct option to complete these sentences.

1. Passepartout was ______________________
   - a. hungry and tired. ☐
   - b. angry and annoyed. ☐
   - c. sad and lonely. ☐
   - d. excited and energetic. ☐
2. Passepartout decided to ______________________ in order to earn money.
   - a. dance ☐
   - b. do acrobatics ☐
   - c. paint ☐
   - d. sing ☐
3. Passepartout wanted to ______________________
   - a. stay in Japan. ☐
   - b. go to the United States. ☐
   - c. go to Paris. ☐
   - d. go to London. ☐
4. The placard was written in ______________________
   - a. English. ☐
   - b. Japanese. ☐
   - c. French. ☐
   - d. Chinese. ☐
5. Batulcar's faithful servants were his ______________________
   - a. two men. ☐
   - b. arms. ☐
   - c. legs. ☐
   - d. ears. ☐
6. Passepartout was given the job because he was ______________________
   - a. humourous and could crack jokes. ☐
   - b. thin and athletic. ☐
   - c. good with disguises. ☐
   - d. strong and could sing. ☐

B Answer these questions in your own words.

1. Why did Passepartout think that the Japanese loved music?
2. Why did Passepartout decide to exchange his clothes? What clothes did he obtain?
3. What did William Batulcar do for a living?
4. When Batulcar realised that Passepartout was French, what question did he ask him? What reply did he receive?
5. What job did Batulcar give him? What did he want Passepartout to do at the show?
6. What made Passepartout take up the job, even though it was 'not a very dignified position'?

C Write the meanings of these words from the passage. You can use a dictionary if necessary.

1. foreign
2. exhibit
3. robust
4. melodious
5. wandering
6. immense
7. trickster
8. adorned

D Write whether the verbs in these sentences are transitive or intransitive. Underline the object of the transitive verbs.

1. Passepartout would leave the country within a week.
2. He wanted to cross the Pacific with Batulcar.
3. Passepartout stopped before a large cabin.
4. Batulcar gave the man a job.
5. It was the last performance of the Japanese troupe.
6. He saw something advertised on the placard.
7. He once sang in the streets.
8. Passepartout balanced a sword on his right foot.

E Correct the errors in the usage of prepositions in these sentences.

1. They ordered for three new shirts.
2. Her face turned pale in fear.
3. They told to me to apply for the job.
4. It becomes terribly cold in night.
5. Run through the road and get the ball.
6. My favourite channel in TV is *Animal Planet*.
7. Mohit prefers sweets for savoury items.
8. Enter the room in your own risk.

28 Travels in Venice

Read this letter by Russian writer Anton Chekov to his brother, Ivan.

24 March, 1891

I am now in Venice. I arrived here two days ago from Vienna. One thing I can say: I have never in my life seen a town more marvellous than Venice. It is perfectly enchanting. Instead of streets and roads, there are canals; instead of cabs, gondolas. The architecture is amazing, and there is not a single spot that is not of some historical or artistic interest. You float in a gondola and see the Palace of the Doges, the house where Desdemona lived, homes of various painters, churches. And in the churches there are sculptures and paintings such as we have never dreamed of.

All day from morning till night I sit in a gondola and glide along the streets, or I walk about the famous St Mark's Square. The square is as level and clean as a parquet floor. Here there is St Mark's, the Palace of the Doges - I feel their amazing beauty and revel in it.

And the evenings! One goes about in a gondola, [there is] warmth, stillness, stars. There are no horses in Venice. So there is a silence here as in the open country. Gondolas flit to and fro. Then a gondola glides by, hung with lanterns. In it are a double-bass, violins, a guitar, a mandolin and cornet, two or three ladies, several men, and one hears singing and music. They sing from operas. What voices! One goes on a little further and again meets a boat with singers, and then again. The air is full, till midnight, of the mingled strains of violins and tenor voices. Merezhkovsky, whom I have met here, is off his head with happiness. For us poor and oppressed Russians, it is easy to go out of our minds here in a world of beauty, wealth, and freedom. One longs to remain here forever, and stand in the churches and listen to the organ.

The tombs of Canova and Titian are magnificent. Here they bury great artists like kings in churches; they do not despise art, as with us. The churches provide a shelter for pictures and statues. In the Palace of the Doges, there is a picture in which there are about ten thousand human figures.

Today is Sunday. There will be a band playing in St Mark's Square. If you ever happen to come to Venice, it will be the best thing in your life. You ought to see the glass here! Your bottles *(His brother Ivan was teaching in a school attached to a glass factory)* are so hideous compared with the things here that it makes one sick to think of them. I will write again.

Meanwhile, goodbye.

A **Answer the questions.**

1. How is Venice different from other cities?
2. Explain the meaning of the phrases 'to be off one's head' and 'to go out of one's mind'.
3. What are some of the sights and sounds that can be experienced in the evenings from a gondola?
4. Who is Merezhkovsky? What makes him go out of his mind and why?
5. List all the places one can visit in Venice.
6. The author says, 'they do not despise art, as with us'. Whom do 'they' and 'us' refer to? What does the word 'despise' mean?
7. Where are the great artists of Venice buried?
8. What is special about the churches in Venice?
9. What was happening on Sunday in St Mark's Square?
10. Who is writing this letter to whom? What does the recipient do?

B **Find words from the passage which have the following meanings.**

1. extraordinary, causing great wonder
2. charming and attractive
3. a light, flat-bottomed boat
4. move with a smooth, quiet, continuous motion
5. enjoy oneself in a noisy way
6. subject to strict treatment
7. deeply hate
8. extremely ugly

C **Use these phrases in sentences of your own.**

1. often scolds
2. glide along
3. amazing beauty
4. poor and oppressed
5. flit to and fro
6. provide a shelter

D **Identify the sentences as simple, compound or complex.**

1. The architecture is amazing, and there is not a single spot that is not of some historical or artistic interest.
2. You float in a gondola and see the Palace of the Doges.
3. All day from morning till night I sit in a gondola and glide along the streets.
4. There are no horses in Venice, and so there is a silence here as in the open country.
5. In it are a double-bass, violins, a guitar, a mandolin and cornet, two or three ladies, several men, and one hears singing and music.
6. Merezhkovsky, whom I have met here, is off his head with happiness.
7. For us poor and oppressed Russians, it is easy to go out of our minds here in a world of beauty, wealth, and freedom.
8. If you ever happen to come to Venice, it will be the best thing in your life.

29 The Cobbler

Read the passage carefully.

He sat a few furlongs away from the teashop, just where the footpath takes a bend. A spot where no one could miss him as they walked by. To anyone who did pass by, ignoring him, he would tap his brush and shout 'Polish, sir?'

He was always sipping his tea. His eyes were always glued to the feet of those who passed by, summing them up.

Shining shoes, slippers or dirty ones, whoever walked past would be greeted by his 'Polish, sir!'

I spotted him on my first day to office. I had to pass him from the bus stop. I had brand new shoes on. Getting down from the bus, I had managed to keep the shoes shining bright. As I walked past, lost in my thoughts, I was startled by his 'Polish, sir!'

Ever since that day, I made sure my shoes – if not shining bright – were in good condition.

When the monsoons came, he would add some broken umbrellas to his kit and move in to the shelter of a shop if it rained. His eyes however, would always be glued to footwear.

His reputation was not very good. 'He charges too much. And he is far too rude,' my friend once told me, though he grudgingly admitted that he was 'good at his job'.

'Someday,' I told myself, 'I will get him to do my shoes.' And all through I enjoyed passing by him playing my little game of 'I don't need you.' I wondered at times if he caught on to my game or if I was just another pair of feet passing by.

Years rolled by and yet the game never changed. He was always at the same spot, with his tools and knick-knacks, having a good time with his fellow vendors and never failing to call out to customers.

All through I kept my shoes in prime condition.

One day, fate made me keep my word. Getting down from the bus, my soles opened up. I could not walk further without getting them mended. Did I feel relieved to see my cobbler!

I stood before him. He looked at the shoes and looked me in the eye but before I could say anything further, said, 'Sorry sir, I am closing the shop now. Come tomorrow.'

A Answer the questions in brief.

1. How did the cobbler make sure that he was visible? How did he attract customers' attention?
2. What does the phrase 'summing them up' mean? Who was the cobbler summing up and why?

3. The cobbler rarely missed greeting the passers-by. How do we know this?
4. When and where did the author first spot the cobbler?
5. Why did the author make sure that his shoes were in a good condition whenever he passed by the cobbler?
6. How did the cobbler manage his business during the rainy season?
7. Why did the cobbler not have a good reputation?
8. 'Years rolled by and yet the game never changed.' What was the game? Who were the players?
9. 'One day fate made me keep my word.' Explain this sentence.
10. Who won the game finally? How can we say so?

B Find the meanings of these words from the story and write what part of speech they are. Then, use them in sentences of your own. Use a dictionary if necessary.

1. *Reputation: (abstract noun) The opinion people have about someone or something, based on what happened in the past. Sentence: He had a **reputation** for being fast and efficient.*
2. rude
3. grudgingly
4. knick-knacks
5. vendors
6. mended
7. relieved

C Say whether the italicized parts of these sentences are phrases or clauses. If clauses, say whether they are the main clause or the subordinate clause.

1. He sat a few furlongs away from the teashop, *just where the footpath takes a bend*.
2. His eyes were always glued to the feet of those who passed by, *summing them up*.
3. *Shining shoes, slippers or dirty ones*, whoever walked past would be greeted by his 'Polish, sir!'
4. *Getting down from the bus*, I had managed to keep the shoes shining bright.
5. *As I approached him*, lost in my thoughts, I was startled by his 'Polish, sir!'
6. When the monsoon came, he would add some broken umbrellas to his kit and *move into the shelter of a shop* if it rained.

D Convert the following sentences as directed.

1. I had brand new shoes on, it being the first day at my job. (compound sentence)
2. Years rolled by and yet the game never changed. (complex sentence)
3. He would move in to the shelter of a shop if it rained. (simple sentence)
4. I could not walk further without getting them mended. (complex sentence)
5. He looked at the shoes and looked me up in the eye. (simple sentence)

30 A Plague of Locusts

Read the passage carefully.

While India was battling the coronavirus pandemic during a scorching summer, there came the desert locust, travelling in huge swarms from eastern Africa and Southeast Asia. Millions of locusts damaged crops across 13 countries before entering Rajasthan on 13 May 2020. The attack was the worst in 27 years and scientists said that the crisis would worsen in the monsoons.

Desert locusts appear in *The Bible*, as part of the story of the prophet, Moses. A plague of locusts ravages Egypt as God's punishment upon the Pharaoh for not allowing the enslaved people of Israel to leave Egypt. The 2020 locust attack seemed to be of Biblical proportions too.

Locusts are a type of short-horned grasshoppers, thought to be the most dangerous migratory pests in the world. They consume everything in their path, eating as much as their own body weight daily. They damage crops by consuming every part of the plant, and can even break trees by their sheer weight when they settle down on one in huge numbers.

This calamity has been caused by the warming of the Indian Ocean due to climate change. The rising temperatures have caused cyclones and torrential rainfall, often in traditionally desert areas in eastern Africa and the Middle East. These moist deserts became the ideal breeding ground for locusts.

Locusts can cover distances up to 150 km every day. Their migration area covers about 30 million square kilometre in nearly 64 countries, including parts of the Indian subcontinent. One square kilometre of a locust swarm contains up to 80,000 adults that, each day, eats as much food as 35,000 people. By ruining cropland and leaving pastures barren, they create food scarcity for local grazing animals and other insects. They also pose a threat to livestock grazers and rob farmers of their livelihood. In Kenya, locust plagues threaten the habitat of the endangered Grévy's zebra. By May 2020, locusts had destroyed crops in 18 districts of Rajasthan and 12 districts of Madhya Pradesh.

India has been managing locust attacks since colonial times. Today, the Locust Control and Research initiative by the Indian government monitors the swarms and the areas they pass through, and sprays infected areas with insecticides. Aerial sprayers and even drones have been used in 2020 for surveys and to spray insecticides. Experts say that protecting creatures who feed on locusts, including birds like the myna, will also help control the pests.

As our planet gets warmer due to climate change, chances are that locusts will continue to arrive in the numbers seen in 2020. Preparedness holds the key to fighting the locusts.

A **Match the figures in Column A with the information in Column B correctly. One is done for you.**

Column A	Column B
1. 150km	a. the number of adults that one square kilometre of a locust swarm contains
2. 13	b. the distance that locusts can cover in a day
3. 35,000	c. the date on which the desert locust storm entered India
4. 13 May 2020	d. the distance which makes up the migration area of locusts
5. 30 million square km	e. the number of countries the locusts passed through before entering India
6. 80,000	f. one square km of a locust swarm eats as much food in a day as this number of people would

B **Answer these questions in your own words.**

1. What are locusts? How do they damage crops and trees?
2. Which ancient book do locusts appear in? What do they do in the story?
3. How has climate change caused the calamity of the locust attacks?
4. What measures are taken to control locust attacks?

C **Match the words in Column A with their meanings in Column B.**

Column A	Column B
1. pandemic	a. dry, bare and not fertile
2. scorching	b. chemical substances used to kill insects
3. migration	c. a disease that affects many people over a very wide area
4. barren	d. movement of a large number of animals, birds or insects during a particular season from one part of the world to another
5. insecticides	e. very hot

D **Fill in the blanks with suitable words from Column A of the previous exercise.**

1. Farmers who follow organic farming methods do not use any ____________.
2. The flood left the old man's fields ____________ and he was unable to grow anything in them.
3. It is difficult to be out in the ____________ afternoon sun during summer.
4. The ____________ of flamingos to Pulicat Lake in Andhra Pradesh is an annual event which attracts many birdwatchers.

5. One of the safety measures followed during the coronavirus ____________ is the frequent washing of hands.

E Choose the correct option.

1. A swarm of locusts ____________ (have/has) arrived in India recently.
2. Each of us ____________ (is/are) responsible for maintaining cleanliness in our neighbourhood.
3. Many students ____________ (feel/feels) that mathematics is a tough subject.
4. The members of the committee ____________ (do not/does not) want to discuss this matter further.
5. Either my father or my brother ____________ (is/are) going to pick me up from school.
6. Athletics ____________ (refer/refers) to physical activities that require stamina and fitness.

F Fill in the blanks with the correct modals.

1. A locust ____________ (can/shall) consume as much food as its body weight.
2. Scientists said that the crisis ____________ (must/may) worsen in the monsoons.
3. Locusts ____________ (should/will) continue to arrive in more numbers.
4. India ____________ (must/would) manage locust attacks proactively.
5. Certain birds like the myna ____________ (can/should) help in pest control.
6. Farmers ____________ (should/might) be prepared to fight the locust swarms.

31 The Ransom of Red Chief

Read the passage carefully.

It seemed like a good idea at the time. We were in Alabama, Bill Driscoll and I, when this kidnapping idea struck us. It was, as Bill afterwards said, 'a moment of temporary madness'.

There was a town of honest farmers there called Summit. We selected for our victim a boy of ten, with freckles and bright red hair, the only child of a prominent citizen named Ebenezer Dorset.

About two miles from Summit was a little mountain covered with cedar trees. Behind it was a cave. There, we stored provisions.

One evening after sundown, we drove past old Dorset's house. The kid was on the street, throwing rocks at a frog.

'Hey, little boy!' said Bill, 'do you want a bag of candy and a nice ride?'

The boy caught Bill neatly in the eye with a piece of brick.

'That just raised the ransom by five hundred dollars,' said Bill, climbing out.

The boy put up a fight like a bear, but we got him inside and drove away. We took him up to the cave.

When I returned after an errand, Bill was applying a plaster over his scratches and bruises. A fire was burning at the entrance of the cave, and the boy was keeping watch, with two buzzard tailfeathers stuck in his red hair. He pointed a stick at me and said:

'Ha! cursed white man, do you dare to enter the camp of Red Chief, the terror of the plains?'

'We're playing Indian,' said Bill. 'I'm Old Hank, the trapper, Red Chief's captive, and I'm to be scalped at daybreak.'

The boy seemed to have forgotten that he was a captive himself.

After supper, he began to talk.

'I never camped out before, but I had a pet opossum once. I hate going to school. Are there any real Indians in these woods? Does the moving of the trees make the wind blow? Have you got beds to sleep on in this cave?'

Every few minutes, remembering he was a Red Indian, he would pick up his stick rifle and tiptoe to the mouth of the cave to look out for spies. He also let out sudden war whoops that made 'Old Hank' shiver.

'Red Chief,' I asked, 'would you like to go home?'

'Aw, what for?' said he. 'I don't have any fun at home. You won't take me back again, will you?'

At night, we spread down some quilts and put Red Chief between us. He kept us awake for three hours, jumping up and reaching for his rifle at the imagined crackle of a twig or the rustle of a leaf. When I fell into a troubled sleep, I dreamed that I had been kidnapped and chained to a tree by a ferocious pirate with red hair.

A Fill in the blanks with words from the passage.

1. The town of honest farmers was called ________________.
2. The name of the narrator's friend was ________________.
3. Ebenezer Dorset was a ________________ citizen of the town.
4. Bill had to play the role of ________________, the ________________ to entertain the boy.
5. The boy once had a pet ________________.
6. The boy imagined that he was ________________, the ________________ of the plains.

B Answer these questions in your own words.

1. Whom did the narrator and his friend kidnap? How did he look?
2. What was the boy doing when the kidnappers spotted him?
3. What did the boy do when Bill offered him candy and a ride?
4. What did the narrator see when he returned from an errand?
5. What did the boy do every few minutes, after supper?
6. What dream did the narrator have that night?

C Find words from the passage which mean the same as these phrases. Then make sentences of your own with any four of the words.

1. take someone away by force and keep them captive
2. money demanded to release a captive
3. a short trip undertaken to perform a necessary task
4. people who find out secret information about another country or organization
5. a thick, warm cover for a bed
6. someone who attacks and robs ships at sea

D Add suitable question tags to these statements.

1. The Red Chief did not like to go to school, ________________?
2. The kidnappers had a tough time with the boy, ________________?
3. You have got beds to sleep on in this cave, ________________?
4. The boy has bright red hair, ________________?
5. It seemed like a good idea at the time, ________________?
6. The cave is behind the mountain, ________________?
7. We will store our provisions here, ________________?
8. You would like to go home, ________________?

E **Punctuate the following passage.**

every few minutes, remembering that he was a red indian, he would pick up his stick rifle and tiptoe to the mouth of the cave to look out for spies he also let out sudden war whoops that made 'Old Hank' shiver

red chief i asked would you like to go home

aw what for said he i don't have any fun at home you wont take me back again will you

at night we spread down some quilts and put red chief between us he kept us awake for three hours jumping up and reaching for his rifle at the imagined crackle of a twig or the rustle of a leaf

32 Mr Franks

Read the passage carefully.

I met Mr Franks at Susie's birthday party. 'See that gentleman over there, blowing up balloons,' Susie had told me, 'He is old Frankie, my grandpa's closest friend - lives in the Home for the Aged. He must be eighty at least!'

I took a great liking to Mr Franks the moment I started talking to him. He had a lot of enthusiasm for life, despite his failing health. His anecdotes kept us laughing and amused throughout the evening.

As I rose to get back to my school hostel, he said, 'Why don't you come and see me at the Home sometime?'

I met Mr Franks the next Wednesday, my day off from the school hostel and every Wednesday thereafter. I would spend the morning at Susie's and after lunch, I'd walk down to the Home, sometimes with Susie and sometimes on my own. He would be relaxing in his tiny doll's home garden, his lanky frame curled up in a cane chair and soaking in the warm winter sunshine. Susie and I would troop in, chattering shrilly like a couple of magpies.

'Ah! Come in, ladies,' Mr Franks would say, straightening up and asking us to sit down. 'Do mind that flower bed! I've just planted the sweet peas!' That he had been an expert gardener in his younger days was no empty boast. He had a beautifully kept garden and a large number of certificates to prove it. Some of the certificates had been framed and they now hung on his veranda walls, yellow and dusty with age.

Mr Franks had served in the army, and somehow most of his anecdotes were a hilarious mixture of botanical and military life. 'You know, young ladies,' he told us one day, 'Misunderstandings can be quite embarrassing sometimes! Once when I was away on leave, our unit mess got the electricity connection they had been wanting for quite some time. I was in the dark about this latest development. When I came back, the colonel called me and asked me to get new bulbs put in the entire mess. I informed him that I had already put in the bulbs, and could not now put in new ones. He was extremely angry at me for disobeying orders and we continued arguing. It was only much later that we realised that he was talking of the electric bulbs and I of the lilies!'

Most times that I went to visit Mr Franks, I took something for his garden - a packet of seeds or a couple of small terracotta pots. Or it would be a bougainvillea cutting of a colour which he didn't already have.

Mr Franks waited for Wednesday as much as I did. One day I fell ill with viral fever and was taken to the infirmary with high temperature. Lying in bed, I realised it had been almost two weeks since I had seen Mr Franks. Just then the nurse walked in. 'Someone to see you, miss!' Behind her ambled in old Mr Franks.

'So the bug got you too! How do you feel now, lady?' he said, handing me a bunch of dahlias. 'Thought something must have gone wrong, so I asked Susie and came along to see you. These flowers are from my garden.'

I thanked him for the flowers and for coming to see me. 'Oh, not at all! Now get well soon, and then we can prune the roses together.'

Before going home to Gorakhpur in December, I would take for Mr Franks a small box of decorations for his Christmas tree, bought from my pocket money. 'Thank you, my dear,' he would say. 'I'll leave them on the tree till you come back!' I'd wish him a merry Christmas and ask him to take care. 'I will, my child, and come back soon!'

And so two years passed. Then one day, just before school was to break up for the winter vacations, I got a letter from Daddy. He had been transferred to Delhi, and I was to complete my last two years of school there. He would be coming to Lucknow the following week to complete the formalities at my school and to take me home.

I was very sad. I thought of my school and my friends and knew I would feel terrible leaving them. But at the top of my mind was leaving Mr Franks.

A Choose the correct option to complete these sentences.

1. The narrator met Mr Franks at ________

   a. her birthday party.
   b. Susie's birthday party.
   c. Mr Frank's birthday.
   d. a school function.

2. The narrator took an instant liking to Mr Franks because ________

   a. he was young and handsome.
   b. he resembled her grandfather.
   c. he blew up many balloons.
   d. he had great enthusiasm for life and told interesting tales.

3. The narrator met Mr Franks on Wednesdays because ________

   a. Mr Franks was free on that day.
   b. Susie was free on that day.
   c. the narrator was free on that day.
   d. Wednesdays were special days.

4. The narrator could not meet Mr Franks for a long time because ________

   a. the narrator fell sick.
   b. Mr Franks fell sick.
   c. the narrator relocated to another place.
   d. Mr Franks relocated to another place.

5. The author compares the narrator and her friend to ________

   a. noisy crows.
   b. shrilly chattering magpies.
   c. singing koels.
   d. mynahs.

6. The narrator's home town was ________

   a. Delhi.
   b. Lucknow.
   c. Gorakhpur.
   d. Dehradun.

(B) Answer the questions in a few lines.

1. How do we know that Mr Franks was an expert gardener?
2. What were some of the things which the narrator took with her when she went to visit Mr Franks?
3. Why did Mr Franks and the colonel have an argument?
4. What would the narrator do for Mr Franks before going home in December?
5. What happened after two years that was a break from the regular routine of Mr Franks and the narrator?

(C) Find words from the passage which mean the following.

1. a strong feeling of excitement and interest in something ____________
2. short amusing stories about people or incidents ____________
3. tall and thin ____________
4. loudly ____________
5. something that a person talks about with excessive pride ____________
6. funny and entertaining ____________
7. to walk in a slow, easy pace ____________
8. to cut off branches from a plant to make it grow better ____________

(D) Rewrite the sentences in indirect speech.

1. As I rose to get back to my school hostel, he said, 'Why don't you come and see me at the Home sometime?'
2. 'You know, child,' Mr Franks would tell me as we worked, 'Plants too have feelings.'
3. 'It's time for you to go! Shall I see you again next week?' Mr Franks asked.
4. 'So the bug got you too! How do you feel now, lady?' he said, handing me a bunch of dahlias.
5. 'Now get well soon, and then we can prune the roses together,' he said.

(E) Write whether the italicized verbs are infinitives, participles or gerunds.

1. He would be coming to Lucknow the *following* week.
2. We continued *arguing*.
3. '*Misunderstandings* can be quite embarrassing sometimes!'
4. I was delighted *to see* him.
5. Other than *gardening*, Mr Franks had a great liking for one more thing.

33 Count Your Jumbos

Read the news report carefully.

Jan 15: Migrating elephant herds appear to like Bengal so much that they spend more time here than in the neighbouring states from where they cross over.

In the 2014 census, the south Bengal districts of West Midnapore, Bankura and Purulia were found to have an elephant population of 150, of whom around 100 had crossed over from adjoining Jharkhand. 'These herds are now spending close to 10 months in Bengal and only two in Jharkhand,' Subhankar Sengupta, conservator of forests (wildlife), said.

This and other such curious facts will be proved by a field estimate of the country's elephant population, to be carried out in phases by clubbing together states that share boundaries and wildlife corridors.

The survey will start in the south Bengal districts in April along with Jharkhand, Odisha, Chhattisgarh, Bihar and Andhra Pradesh. The north Bengal districts of Jalpaiguri, Alipurduar and the foothills of Darjeeling have been grouped with Assam, said Pradeep Vyas, the principal chief conservator of forests (wildlife).

The last census in north Bengal, which has several national parks and the Dooars forests, had pegged the elephant population there at 650.

Population counts carried out every five years have so far not followed a uniform method before. This time, all states have been asked to not only map the population distribution but also create a database split into various sections - males, females, adults, calves and tuskers.

The aim of the programme is to reduce overcounting or undercounting when states with boundaries do field-level counting on different days. 'Since elephants cross over in search of food or favourable climate, we can do a simultaneous head count in neighbouring habitats,' said an official of the wildlife division.

The forest departments of the participating states have to pass on the field data to the central government. The final figures will be published about three months after all states submit their data.

India's elephant population during the last such count in 2012 was estimated to be 30,000.

Raman Sukumar, a professor at the Indian Institute of Science, Bangalore, and founder of the Asian Nature Conservation Foundation, is co-ordinating plans for the survey on the central government's behalf. 'Besides the standard headcount, all states will have to report figures based on the dung decay method. Field work will be done in the dry season when most elephants stay inside the forests,' Sukumar told Metro.

The dung decay method is an indirect way of estimating the elephant population in a location by tracking excreta.

A **Answer these questions.**

1. What were the elephants who had crossed over from south Bengal into Jharkhand now doing?
2. Name the states and the districts in north Bengal which would be surveyed.
3. What is the aim of the programme?
4. What are the two methods that will be used to count the number of elephants?
5. What is the dung decay method?

B **Find words from the passage which mean the following.**

1. an official count of a population
2. occurring at the same time
3. combining many things for a particular purpose
4. sharing a common border
5. a number which forms part of official statistics
6. the act of following an animal, person or thing

C **Underline the gerunds, tick the infinitives and circle the present participles in these sentences.**

1. Migrating elephant herds appear to like Bengal so much that they spend more time here than in the neighbouring states from where they cross over.
2. Grouping the north Bengal districts of Jalpaiguri, Alipurduar and the foothills of Darjeeling with Assam was decided by Pradeep Vyas.
3. The survey is scheduled to start in the south Bengal districts in April.
4. The forest departments of the participating states have to pass on the field data to the central government.
5. Tracking elephants accurately is important for the national survey.

D **Write whether these sentences are in the active or passive voice. Then, change the ones in active voice to passive and vice versa.**

1. This would be proved by a field estimate of the country's elephant population.
2. The last census in north Bengal had pegged the elephant population at 650.
3. The final figures were published by the central government.
4. The dung decay method estimates the elephant population in a location.
5. Population estimations have not followed a uniform method.
6. The forest departments of the participating states need to pass on the field data.

34 The Storyteller

Read the passage carefully.

It was a hot afternoon. Inside a railway carriage travelled a small girl, a smaller girl and a small boy with their aunt. The further corner seat was occupied by a young man who was a stranger to their party. Both the aunt and the children spoke continuously. Most of the aunt's remarks began with 'Don't,' and nearly all of the children's remarks began with 'Why?'

'Don't, Cyril,' exclaimed the aunt, as the small boy began beating the cushions, producing a cloud of dust at each blow.

'Come and look out of the window,' she added.

The child moved unwillingly to the window. 'Why are those sheep being driven out of that field?' he asked.

'I guess they are being driven to another field where there is more grass,' said the aunt weakly.

'But there is a lot of grass in that field,' said the boy.

'Perhaps the grass in the other field is better,' suggested the aunt pointlessly.

'Why is it better?' came the swift question.

'Oh, look at those cows!' exclaimed the aunt. Nearly every field along the line had cows or bullocks, but she spoke as though it were something not seen before.

There was a deep frown on the young man's face. He was a cruel, unkind man, the aunt decided.

The smaller girl now began to recite 'On the Road to Mandalay'. She only knew the first line, but she repeated it over and over in a dreamy but determined and loud voice.

'Come over here and listen to a story,' said the aunt, when the man had looked twice at her pointedly.

The children moved uninterestedly towards the aunt.

In a low, secretive voice, interrupted frequently by loud, grumpy questions from her listeners, she began an extremely boring story about a little girl who was good. She made friends with everyone because of her goodness and was saved from a mad bull by a number of rescuers who admired her moral character.

'Wouldn't they have saved her if she hadn't been good?' asked the older girl. It was exactly the question the man had wanted to ask.

'Well, yes,' admitted the aunt, 'but I don't think they would have run quite so fast to her help if they had not liked her.'

'It's the silliest story I've ever heard,' said the girl.

'I didn't listen after the first bit,' said Cyril.

The smaller girl made no comment, but she had restarted a murmured repetition of her favourite line.

'You don't seem to be a success as a storyteller,' said the man suddenly from his corner.

'It's very difficult to tell stories that children can both understand and appreciate,' the aunt said stiffly.

'I don't agree with you,' said the man.

'Perhaps you would like to tell them a story.'

'Tell us a story,' demanded the bigger girl.

'Once upon a time,' began the man, 'there was a little girl called Bertha, who was extraordinarily good.'

The children's interest began at once to dim.

'She did all that she was told, was always truthful, kept her clothes clean, learned her lessons perfectly, and was polite in her manners. She was not as pretty as any of you, but she was horribly good.'

There was a wave of appreciation for the story. The listeners liked the word 'horrible' in connection with goodness. It had a ring of truth that was absent from the aunt's tales about how children behaved.

A Complete the following sentences with words and phrases from the passage.

1. The boy began ________________________________ producing ________________________________.
2. The aunt said that the sheep were being driven to another field because ________________ ________________________________.
3. The aunt felt that the stranger was a ________________________________.
4. The older girl thought that her aunt's story was ________________________________.
5. The aunt felt that it was difficult to tell stories that ________________________________.
6. Bertha was a ________________ who was ________________ good.

B Answer these questions in your own words.

1. Who were the occupants of the railway carriage?
2. What questions did Cyril ask his aunt?
3. Describe the smaller girl's recitation.
4. What story did the aunt tell the children?

5. What question did the older girl ask about the story? What was her aunt's response?
6. Why did the children appreciate the man's story?

C Fill in the blanks with the given words and phrases.

unwillingly truth moral wave of appreciation interrupted cloud of dust admired

1. When the bowler took the third wicket in a row, there was a ______________ from the audience.
2. A ______________ rose from the road when the car came to a sudden halt.
3. Don't believe him; there is no ______________ in what he said.
4. What is the ______________ of the story?
5. Everyone ______________ the young girls for their act of heroism.
6. As Pia was already quite busy, she took on the extra projects ______________.
7. My flow of thoughts was ______________ by a sudden knock at the door.

D Make new words from each of the given words. One is done for you.

1. appreciation: *ape*, ______________
2. pointless: *top*, ______________
3. character: *hat*, ______________
4. uninterestedly: *line*, ______________
5. connection: *net*, ______________

E Identify the types of sentences and write A for assertive, I for interrogative, E for exclamatory and IM for imperative.

1. Come and look out of the window. ☐
2. Why are those sheep being driven out of that field? ☐
3. It's the silliest story I've ever heard! ☐
4. Wouldn't they have saved her if she hadn't been good? ☐
5. I don't agree with you. ☐
6. Tell us a story, please. ☐
7. There was a deep frown on the young man's face. ☐
8. Oh, look at those cows! ☐

35 Stopping by Woods on a Snowy Evening

Read this poem.

Whose woods these are I think I know.
His house is in the village though;
He will not see me stopping here
To watch his woods fill up with snow.

My little horse must think it queer
To stop without a farmhouse near
Between the woods and frozen lake
The darkest evening of the year.

He gives his harness bells a shake
To ask if there is some mistake.
The only other sound's the sweep
Of easy wind and downy flake.

The woods are lovely, dark and deep,
But I have promises to keep,
And miles to go before I sleep,
And miles to go before I sleep.

— *Robert Frost*

A Answer the questions.

1. Where is the poet? What is he doing there?
2. What season is it? How do we know?
3. What surprised the poet's horse?
4. What does the poet think that the horse wants to ask him? What action of the horse suggests this to the poet?
5. Write about the sights and sounds described in the woods.
6. Do you think the line, 'And miles to go before I sleep' has more than one meaning? What are they?

B Make sentences using the given phrases.

1. darkest evening
2. frozen lake
3. easy wind
4. harness bells
5. downy flake
6. promises to keep

C Pick out all the nouns from the poem. Then, underline those nouns which are qualified by adjectives. Write the adjectives.

36 Letters, Emails, Messages

As you know, letters can be categorized into two types.

Informal or personal letters are written to parents, siblings, relatives and friends.

Formal or official letters are written to government officials, business enterprises, editors of newspapers. These can be applications, invitations or complaints.

Informal letters

Informal letters are written in a conversational style. They express warmth and intimacy. Keep these points in mind while writing an informal letter:

1. The address of the sender should be written on the upper left hand side of the page, followed by the date.
2. The greeting can be written as: *Dear Father, My dear Uncle, Dear Savita*
3. The letter should be divided into at least three paragraphs: the introduction, the body (this can be of more than one paragraph) and the conclusion.
4. End the letter with a closing salutation.

   Examples: *Yours affectionately, Yours lovingly, Your loving friend*

Watch Out!

Remember not to use apostrophe with *yours.*

Read this sample informal letter.

Write a letter to your mother about your first day at your new boarding school.

Room A 301
Triveni Hostel
Hyderabad 500014

18 June 2017

Dear Mummy,

I had been waiting to sit down and write to you, but it has been very rushed since I arrived. I am still finding my way around the school and the hostel, and getting to know my classmates and teachers.

This is the first time in my life that I'm away from home with totally new people. I know you said that it takes time to settle in, but at the moment, I miss home terribly. I long to come home.

Going on to better things: our dormitory is quite comfortable. I have already started to make friends. One of the girls in my dormitory, Nasreen, is very friendly. She has been studying here for the past four years and tells me that I will soon get over this homesickness. She has been showing me around the school. We go to the hostel mess together to have meals. The food is good. The breakfast, especially, reminds me of your breakfasts at home, though yours are the best. Today, we were served masala dosa with chutney and sambar, just like in a restaurant.

I did not have many classes today since it's the first day. I met some of my teachers. They all seem knowledgeable and approachable. The library is very good. There are books by all my favourite authors, as well as reference study material on all subjects. I'm sure I'm going to spend a lot of time there.

In the evening, I got a bit bored. I remembered being at home in the evenings, with you, Papa and Vikrant. Vikrant must be happy that he does not have to share the room with me anymore! Please remind him to write to me, as he had promised, and also to send me the *Harry Potter* books which I had left behind.

It's time for bed now, and the matron will soon come to switch off the lights. I will post the letter tomorrow. I am looking forward very much to your visit next month.
Missing all of you!

Yours lovingly,
Sandhya

A Write informal letters on these topics.

1. Write a letter to your cousin congratulating him/her for leading the school football team to victory in the inter-state football tournament.
2. You are living in a hostel. Your mother has given you her expensive wristwatch and the watch is lost. Write a letter to your mother apologizing to her about it.
3. Write a letter to your friend telling her about a summer camp you attended during your vacation. Mention the various activities you participated in and what you learnt.
4. You have been facing problems at school, including bullying and difficulty in concentrating on your studies. Write a letter to your elder brother, who you are close to and who goes to college in another city, asking for his advice on dealing with the problems.
5. You are a keen photographer who plans to take part in a national-level photography competition. Write a letter to your friend describing your love for photography and your plans for the competition.
6. Your uncle is a novelist. His latest book has won one of the highest literary awards in the country. Write a letter congratulating him on his achievement. Mention how he is an inspiration to you and the younger generation in the family.
7. You are planning to take up a new hobby, and you would like your friend to join you. Write a letter to your friend telling him/her about the hobby and why it would be fun to pursue the hobby together.

Formal letters

A formal letter can be written to make requests, suggestions, proposals, enquiries and complaints. They may be addressed to heads or officers of institutions such as banks, railways and municipal corporations. You may also write to place/cancel an order, and acknowledge receipt of consignments.

Keep these points in mind while writing a formal letter.

1. Formal letters are brief and to the point and are written in a neutral tone.
2. The sender's address and the date are written on the upper left hand side.
3. The recipient's name, designation and address are written on the left hand side, below the sender's address.
4. A formal letter always mentions the subject at the beginning. It comes after the initial salutation and captures the objective of the letter in a single short sentence.
5. The subscription, or the sender's name and signature come on the left at the end of the letter.
6. The common forms of leave-taking used are *Yours faithfully* and *Yours sincerely*.

Read these sample formal letters.

Letter to the Editor

Write a letter to the editor of your local newspaper, on the rising levels of air pollution caused by the excessive bursting of crackers during Diwali.

F 433
Komal Apartments
Kalkaji
Delhi 110029 ← Writer's address

21 October 2017 ← Date

The Editor
The Daily Sun
12, Royd Street
Delhi - 110098 ← Receiver's address

Subject: Rising levels of pollution during Diwali

Madam, ← Salutation

Diwali celebrations in the capital have been getting progressively more taxing each year. However, this year was the very worst that I have ever seen in the two decades that I have resided in this city, both in terms of the noise and smoke.

The noise caused by the bursting of crackers always goes well above the permissible limit and can cause serious harm to the elderly and the very young. This year, I was at home with my ailing mother, who was suffering from palpitations as a result of the noise. Animals, whose hearing is more sensitive than ours, are also badly affected by it. ← Body

The air, too, has become so polluted that it is a struggle to breathe when one steps out of the house. The smog continues to hang in the Delhi air two days after the celebrations. I would like to ask my fellow citizens whether such reckless celebrations are worth the price we pay by endangering our own health and that of our loved ones.

In future, the Delhi government should ban the use of fire crackers that emit noise and ensure strict punishment for those who go beyond the permitted noise levels.

Yours faithfully,
Sonali Mehta ← Subscription

Letter of Complaint

Write a letter to the Municipal Commissioner of your city, about the overflowing drainage lines in your locality as a result of heavy rains the previous week.

MIG 524
Doctors' Colony
Kurnool 518001

To
The Commissioner
Kurnool Municipal Corporation
N R Peta
Kurnool 518004

12 August 2017

Subject: Overflowing drainage lines in Doctors' Colony

Sir,

I write this letter with great concern and worry. We know that our city does not have an efficient drainage system, especially in some localities. During the recent rains, the drainage lines in our colony overflowed and some gave way completely, unable to take the pressure and volume of the heavy rain water. All the by-lanes were waterlogged and there was no way people could go to their offices, or children, to their schools. Public life came to a standstill.

I request you to take measures to undertake the repair of the drainage lines as well as that of the damaged roads at the earliest before another heavy downpour occurs.

Yours faithfully,
Mini Mathews

B Write formal letters on these topics.

1. The local city buses are never on time. They never stop at the bus stop and when they do, it is only for a few minutes. This is causing a lot of inconvenience for office goers and college students. Write a letter to the manager of the city bus service complaining about this issue and request him to take steps about such behaviour.
2. The footpaths on several roads in your city have been occupied by hawkers and tea sellers, causing pedestrians to walk on the roads, which has led to several accidents. Write to the Municipal Commissioner of your city requesting him to relocate the vendors and ensure proper maintenance of footpaths.
3. Write a letter to your father requesting him to allow you to go on an excursion organized by your school. Mention where you are going, for how many days and request him to send you the money required for the trip.
4. Your school has recently completed the team selection for an upcoming tournament. You missed the selection because you were sick. Write a letter to your sports teacher requesting him/her to allow you the chance to appear for the selections again. Mention how you will be an asset to the team.

5. You are the secretary of your school's book club. Write a letter to the school librarian with a list of books that you would like the library to purchase. Explain why you think they would be a good addition to the current collection and how they would be of use to the students.
6. You cannot go to school on the day it reopens after the summer vacations because a close family member is unwell. You have to travel out of the city with your family to take care of them. Write a letter to the principal of your school requesting her/him to grant you leave for a week.

Emails

Traditional forms of letter writing are increasingly being replaced with **emails** today. All it requires are a computer and an internet connection. Emails can be both formal and informal.

Many of the rules for writing emails are the same as that for writing formal and informal letters. Keep the following points in mind while writing an email.

1. The email ID of the recipient should be included correctly in the 'To' field.
2. Mention the subject of the email in the 'Subject' field. It should be short and to-the-point.
3. Do not mention the postal address or date of the sender or recipient in an email.

Read these sample emails.

Write an email to a friend inviting him to join you at your ancestral village for the summer vacation.

From paul09@smail.com
To kiransv@smail.com
Subject Spending the summer vacation at my ancestral village

Dear Kiran,

You have always told me that you have never been to a village. Why don't you join me for a visit to our village near Kottayam, Kerala during this vacation? I'm planning to leave on 10 June and will be back by 17 June. We will go by our car with my parents.

Our village is located near the backwaters of Kerala. Here, the freshwater from the rivers meets the seawater from the Arabian Sea. You can see an expanse of coconut fields, farms growing spices and mangroves too. We could explore the village and neighbouring areas and give you a taste of village life. You will love the food and the people. I could also teach you how to fish! This is also the time when the famous snake boat races are organized in Kerala. We could attend one of them too.

Please do come with us. We will have a great time.

Looking forward to hearing from you soon.

Paul

Write an email to your class teacher requesting for permission to organize a cleaning drive.

From: vivek05@smail.com
To: minimathew@smail.com
Subject: Request for permission for a cleaning drive

Dear Madam,

My name is Vivek Saran. I am a student of Class VII, section A, and a member of our school's Nature Club. I, along with a few club members, wanted to organize a cleaning drive in the park adjoining the school. The park is littered by visitors and the local municipality workers have not been regular in cleaning it either.

We would like to undertake the drive next Friday from 2 p.m. to 5 p.m. We will ensure proper safety for all of us during the drive. Ms Mishra, our biology teacher, who has been our guide in the activities of the Nature Club, would also be present.

We would be grateful if you could kindly grant us permission for the drive and excuse us during the time that we would be away.

Warm regards,
Vivek Saran

C Write emails on these topics.

1. You had gone on a school excursion to a hill station, but your return has been delayed because of a landslide. Write an email to your father informing him of the situation. You should mention that you and your friends are safe and that he should not worry.
2. Write an email to your friend expressing your regret for not being able to attend his birthday party.
3. Write an email to your elder brother asking for his advice on what to take with you on your upcoming school trip to Mysore and Hampi.
4. Write an email to your friend, who lives in another city, telling her about a news article you read recently about the threat to polar bears because of melting ice, and asking her opinion about it.
5. Write an email to your cousin telling him about your performance in a play on your school's Annual Day celebrations.
6. Your uncle lives in another country. Write an email to him, thanking him for the birthday gift he sent you.
7. Write an email to a friend about how and why you decided to avoid junk food.
8. Your sister has just completed her higher education in another city. Write an email congratulating her on getting a job in a prestigious company.
9. Write an email to the principal of your school, with a copy to your class teacher, requesting for leave of absence, because you are suffering from chicken pox.
10. Write an email to your music teacher stating that you would not be able to attend music classes for one month as you are going to your aunt's place for a vacation. Mention that you would make up for the lost time upon your return.

Messages

Messages are short letters sent to communicate with people briefly. Messages of invitation, acceptance and regret are more detailed, including the address of the sender, the date and the signature.

Read these sample messages.

Informal Message of Invitation

C 401
Crown Signature Apartments
Sitaphalmandi
Hyderabad - 500007

Dear Vandana and Sampath,

We are celebrating my father's eighty-fifth birthday at Diamond Function Hall, Nallakunta, on Friday, 5 September. He still remembers teaching Vandana at Jubilee School. We cordially invite you to the party at 8 p.m.

Yours sincerely,
Megha Anup

Informal Message of Acceptance

Flat 112
Sai Sankalp Apartments
Miyapur
Hyderabad - 500049

Dear Megha,

Thank you for your kind invitation. It will be our pleasure to attend Sir's birthday party. I am so glad to know that he remembers me. He was one of my favourite teachers in school. We will certainly be there at the party.

Yours sincerely,
Vandana and Sampath

Informal Message of Regret

Flat 112
Sai Sankalp Apartments
Miyapur
Hyderabad - 500049

Dear Megha,

Thank you for your kind invitation. I am very glad to know that your father remembers me. He was one of my favourite teachers in school. However, we will be unable to attend the party, as Sampath's father is very unwell, and we are busy taking care of him. Do convey our regards to Sir.

Yours sincerely,
Vandana and Sampath

D Write messages on these topics.

1. Write an informal message inviting your cousin for the Annual Sports Day celebrations at your school.
2. Write a message of acceptance to a birthday party invitation.
3. Write a message of regret for a birthday party invitation that you are unable to attend.
4. Write a message to your friend inviting him/her to the New Year's eve celebration at your house.
5. Write a message of acceptance to the invitation in question 4.
6. Write a message expressing your regret in response to the invitation in question 4.

37 Essay and Biography

An **essay** is a piece of writing on a given topic. In an essay, we can narrate an incident or take a stand and argue for or against an idea.

An essay has three parts.

Introduction: It sets the tone for what the essay is about. It should be brief and to the point.
Body: It consists of two or three paragraphs. Each paragraph is devoted to discussing a single idea.
Conclusion: This is short and thought-provoking, and should leave a lasting impression on the reader.

Read these sample essays.

My Best Childhood Memories

Memories are the milestones that help us find our way through the past, when we sit down to remember it. I have so many wonderful memories from my childhood that it is difficult to decide which ones to pick.

One of my most cherished memories is from the time when I was seven years old. I used to love playing computer games. The game that I loved most was *Prince of Persia*. I would invite all my friends home and we would play together for hours on end. Morning would stretch into afternoon as we got lost in the world of the game. Those afternoons were memorable for the delicious food that my mother would dish out for all of us. I wish now that we had taken a break and offered to help her while she worked so hard in the kitchen for us.

Not all memories are special moments, however. When I was five, my father was posted to a small town in the hinterlands of Hyderabad. There were none of the distractions of the city, but we were surrounded by nature, and the cacophony of birds and small animals. Though I was really young, I remember my mother teaching me to recognize various trees, birds and their calls, flowers, insects. Even today, I can recognize the harsh call of the Coucal, a big brown and black bird, and the sweet notes of the Ashy Prinia, a tiny bird with a tail as long as its body, whenever I hear them.

The most cherished moment of my life was the day I first held my baby brother. I was seven at the time. I had gone to the hospital with my aunt to meet my new-born brother. I had been excited about meeting him, my very own sibling, who would be mine to play with. But I had not expected him to be so very small and adorable, a sleepy little morsel who let out a giant yawn, blinked and looked up at me with eyes that seemed to fill his face. I knew, then, that he would always be special for me.

The arrival of my brother brought about a series of changes in our family. My mother got a job in the University and we left Kurnool, where she had been working and went to live in Hyderabad. It was my first time in a city as big as Hyderabad. I joined a new school. Though it was a good school, I would often feel a little lost. The students at my new school seemed to have an opinion on everything and were all too ready to voice them, while I would hesitate to speak even though I knew what I wanted to say. It was at this time that I became friends with Joy, Samu, Aditya,

Sandeep and Rohan. They helped me find my way around my new school and have always stood by me during difficult times. The high points of our friendship over the past three years, whether it is our epic cricket matches, our first film in a movie theatre together, or our joint study sessions, form some of my dearest memories.

We continue to build memories as we go on in life. Some are happy, many less so. But whether happy or sad, I hope my memories will remind me of a life lived well and to the fullest.

The Role of the Internet In Modern Life

Technology makes the world go around today. It has progressed exponentially in the past two decades and now, we can't imagine a world without computers and smartphones.

The last century saw rapid advancements in technology and science which were unheard of before. The invention of the Internet is perhaps the biggest of these. Today, communicating with people, irrespective of how far away they live, is no longer something in the realm of science fiction. Today, we depend on the Internet to pay our bills, book tickets, travel, do banking transactions.

While we are always connected with the virtual world thanks to smartphones, wireless Internet has done away with the need to use a physical wire to connect with this world. A new technology is in the works named as Li-Fi which uses light signals to transmit the data and reduce the interference caused by external factors.

On the flip side, there are some disadvantages to such rapid progress. A new type of crime, known as cyber crime, is the biggest threat to security today. One of the biggest recent cyberware attack was WannaCry, which infected more than 230,000 computers in over 150 countries, threatening to erase valuable data unless ransom payments were made. Confidential and personal data continue to be stolen regularly and cyber security is still lax in our country.

It could also be said that because people spend so much time in the virtual world, they lose out on important experiences in the real world. With the spread of social media, especially, the difference between the real and the online world sometimes seem to blur. In China, for example, the Internet was said to have developed into such an addiction that there were programmes to wean people off it.

However, the advantages of technology outweigh the disadvantages. It all depends on what use we put it to. One thing we should remember is that technology is a good servant but a bad master.

Write an essay on each of these topics.

1. A bad workman complains about his tools
2. Children's role in protecting the environment
3. The importance of road safety
4. Bullying in schools
5. The President of the United States is said to be one of the most powerful people in the world. If you were to be the American President for a day, what would you do?
6. An unexpected turn of events
7. A special day in my life
8. *It was a chilly night. My parents had gone to attend my sister's annual concert. I was alone at home. I was walking to the kitchen to get myself a glass of water when ...*

   Write what happens next.

A **biography** is the story of a person's life. It is based on the real experiences and achievements of a person.

A biography should include these details about a person.

early life	family	childhood	education	hobbies/interests
profession	experiences	achievements	awards	demise

Remember, however, that a biography should not merely be a list of facts about a person's life. You should include interesting stories and tidbits that bring the person to life.

Look at these details about the life of A. P. J. Abdul Kalam, the late President of India. Then, read the biography based on them.

Best known as	: 11th President of India, scientist and author
Birth	: 15 October 1931, Rameswaram, Tamil Nadu
Parents	: Jainulabdeen and Ashiamma
Education	: Schwartz Higher Secondary School, Ramanathapuram, Tamil Nadu; St Joseph's College; Madras Institute of Technology
Career	: In 1960, joined as scientist in the Aeronautical Development Establishment, Defence Research and Development Organisation (DRDO), went on to work at Indian Space Research Organisation (ISRO)
Awards	: Padma Bhushan 1981, Padma Vibhushan 1990, Bharat Ratna 1991
Honours	: Seven doctorates and several awards, commemorative postal stamps released by the Government of India in 2015
Books	: *Ignited Minds*, *Wings of Fire*, *India 2020*
Death	: 27 July 2015, due to cardiac arrest

Dr Avul Pakeer Jainulabdeen Abdul Kalam was the eleventh President of India, remaining in office from July 2002 to 2007. Born on 15 October, 1931 in Rameshwaram, Tamil Nadu, he came from a humble family which had once seen better days. His father Jainulabdeen was a boat owner while his mother Ashiamma was a homemaker. He was the youngest of four brothers and a sister. He studied in Schwartz Higher Secondary School, Ramanathapuram, Tamil Nadu. As a youngster, Kalam sold newspapers to support his family. But he was determined to get a higher education and went to Saint Joseph's College, Thiruchirapalli, to study physics. This was followed by a degree in aerospace engineering from Madras Institute of Technology.

In 1960, he joined as a scientist at the Aeronautical Development Establishment, a laboratory of Defence Research and Development Organisation (DRDO). In 1969, he was appointed as the Project Director of India's first Satellite Launch Vehicle at ISRO and went on to become the Director of the Advanced Missile Programme for developing missiles. He was the Chief Scientific Advisor to the Prime Minister from July 1992-1999.

In 1998, along with cardiologist Dr Soma Raju, Kalam developed a low-cost coronary stent. In 2012, they went on to develop a tablet computer for health care in the rural sector.

He was a visiting professor at many universities, including the University of Shillong, Indian Institute of Management, Ahmedabad and Indore and Indian Institute of Science, Bangalore.

Kalam received many accolades throughout his long career. He was honoured with the Padma Bhushan (1981), the Padma Vibhushan (1990) and the Bharat Ratna (1991). He also received seven doctorates and honours from many organizations, including NASA. Some of his well-known books include *Ignited Minds*, *Wings of Fire*, *India 2020*.

Kalam breathed his last on 27 July 2015 due to a cardiac arrest, while delivering a lecture at IIM, Shillong. The Tamil Nadu government instituted the 'Dr APJ Abdul Kalam Award' for meritorious service in the field of higher education. The Government of India also released a postal stamp in his honour on 15 October 2015.

Write biographical sketches on these personalities. Include relevant and interesting details.

1. Indra Krishnamurthy Nooyi, an Indian American businesswoman who is the first female CEO of PepsiCo
2. P. V. Sindhu, the badminton player who won a silver medal at the 2016 Rio Olympics
3. J. K. Rowling, the world-renowned author of the *Harry Potter* series

38 Report Writing

A **report** is an account of an event. It has a clear purpose and a specific audience in mind.

When you write a report, ensure that it answers these questions.
What are we writing about? (event/occasion)
When and where did the incident happen? (date, time, venue)
Who was involved? (the people in the scene)
How did it happen and why? (description of the event)
Keep these points in mind while writing a report.

1. Write to communicate, not to impress. Adopt a neutral tone.
2. Write in short and simple sentences.
3. Give only those details which are essential.
4. Use active voice.
5. Give a title to your report.

Read this sample report.

International Girl Child Day at Arundhati High School

Arundhati High School celebrated the International Girl Child Day on 11 October with great fervour. The venue was the sprawling Pearl Gardens in the heart of the city. The programme was the culmination of a week-long celebration at the school. Several competitions were held through the week and prizes for the winners were distributed. Sneha Lakra, Director General of Police, was the Chief Guest. Preetha Sethuram, Member of Parliament was the Guest of Honour.

The Chief Guest, in her address, spoke about the issues that girls usually face. She deplored the inequality meted out to girls in education, nutrition, medical care and legal rights. During the cultural programmes that followed, all based on the theme of the girl child, Class 3 student Bhavana Shetty enthralled the audience with her dance performance. She portrayed the woes of a girl married at a very young age. The play performed by students of Class 8 depicted, through the inspiring story of a young ragpicker, how girls can fight for their rights and achieve their dreams. The auditorium rang with applause after the play was over.

'We plan to make the celebrations an annual affair. It is important to educate our children on the issue. Only then can they spread awareness in their turn and grow up to be responsible citizens,' said the school Principal, Reena Raman.

Write reports on these topics.

1. Use the given points to write the report. Remember to include other relevant details.
   International Yoga Day - 21 June - Master Minds School - week long yoga practice -

inter-school yoga competitions - the Yoga Ambassador selected to promote yoga among children - posters on importance of yoga in everyday life - make yoga practice three-days-a-week part of the curriculum

2. As part of encouraging the habit of reading in children, your school has started an initiative called *Children and Reading*. The school has asked students to donate one book each. The books will be given to children in less privileged schools. You are one of the volunteers. The initiative witnessed great participation and became a success. Write a report about how it received appreciation from everyone.
3. You and your friends visit an old age home regularly. The elderly people at the home look forward to meeting you every second Saturday of the month. Recently, with the help of your parents, you organized a gift and essential goods giveaway for the inmates of the home. Write a report about it for your school newspaper.

Newspaper Reports

A **newspaper report** may cover matters or incidents which affect the larger public as a whole. It may be a short report about a notable incident, or a longer essay-like piece discussing an issue in detail.

Keep the following points in mind while writing a newspaper report.

The title/headline of your report should be short and catchy, so that it immediately grasps the reader's attention.

It should start with the date and place.

The most important information should come in the first sentence.

It should be to-the-point and not be vague or beat around the bush.

It should be objective and avoid expressing personal opinions.

Look at this sample newspaper report.

Carry Your Ride in Your Bag

26 August, Hyderabad

Technology can come up with advancements that one would never have thought possible. An example of that is the Smartbike, an electronic bike manufactured by a Chinese company that will soon hit the markets. Can you imagine folding and coolly putting your bike away in your backpack? This is what you can do with the Smartbike, made of hi-tech carbon material and weighing only 7 kg. The bike was launched in India at the World Trade Business Complex on Tuesday, by the state minister for technology, Raghav Reddy and the CEO of SmartBike, Li Hua. 'We provide a simple, easy and stylish way for a short commute,' he said.

Capable of carrying a load of 100 kg, it runs on lithium battery, which gets fully charged in two hours. If the bike is ridden at a speed of 20 km per hour, the battery runs out after an hour of travel. Instead, if the speed is reduced to half, it can go double the distance. The bike can be folded in 10 seconds and can be assembled in five easy steps. The battery also doubles up as the seat!

The bike has an app which can be downloaded and linked to the bike. Then, a screen fitted to the bike can show details such as battery remaining and speed. The bike can be locked by pressing the lock button on the screen. It will hit the Indian market early next year.

By a Staff Reporter

Write newspaper reports on the given topics using the hints provided.

1. 75 year old Lachumamma shot to fame - makes delicious dishes both vegetarian and non-vegetarian - cooks on traditional earthen cookware - charcoal stove and firewood stove - specialty curries and chutneys - grandson starts a YouTube channel - uploads recipes every week - lots of subscribers - channel receives many advertisements - Lachumamma knows nothing about computers and internet - but she is happy making money and supporting herself
2. A blockbuster film of a famous actor released two weeks ago - pirated CDs available everywhere in the market - producer files a case - Film Artists Association speaks up about the long-running problem - Mohan Gangaram, 34 years, along with a group of friends, arrested - police discover a large number of yet-to-be delivered CDs - CDs of several other new movies also seized - culprit produced in court - fined and given a six-month sentence
3. Old age home vandalized - attack happened late on Sunday evening -many helpless old people injured - real estate mafia suspected as home was on prime real estate - home was established fifty years ago - said to be one of the best in the entire state - residents are worried, many taken ill - say that their future is uncertain, no place to go - cause taken up by an NGO - police not doing enough as many are in cahoots with the mafia

39 Paragraph and Diary Entry

A **paragraph** is a collection of sentences that discusses a particular topic or describes a particular event.

A good paragraph has these features.
Though a paragraph has limited scope, it should have a clear beginning, middle and end.
The first sentence should clearly indicate what the paragraph is about.
The next few sentences should explain the topic in some detail.

Look at this sample paragraph.

Wasting Food is Wrong

In a country like ours, where a large section of the population lives in abject poverty, wasting food is akin to a crime. Sadly, those of us who live comfortable lives often seem to forget it. At celebrations such as birthdays and weddings, the wastage is boundless, especially among the affluent. It is often a mark of prestige to serve far more dishes than one could ever expect people to eat. The more the number of items served, the 'richer' the celebration is considered. On the other hand, there are poor and needy people who often go without a single meal in a day. A lot of food is also wasted in restaurants and stores which sell pre-cooked items that have to be used within the day. Of late, voluntary organizations have come up which collect excess food from restaurants, and even from celebrations, pack it in a hygienic way and serve them to the needy. However, good deeds should begin at home. While at home, we should take care to serve ourselves only as much as we need, and finish what we have served ourselves.

Write a paragraph in about 150 words on each of these topics. Use the given clues.

1. Books are our best friends
   window to the world – offer knowledge – entertain us – teach values – best way to pass time – plenty of variety in themes – books help us make new friends – reader's clubs – refines and sharpens one's thinking – make a book your friend today
2. My uncle – my role model
   Love and respect my uncle – very kind and understanding – knowledgeable about many things – determination and perseverance to achieve the set goal – fun-loving and jovial – keeps secrets – can be your confidant – the connecting link that unites the extended family – well respected among colleagues – self-made man – an inspiration to youngsters in the family

Write a paragraph in about 150 words on each of these topics.

1. The craze around weight loss
2. If I were the Education Minister
3. My hobby
4. All that glitters is not gold
5. Speed kills
6. Water, the essential commodity

A **diary entry** is a first-person record of events, thoughts and feelings which the writer experiences in the course of a particular day.

A diary entry is written in an informal style and includes short, vivid descriptions. It is most often written in simple past, present perfect or simple future tense. It is about 200 words in length.

The date of the entry is always mentioned on the top left of the page. The place may also be mentioned, if the writer is travelling to another place.

Read the sample entry from the diary of Agastya. He describes his first day of swimming class.

Wednesday, 24 May

The high point of my summer vacation began today. I have written before how much I have wanted to learn swimming for the past couple of years. The water seems to call out to me! This summer, my parents finally enrolled me in a swimming class at our neighbouring swimming club. My best friends, Naren and Shyam and I have joined the class together, hoping to have some fun while we learn.

Today was my first day at the pool. The class was for an hour from 4 p.m. Naren and Shyam were already there when I reached. We were asked to take a shower before we entered the pool. The coach, a rather serious-looking man, asked us to go to the shallow end of the pool. We were asked to hold on to the side of the pool and let our legs float. I was a bit nervous and splashed around for a while. Then the coach came to my side and lightly supported my legs until I got the hang of it. I looked around to see how my friends were doing, and was surprised to find Shyam paddling with his feet quite confidently! I was a little jealous and was planning to ask how he had learnt it, when the coach came around again to see how I was doing. I immediately went back to floating in the water and minding my own business. I think I am a little scared of the coach! We also practised exhaling under water today. Eventually, I also learnt how to paddle and tread water. The coach told us that he would teach us how to come up from the bottom using our arms in a day or two. Shyam boasted later that he already knew how to do the front stroke and backstroke. I wonder if he is bluffing, but then, he goes to his ancestral village every year, where there are a lot of lakes. He might have learnt the basics there.

After the class, we had to shower again. Then, the three of us trooped together to the club canteen. After all the exercise, our stomachs were growling. We polished off the sandwiches and momos we bought in no time.

In spite of the little difficulties, I think I will love swimming. I can't wait to go back tomorrow. I am sure I will be able to swim to the deep end by the end of the season.

Write diary entries about these events.

1. You have recently stopped speaking to a close friend because of a misunderstanding. You realise that it was your fault and that you should apologize, but you are finding it difficult to admit your mistake. Write a diary entry describing what you feel, and what you plan to do.
2. You recently auditioned for a part in a school play, but did not get the role. You wanted the role very much, especially because it was in your favourite play. You are very upset and struggling to accept the situation. Write a diary entry about it, mentioning that you should not give up hope.

3. You went to Goa last winter on a holiday. It was the first time you travelled by air. Write a diary entry describing your experience of flying.
4. You are a good student, but you have been struggling with certain subjects in your new class. You are worried about slipping up and have spoken to your parents. Write a diary entry about how you feel and how you plan to deal with the problem.
5. You recently met your friend's grandfather when you had accompanied your friend on a visit. He left a deep impact on you by his kindness, his willingness to listen to your ideas and his encouragement of them. Write a diary entry describing your experience.

Answers to Self-Assessment

A
1. will move – Intransitive
2. moved – Transitive
3. like – Transitive
4. likes – Transitive
5. baked – Transitive
6. kicked – Transitive
7. laughed – Intransitive
8. have received – Transitive
9. barked – Transitive
10. were received – Intransitive

B
1. to go – to-infinitive; go – bare-infinitive
2. walking – present participle
3. rock climbing – gerund
4. tired and annoyed – past participle
5. carry – bare infinitive
6. finding – gerund
7. hibernating – present participle
8. book – bare-infinitive
9. to attend – to-infinitive
10. making – present participle

C
1. has been working – present perfect continuous; is – simple present
2. had and left – simple past
3. looks after – simple present
4. is writing – present continuous; were; simple past
5. had messaged – past perfect
6. were watching – past continuous; arrived – simple past
7. Had been waiting – past perfect continuous; received – simple past
8. are writing – present continuous
9. have finished – present perfect
10. will have finished – future perfect

D
1. Diya told Dinesh that it was very kind of him to drop her at her place.
2. Mother ordered Meena to polish her shoes
3. Roopa told Mini that she loved her new frock.
4. Tarun said that they should give mummy a surprise gift.
5. Gopal asked Simi when she would come back from Goa.
6. They exclaimed with sadness that they had lost the match.
7. Tabitha asked Robin if he would take Dan to the doctor the next day.
8. Vand ana advised Bhavana to come home early.
9. Sita commanded Lakshman to go and look for his brother.
10. The teacher advised the students to staple the answer scripts carefully.

E
1. Active
2. Passive
3. Passive
4. Passive
5. Active
6. Active
7. Passive
8. Active
9. Active
10. Passive

40 Story Writing

A **story** is an imaginary tale centred on an incident. In a story, there is a build-up of incidents which leads to a climax, or the high point of the story, followed by the resolution.

A story has several characteristic features.

Plot: This is what the story is about. It can be problem or a crisis which is resolved in the end.

Narration: This refers to the way the story is told. It may be told by one of the characters in the story or by a third person.

Characterization: This refers to the traits of the people in the story - what kind of people they are, their temperament, thoughts and appearance. We learn about characters through the description of the author or through the conversations or actions the characters engage in.

Tone: The writer may narrate the story in many ways - humourous, sad, serious or tongue-in-cheek. The language used indicates the tone of the story.

Keep the following points in mind while writing a story.

- Decide on the events in the story beforehand. Ensure that your plot is logically consistent.
- Think about the number of characters the story will have and the relationship the characters share with one another.
- Use dialogues to enliven the action, ensuring that they match the background of the character. An uneducated man would not speak in the same way as an educated person. The dialogue should resemble the way people speak in real life.
- Keep your reader in mind when you write your story. If you are writing a story for young children, the plot should deal with elements that a child of that age group would be familiar with.
- We usually use the past tense for narration. But if you are describing an ongoing action, you can use the present tense to make it more exciting.
- One of the most common plot devices is to end the story with a twist. However, this should not come across as forced, but should flow naturally from the plot.

Read the sample story.

short-tempered king – had a faithful servant – banished servant for a small mistake – servant went to live in forest – years passed – discovered a plot to kill the king – informed king about it using his intelligence – king was sorry – invited him back to the kingdom

The Faithful Servant

Once upon a time, there was a very short-tempered king. Among his many servants, there was one who was very faithful. One day, the king went hunting. At the end of the day, he was tired, thirsty and hungry. The loyal servant fetched him water in a pitcher. While he was handing the pitcher to the king, the servant spilt some water on the king's clothes in his hurry. The king, already touchy and tired, was furious. He immediately banished the loyal servant from the kingdom.

The servant was sad but did not lose heart. He went to live in a neighbouring jungle. He taught himself everything he needed to survive in the forest. When he learnt how to use wood to make things, he built himself a small hut. He planted a garden and started growing vegetables and fruits. He collected the seeds from the trees in the forest and planted them in his garden. He learnt the ways of wild animals and to co-exist with them. He even made friends with some of the wild animals and some, he tamed. Slowly, he made peace with his solitary life in the jungle, but he did not forget the king. He remembered how well the king had looked after him, and waited for an opportunity to prove himself to the king again.

Years passed. By now, the servant knew every nook and corner of the jungle. One day, while he was out gathering wild fruits, he came across a group of soldiers from the kingdom.

'I already have an army assembled outside the city gates. At my signal, they will invade the city,' said one of them.

'Good. Should we do away with the king too?' another asked.

The servant had overheard the conversation, and realized that the soldiers were scheming to attack the kingdom and kill the king.

The servant wanted to alert the king. But how would he do so? If he went back, the king might order him killed. He thought hard. He remembered how pigeons were used as couriers to carry information. He had a pet pigeon whom he had been training to respond to him. He wrote a message on a piece of parchment, signed it with a symbol that he knew the king would remember, and sent it to the king.

The message reached the king. He immediately foiled the plan of his enemy. He also recognized the sender. He realized the mistake he had made by banishing a servant who had remained faithful to him despite his own unjust treatment of the man.

He invited the servant back to the kingdom. He also appointed him minister as a reward for his loyalty and resourcefulness.

A Write stories based on the given outlines.

1. Two year old Surya - loves to eat chips - asks mother to buy him a packet one morning - mother does not buy as she is busy - father and mother sit down to lunch in the afternoon - realise Surya missing - ask in friends' homes - about to search lanes and by lanes - sees a beaming Surya on the road with the packet of chips - with a tall boy - Surya went alone to the nearby shop - shopkeeper knew parents - sends Surya home with his son - relieved parents thank the shopkeeper
2. A university hostel - Sunday afternoon - quiet surroundings - Neha chatting with friends in the lawn opposite the hostel - suddenly a cobra hisses - frightened students run for life - the cobra sleeping happily in the shade - students call Ravi - snake catcher - very skillfully and deftly catches the snake - everyone heaves a sigh of relief

3. Meena working mother - one evening buys groceries, vegetable and fruits - kids happy - Meena tired - everyone has dinner - Meena about to call a colleague - looks for her handbag - can't find it - forgot it in one of the shops - rushes to the market place - inquires in shops - bag safe in one of the shops - kind and honest shopkeeper - Meena is grateful

B Write stories illustrating the following proverbs.

1. Two wrongs don't make a right.
2. The squeaky wheel gets the grease.
3. Fortune favours the bold.
4. Don't judge a book by its cover.
5. Don't count your chickens before they hatch.

C Write stories using the given opening lines.

1. It was a hot summer afternoon. Naren's mother told him to stay indoors. But Naren wanted to go out and play despite the blinding heat. So he quietly ...
2. It was 11 o'clock at night. Shirin's parents had gone to watch a film. Shirin and her brother had gone to sleep, when the doorbell began to ring harshly. Shirin got up with a start ...
3. It was 5:00 in the morning. The hill town of Hrishikesh was slowly waking up. Manoj, a young boy who worked at the temple beside the river, has just stepped outside his room, when he heard a low sound that was distinctly like a leopard's growl ...
4. Jayashree and her parents were travelling by train to Varanasi. When the train stopped at a station, her father got off to buy some magazines. He was paying the shopkeeper when the train started ...
5. Twins Tarun and Siddhanth loved watching horror film. One night the brothers had watched a particularly scary film before they slept. In the middle of the night, Tarun woke up suddenly from a bad dream. He turned to wake up Siddhanth, but he was not in his bed. Then he noticed him shivering in the balcony ...

41 Summary

A **summary** is the summing up of main points from a longer passage.

Remember these points while writing your summary.

- Express the main points in clear and precise language.
- Reduce the length of the passage to one-third.
- Leave out examples, illustrations and long explanations.
- Write the summary in your own words, in third person, using phrases from the text only occasionally.
- Provide a suitable title to the summary.
- Use impersonal language and neutral tone.

Follow these steps while writing a summary.

1. Prepare a rough draft.
2. Read it again to make sure that it is logical and easily understood.
3. Check the length.
4. Ensure correctness of spelling, punctuation and grammar.
5. Write the final draft.

Read the passage and the sample summary that follows.

We have been able to understand our solar system better with the help of NASA's Cassini spacecraft. During the last two decades, the goal of the unmanned spacecraft has been to explore the giant planet Saturn, its ring system and its icy moons. Cassini entered the orbit around Saturn in July 2004, seven years after it was launched in October 1997. In order to reach its destination faster, Cassini first landed on Venus, in April 1998. The probe involved two fly-bys of Venus, Earth and Jupiter. Cassini made its closest approach to Jupiter, the biggest planet of our system, in December 2000.

Over the last 13 years, since landing on Saturn, Cassini has discovered seven new moons orbiting the gas giant. Enceladus and Titan are two of Saturn's biggest moons. Cassini did a fly-by of Enceladus and landed on Titan. Cassini carried a lander called Huygens, built by the European Space Agency. Huygens was designed to enter Titan's atmosphere. It became the furthest landing from Earth that a probe had ever made when it landed on Titan in January 2005.

Cassini flew by Enceladus soon after, and sent back data that indicated a "thin but significant atmosphere". The data also showed water ice geysers erupting at its south pole. Over the years, the spacecraft would return to Enceladus. It was found to have a liquid ocean underneath its surface in addition to hot spots on the ocean floor. These are signs that strongly speak of the existence of life on this moon.

Summary

The Cassini Spacecraft

NASA's Cassini spacecraft has helped us understand our solar system better. Cassini was launched in 1997. Through the fast route from Earth to Venus, it entered Saturn's orbit in 2004. On the way, it went close to Jupiter too, helping us discover new facts about the planet. Cassini carried a lander called Huygens which, in 2005, landed on Titan, one of the seven moons orbiting Saturn. Cassini also flew by Enceladus, another moon. It sent data which showed clear signs of the existence of life on this moon.

Summarize these passages. Give suitable titles.

1. All objects that exist in the sky are called celestial bodies. Sometimes, celestial bodies are also called heavenly bodies. Celestial bodies that we know about include, the sun, the moon, asteroids, meteors, the planets and the stars. Stars are huge celestial bodies. They look small because they are far away from us. They are made of burning gases. When these gases burn, they emit a tremendous amount of heat and light. The star nearest to the Earth is the sun. It is about 150 million km away. There are millions of stars like the sun. The second nearest star is Proxima Centauri, which is 4.25 light years away from the Earth. If you look at the night sky closely, you will see clusters of stars. These groups of stars are called constellations. Some major constellations are Ursa Major, Ursa Minor, Orion, Canis Major and Hydra. Ursa Major is also known as Saptarishi in Hindi. The two stars at the ends are called pointers. The brightest star in the sky is the Pole Star or the North Star. The North Star is almost directly above the North Pole. People in ancient times used to determine the north direction at night with the help of the North Star.

2. In Russia, in 1547, the grandson of Ivan the Great, Ivan IV, was crowned the first czar of undivided Russia. Moscow became the capital for the Holy Russian Empire. Ivan IV ruled with terror and ruthlessness. It is said that he removed the eyes of the architects who built the cathedral of St Basil, so that such a beautiful piece of architecture could never be recreated. Ivan's powers became absolute with the annexation of the remaining independent principalities, such as Siberia. It was at this time that the concept of serfdom emerged in Russia. Under this system of serfdom, a master was appointed over the peasants who cultivated the land around an estate. This master, or feudal lord, controlled all activities of the peasants. Ivan engaged in long and largely unsuccessful wars against Sweden and Poland, and instituted a reign of terror against the hereditary nobility. Ivan organised the Streltsy (members of the army elite) to govern his estates. Since his soldiers served a life-time tenure, their land grants became hereditary, and they formed a new ruling elite class. The Oprichniki, the first police force, was also formed to suppress the boyar or the ruling-class nobles' rebellion. Ivan confiscated the property of the boyars and granted state property to those who served him. In 1582, after the Livonian War with Poland and Sweden, Russia lost her far northern territories and her access to the Baltic Sea. In the same year, the czar also killed his son, Ivan, in a fit of rage. When 'Ivan the Terrible' died in 1584, Russia was left in a state of almost total political and economic ruin.

42 Notice

A **notice** is a formal written communication to inform a group of people about an event.

A notice is short and contains only the essential details of the event, including
- the time, date and venue.
- the people for whom the information is meant and the person giving the information.

Read these sample notices.

Indus Public School
Raj Bhavan Road, Jaipur
NOTICE

Our school is organizing a cultural programme as part of this year's Annual Day celebrations. Poonam Nair, Commissioner of Police, Jaipur is the Chief Guest for the programme. All students are requested to attend the programme and make it a grand success.

Date: 10 February 2020

Time: 10 a.m.

Venue: School auditorium

Swarup Dey

Principal

Nalanda School
Kaveri Marg, Bhopal
NOTICE

Renowned children's writer Robin Smith will visit our school on next week. He will talk about his new book of short stories and will also interact with students. Students from classes VII to IX are invited to attend the programme.

Date: 20 September 2020

Time: 11 a.m.

Venue: H. R. Saini Auditorium

Binita Tiwari

Convener, Literary Club

Write notices on these topics.

1. You are the Sports Secretary of your school. Write a notice requesting students to attend an inter-school table tennis competition to be organized in the main auditorium and cheer the participants of your school.
2. You are the class monitor. Your school is organizing a five day educational tour to Ooty for Classes VI to VIII. Write a notice inviting interested students to register their names for the tour. Give relevant details about the tour, including the dates, accommodation facilities and expenses.
3. You are the organizer of a theatre club in your colony. Your club plans to put up a play during the Durga Puja festivities. You need a few actors for the play. Write a notice inviting interested residents in the colony to audition for certain roles. Mention the details of the play, and the date, time and venue for the audition.
4. You are the cultural secretary of your school. Your school is organizing the annual fete, in which students can create, exhibit and sell their own creations, including paintings, handicrafts and food items. Write a notice inviting students to register their names for the fete.
5. You are the Principal of a school. A few scholarships are available in your school for meritorious students, for the next academic year. Write a notice inviting students to apply for them. Include the eligibility criteria and other necessary details.